## Download Forms on Nolo.com

To download the forms, go to this book's companion page at:

 **www.nolo.com/back-of-book/SPOT.html**

Checking the companion page is also a good way
to stay informed on topics related to this book.

## More Resources from Nolo.com

### Legal Forms, Books, & Software

Hundreds of do-it-yourself products—all written in plain English, approved, and updated by our in-house legal editors.

### Legal Articles

Get informed with thousands of free articles on everyday legal topics. Our articles are accurate, up to date, and reader friendly.

### Find a Lawyer

Want to talk to a lawyer? Use Nolo to find a lawyer who can help you with your case.

# NOLO   The Trusted Name
*(but don't take our word for it)*

*"In Nolo you can trust."*
**THE NEW YORK TIMES**

*"Nolo is always there in a jam as the nation's premier publisher of do-it-yourself legal books."*
**NEWSWEEK**

*"Nolo publications…guide people simply through the how, when, where and why of the law."*
**THE WASHINGTON POST**

*"[Nolo's]…material is developed by experienced attorneys who have a knack for making complicated material accessible."*
**LIBRARY JOURNAL**

*"When it comes to self-help legal stuff, nobody does a better job than Nolo…"*
**USA TODAY**

*"The most prominent U.S. publisher of self-help legal aids."*
**TIME MAGAZINE**

*"Nolo is a pioneer in both consumer and business self-help books and software."*
**LOS ANGELES TIMES**

**13th Edition**

# Law Forms for Personal Use

**The Editors of Nolo**

| | |
|---|---|
| THIRTEENTH EDITION | MARCH 2026 |
| Editor | ILONA BRAY |
| Cover Design | SUSAN PUTNEY |
| Book Design | SUSAN PUTNEY |
| Proofreading | JOCELYN TRUITT |
| Printing | SHERIDAN |

ISSN: 2167-5775 (print)

ISSN: 2330-0434 (online)

ISBN: 978-1-4133-3334-3 (pbk)

ISBN: 978-1-4133-3335-0 (ebook)

This book covers only United States law, unless it specifically states otherwise.

Copyright © 1998, 2001, 2002, 2004, 2005, 2007, 2009, 2011, 2013, 2016, and 2020 by Nolo. Copyright © 2023 and 2026 by MH Sub I, LLC dba Nolo. All rights reserved. The NOLO trademark is registered in the U.S. Patent and Trademark Office. Printed in the U.S.A.

No part of this publication may be reproduced, stored in a retrieval system, or transmitted in any form or by any means, electronic, mechanical, photocopying, recording, or otherwise, without prior written permission. Reproduction prohibitions do not apply to the forms contained in this product when reproduced for personal use. For information on bulk purchases or corporate premium sales, please contact tradecs@nolo.com.

> *Please note*
>
> Accurate, plain-English legal information can help you solve many of your own legal problems. But this text is not a substitute for personalized advice from a knowledgeable lawyer. If you want the help of a trained professional—and we'll always point out situations in which we think that's a good idea—consult an attorney licensed to practice in your state.

MH Sub I, LLC dba Nolo, 909 N. Pacific Coast Hwy, 11th Fl, El Segundo, CA 90245

## About the Editors of Nolo

Nolo's editorial department includes over 15 legal professionals, both editors and legal researchers. Collectively, the department has decades of experience turning legal jargon into plain English. Most of Nolo's editors left careers as practicing lawyers in favor of furthering the company's mission: Getting legal information into the hands of people who need it.

All Nolo editors specialize in certain areas of the law, and many are recognized as national experts in their fields. They write and edit books and articles, develop legal forms, and create the legal content for Nolo's software and online applications.

# Table of Contents

## Introduction

**How to Use This Book** .................................................................................................. 1

Filling In the Contracts and Forms ........................................................................... 3

Editing the Forms ........................................................................................................ 4

Describing People, Property, and Events ................................................................ 5

Signing the Forms ....................................................................................................... 6

Resolving Disputes ..................................................................................................... 8

Do You Need a Lawyer? ........................................................................................... 10

## 1 Caring for Children, Pets, and Property .................................................. 11

Form 1: Temporary Guardianship Authorization for Care of Minor ............... 12

Form 2: Authorization for Minor's Medical Treatment ...................................... 13

Form 3: Authorization for International Travel With Minor .............................. 13

Form 4: House-Sitting Instructions ........................................................................ 14

Form 5: Children's Carpool Agreement ................................................................ 15

Form 6: Pet Care Agreement ................................................................................... 15

Form 7: Authorization to Drive a Motor Vehicle ................................................. 16

Form 8: Power of Attorney for Finances (Limited Power) ................................ 17

Form 9: Power of Attorney for Real Estate .......................................................... 20

Form 10: Notice of Revocation of Power of Attorney ........................................ 25

Form 11: Request to Begin Special Education Process ...................................... 25

## 2 Basic Estate Planning ................................................................................... 27

Form 12: Property Worksheet ................................................................................ 28

Form 13: Beneficiary Worksheet ............................................................................ 29

Forms 14 and 15: Basic Wills .................................................................................. 30

Form 16: Will Codicil ................................................................................................ 34

## 3 Things to Do After a Death: Documents for Executors ............ 35
Form 17: Notice to Creditor of Death ............ 36
Form 18: Executor's Checklist ............ 37
Form 19: General Notice of Death ............ 37
Form 20: Obituary Information Fact Sheet ............ 38
Form 21: Notice to Deceased's Homeowners' Insurance Company ............ 38
Form 22: Notice to Deceased's Vehicle Insurance Company ............ 39

## 4 Renting a Place to Live ............ 41
Form 23: Rental Application ............ 43
Form 24: Tenant References ............ 43
Form 25: Landlord-Tenant Checklist ............ 44
Form 26: Move-In Letter ............ 45
Form 27: Resident's Maintenance/Repair Request ............ 46
Form 28: Semiannual Safety and Maintenance Update ............ 47
Form 29: Landlord-Tenant Agreement to Terminate Lease ............ 47
Form 30: Consent to Assignment of Lease ............ 48
Form 31: Month-to-Month Tenant's Notice of Intent to Move Out ............ 49
Form 32: Demand for Return of Security Deposit ............ 49

## 5 Borrowing and Lending Money ............ 51
Form 33: Loan Comparison Worksheet ............ 52
Form 34: Authorization to Check Credit and Employment References ............ 52
Form 35: Monthly Payment Record ............ 54
Forms 36–40: Promissory Notes ............ 54
Form 41: Cosigner Provision ............ 59
Forms 42–45: Security Agreements ............ 59
Form 46: Agreement to Modify Promissory Note ............ 62
Form 47: Overdue Payment Demand ............ 62
Form 48: Demand to Make Good on Bad Check ............ 63

## 6 Buying a House .......................................................................................... 65

Form 49: Ideal House Profile .......................................................................... 66
Form 50: House Priorities Worksheet ............................................................ 67
Form 51: House Comparison Worksheet ....................................................... 67
Form 52: Family Financial Statement ............................................................ 68
Form 53: Monthly Carrying Costs Worksheet ............................................... 70
Form 54: Mortgage Rates and Terms Worksheet .......................................... 71
Form 55: Moving Checklist ............................................................................ 74

## 7 Buying or Selling a Car, Dog, or Personal Property ........................................ 75

Form 56: Motor Vehicle Bill of Sale ............................................................... 76
Form 57: Boat Bill of Sale .............................................................................. 78
Form 58: General Bill of Sale ......................................................................... 78
Form 59: Bill of Sale for Dog ......................................................................... 78

## 8 Renting Personal Property and Storing Goods ............................................... 81

Form 60: Personal Property Rental Agreement ............................................. 82
Form 61: Notice of Termination of Personal Property Rental Agreement ... 83
Form 62: Storage Contract ............................................................................ 83

## 9 Home Repairs and Maintenance ................................................................... 85

Form 63: Home Maintenance Agreement ..................................................... 87
Form 64: Home Repairs Agreement .............................................................. 88
Form 65: Contractor Mid-Job Worksheet ..................................................... 88

## 10 Handling Personal Finances ........................................................................ 91

Form 66: Daily Expenses ............................................................................... 92
Form 67: Monthly Income ............................................................................ 93
Form 68: Monthly Budget ............................................................................. 93
Form 69: Statement of Assets and Liabilities ................................................ 94

Form 70: Assignment of Rights .......................................................................................................... 94

Form 71: Notice to Terminate Joint Account ................................................................................ 96

Form 72: Notice to Stop Payment of Check .................................................................................. 96

Form 73: Request for Credit Report ................................................................................................ 97

Form 74: Request Reinvestigation of Credit Report Entry ........................................................ 98

Form 75: Dispute Credit Card Charge .......................................................................................... 100

Form 76: Demand Collection Agency Cease Contact .............................................................. 101

## 11 Hiring Child Care, Elder Care, or Household Help ........................................................... 103

Form 77: Child Care Agreement .................................................................................................... 106

Form 78: Child Care Instructions .................................................................................................. 108

Form 79: Elder Care Agreement .................................................................................................... 109

Form 80: Housekeeping Services Agreement ............................................................................ 109

## 12 Handling Legal Disputes ............................................................................................................. 111

Form 81: Demand Letter ................................................................................................................. 112

Form 82: Online Auction Buyer Demand Letter ........................................................................ 113

Form 83: Request for Refund or Repair of Goods Under Warranty ...................................... 113

Form 84: Accident Claim Worksheet ........................................................................................... 116

Forms 85–90: Releases .................................................................................................................... 116

Form 91: Complaint Letter to a Government Agency ............................................................. 119

Form 92: Notice to Cancel Certain Contracts ............................................................................ 121

Form 93: Identity Theft Worksheet .............................................................................................. 122

# Appendixes

## A How to Use the Downloadable Forms on the Nolo Website ........................................... 125

Editing RTFs ....................................................................................................................................... 126

List of Forms Available on the Nolo Website ............................................................................ 127

## B Forms in This Book ........................................................................................................................ 131

# How to Use This Book

Filling In the Contracts and Forms ........................................................................................3
Editing the Forms .....................................................................................................................4
    Selecting From Several Choices ......................................................................................4
    Deleting Clauses or Phrases .............................................................................................5
    Adding Clauses or Language ...........................................................................................5
Describing People, Property, and Events ..............................................................................5
Signing the Forms .....................................................................................................................6
    Notarization ........................................................................................................................7
    Spouse's Signature .............................................................................................................8
Resolving Disputes ...................................................................................................................8
Do You Need a Lawyer? ........................................................................................................ 10

This book provides dozens of ready-to-use forms and contracts for a variety of everyday legal and practical transactions. These are the types of transactions that most people can safely handle themselves, without formal legal help. Among the forms are those necessary to write a simple will, settle minor legal disputes, prepare a power of attorney, lend or borrow money, rent a place to live, request a credit report, and sell a used car. Forms are also included to hire someone to do home repairs, to care for your children, and more.

Many of the forms in this book are primarily designed for your personal, individual use, such as the Landlord-Tenant Checklist or Loan Comparison Worksheet. But other forms, such as the Elder Care Agreement, are contracts, designed to allow two or more parties to create a legally enforceable agreement.

Unlike many commercial contracts you might encounter, the ones in this book are written in everyday (but legal) language. They are designed to describe and define a transaction, such as designating a temporary guardian for your child, with a reasonable level of specificity—without sacrificing clarity and simplicity.

Don't worry that because our contracts are jargon-free they might be less valid than others. In general, as long as two parties—business entities or people—exchange promises to each do something of benefit for the other, a valid contract is formed. A contract will usually be enforced as long as all of the following requirements are met:

- **The terms are specific enough.** The contract must be sufficiently clear and detailed that an arbitrator or judge can sensibly decide who is right if there's a dispute later. For example, a house-painting agreement that says "John the Painter shall paint Sally the Homeowner's house" provides so little guidance that it probably would not be enforced. At the very least, to be enforceable, the contract should state how much John is to be paid for his work. Of course, you'll want to create a contract that not only defines who and what is involved but also anticipates problems that are likely to arise. To be of real value, the contract should include key details such as the type of paint to be used, the work schedule, how and when payment is to be made, and what happens if John and Sally disagree about something.

- **The contract is for a legal purpose.** A contract formed to accomplish something illegal is not enforceable in court. For instance, if two people sign a contract to transfer an illegal gambling operation, and they later have a falling out, a judge will refuse to order compliance with the agreement.

- **Enforcement would not be grossly unfair.** The contracts you make using the forms in this book are unlikely to be challenged on the grounds of fairness. But in extreme situations, if a contract is both unfair and the result of one party's superior bargaining position (such as a one-sided premarital agreement between a millionaire and a recent immigrant who is still learning English), a court might not enforce it. If you keep in mind that the best contracts substantially benefit both parties, you should have no problems.

> **The Importance of Getting Contracts in Writing**
>
> The most important rule when entering into any business agreement or transaction is this: Get it in writing. In a few situations—such as a contract to buy or sell real estate—you must have a written agreement for it to be legally enforceable. Similarly, a contract usually must be written if it can't be performed within one year of when it's made.
>
> But even when an oral contract is legal, there are many practical reasons why a written contract is preferable. Two years from now, you and the other people involved in any transaction might have significantly different recollections about what you agreed to. So putting your agreement into black and white is an important memory aid.
>
> A well-drafted contract has several other important benefits. For one, it serves as a framework for settling disputes. And if settlement proves impossible and a court contest ensues, it will be far easier to prove the terms of a written contract than an oral one.
>
> Another important benefit of drafting a written agreement is that the act of putting a contract together can help you and the other parties focus on key legal and practical issues, some of which might otherwise be overlooked. By starting this process with a well-designed form—like those in this book—you increase your chances of creating a thorough and useful document.

## Filling In the Contracts and Forms

The forms in this book are designed to be used as needed; we don't expect you to read the book from start to finish, or to need every form. But we do ask one thing: Read this introduction, all of the introductory material at the beginning of any chapter containing a form that you will use, and the instructions for completing the form itself.

Readers who have a print version of this book can use the forms provided in the book in at least three ways:

1. **Use the companion page on Nolo.com.** All of the forms and contracts in this book are available for you to download on this book's online companion page (see Appendix A for the link). For a list of all forms as well as step-by-step instructions on accessing, using, and saving them, see Appendix A.
2. **Fill out the forms in this book.** You can get the job done the old-fashioned way—by photocopying a form out of the book and filling it in with a typewriter or pen. *Don't*, however, use the original form from the book, or you'll be left without a clean copy. Although you'll be fine filling in some forms in this book by hand, such as the Property Worksheet, we suggest that you type the agreements whenever possible. While typing is not legally required, a typed document usually carries more weight than a handwritten one and is more legible. But if convenience or cost dictates that you fill in a contract or form by hand, do it neatly and you should be fine.

 CAUTION

**Do not just fill in a will form by hand.** Unlike the rest of the forms in this book, a will form cannot be completed by hand. Legally, a valid will cannot contain a mix of handwritten and machine-printed material. To make a legally valid will, use one of the downloadable forms on this book's companion page. Use your word processing program to enter the personal information called for and to delete any clauses you don't need. If you don't have a computer, you can use a typewriter to type the entire will document.

3. **Use the forms in this book to evaluate similar forms and contracts.** If someone drafts a contract and presents it to you to sign, you can use a corresponding form in this book as a checklist to make sure that the proposed contract has all the recommended ingredients. If it doesn't, use the form in this book as a model to suggest modifications or additions.

## Editing the Forms

Many of the forms in this book might meet your needs perfectly. All you will need to do is fill in a few blanks and sign. But for some forms, you'll want to make some changes—such as adding or deleting language or clauses. Here's how.

## Selecting From Several Choices

Many of our forms require that you choose among options, such as the method of payment for work being performed. When you see a clause like this, simply check the correct box on the form and provide any requested additional information.

On several of our forms, you might encounter language that's too cut and dried for your purposes, or wording that ends up sounding awkward, such as ☐ Yes ☐ No or ☐ "his/hers." In these situations, you can easily clean the form up by deleting words that don't apply or substituting more appropriate language (assuming you're using a downloadable form). If you're filling in a hard-copy form, leaving in unneeded words will not affect the validity of the contract. If you prefer, however, you can ink out the portion that doesn't apply.

**Example of Clause With Several Options (Clause 2 of Home Repairs Agreement)**

---

2. **Payment**

    In exchange for the work specified in Clause 1, Homeowner agrees to pay Contractor as follows [*choose one and check appropriate boxes*]:

    ☐ $ _____ , payable upon completion of the specified work by ☐ cash ☐ check.

    ☐ $ _____ , payable by ☐ cash ☐ check as follows:
    _____ % payable when the following occurs: _____
    _____ % payable when the following occurs: _____
    _____ % payable when the following occurs: _____ .

    ☐ $ _____ per hour for each hour of work performed, up to a maximum of $ _____ , payable at the following times and in the following manner: _____
    _____
    _____ .

    ☐ Other: _____
    _____ .

## Deleting Clauses or Phrases

Some individual clauses or phrases in our forms and agreements might not apply to your situation. If you're using the downloadable forms, making changes is easy—simply delete those clauses and renumber the remaining clauses as appropriate.

If using the hard-copy forms, draw lines through the clause you want to delete and have all parties put their initials next to it. If deleting a complete clause, you'll need to renumber the clauses to avoid confusion. For example, if you don't want your lease assignment consent contract to include a clause on "Tenant's Future Liability" (Clause 4 of the Consent to Assignment of Lease), make the modifications as shown below.

## Adding Clauses or Language

Adding extra terms to a contract is easy if you're completing the forms on your computer: Simply add the new language or clauses and renumber the remaining clauses as appropriate.

If you are using the hard-copy forms and want to add words to a clause, use the space provided. If we didn't leave enough room, or if you want to add a new clause, you should prepare a separate addendum sheet or attachment. See "How to Prepare an Attachment Page," below, for details.

 CAUTION

**Be sure your changes are clear, easy to understand, and legal.** If you add a list of property or work specifications to a contract, your contract should still be fine. But if you delete one of our clauses and substitute your own, make sure your language is easy to understand, free of ambiguity, and consistent with the rest of the contract. Also, if you have any doubt about the legal validity of language you want to add or delete—especially if significant amounts of money or property, or the personal rights of the other person, are involved—have the changes checked by a lawyer.

## Describing People, Property, and Events

Some forms ask you to name people or describe events or property. Here's the best way to do this.

**People.** Where you are asked to insert someone's name, address, and other identifying information, use that person's legal name—the name on a driver's license—and home street address. If a person commonly uses two names (not including a nickname), include both, for example, "Alison Johnson, a.k.a. Alison Walker-Johnson."

**Property.** To identify property, be as specific as you can. There are no magic words. Your goal is simply to identify the property clearly

**Example of How to Delete a Clause (Clause 4 of Consent to Assignment of Lease)**

so that no misunderstanding will arise later. Normally, this means listing the make, model, type, color, identifying number if the item has one, and any other identifying characteristics that come to mind. For instance, if you're requesting repair of a computer under warranty, you might say "Dell XPS 13 laptop, ID # 445556."

**Events.** Take a similar approach when describing events, such as payment for a house cleaner. As long as you identify the date, time (if appropriate), and location, and include a clear description of what happened or what is supposed to happen, your description should be adequate.

## Signing the Forms

Each form has specific signing instructions, including who must sign, how many copies to make, whether notarization is required or recommended, requirements for a spouse's signature, or the need for witnesses.

> **CAUTION**
> **Always keep your signed copy in a safe place, along with any related documents or correspondence.** You might need this at some point—for example, if you end up in court over a dispute concerning an agreement or contract.

### How to Prepare an Attachment Page

If you need to add anything to a copy of one of the forms or agreements in this book, take the following steps:

1. If you want to add words to a clause and there's not enough space to insert the new language into the specific clause of the agreement, you can refer to it as an attachment by adding the words: "Clause [number] continued on Attachment A [or B or C and so on] of [name of agreement or form]."

    **EXAMPLE:** Clause 1 of the General Bill of Sale provides space for you to list the items you're selling. If there is not enough room to list all these items on the form, write the words "Clause 1 continued on Attachment A of the General Bill of Sale."

    Similarly, if you want to add a new clause, insert the words "Agreement continued on Attachment A of [name of agreement or form]" after the last clause of the agreement and before the place where the agreement gets signed. Use a separate attachment each time you need more room.

2. Make your own attachment form, using a sheet of blank white 8½" by 11" paper. At the top of the form, write "Attachment A [or B or C and so on] to [name of agreement or form] between [insert names of all parties]" for the first attachment, and so on. Then add the words "a continuation of [number clause]" if you're continuing a clause, or "an addition to [number clause]" if you're adding a new clause.

    **EXAMPLE:** "Attachment A to General Bill of Sale between Beth Spencer and Rich Portman. A continuation of Clause 1."

3. Type or print the additional information on the attachment.
4. Have both parties sign or initial the attachment at the bottom of each page.
5. Staple all attachments to the end of the main agreement or form.

## Notarization

When this book tells you that a form can (or should) be "notarized," it means that you can (or should) take your form to a notary public (or have one come to you) so that the notary can certify in writing that:

- you're the person you claim to be, and
- you've acknowledged under oath signing the document.

When having a form notarized, who needs to be present depends on the circumstances. If you're preparing a form that must be both witnessed and notarized (like the Power of Attorney forms in Chapter 1), you and your witnesses must appear together before the notary public so the witnesses can watch you sign the form. In other cases where more than one person signs the document, you can each visit the notary on your own, if you prefer. In that case, each signer will get a separate notarization certificate and you'll attach all of them to the document.

Very few legal documents need to be notarized or witnessed. Notarization and witnessing are usually limited to documents like a power of attorney involving real estate, which are going to be recorded at a public office charged with keeping such records—for example, a county land records office or registrar of deeds. Occasionally—but very rarely—state laws require witnesses or notaries to sign other types of documents.

The notary will want proof of your identity, such as a driver's license that bears your photo and signature. The notary will watch each of you sign (or, in some circumstances, you can simply acknowledge that you signed the document already) and then will complete an

**Sample Notarization Language**

---

**Certificate of Acknowledgment of Notary Public**

State of _____

County of _____ } ss

On _____, _____, before me, _____
_____, personally appeared _____
_____,
who proved to me on the basis of satisfactory evidence to be the person(s), whose name(s) is/are subscribed to the within instrument and acknowledged to me that he/she/they executed the same in his/her/their authorized capacity(ies) and that by his/her/their signature(s) on the instrument, the person(s), or the entity upon behalf of which the person(s) acted, executed the instrument.

I certify under PENALTY OF PERJURY under the laws of the State of _____
that the foregoing paragraph is true and correct.

WITNESS my hand and official seal.

[NOTARY SEAL]

Notary Public for the State of _____
My commission expires _____

acknowledgment, including a notarial seal or stamp. In some states, the notary may take your thumbprint for documents that affect real estate.

Your state might also have special requirements for the form or language of the notary certificate. A competent notary will know and follow your state's requirement. A sample notary acknowledgment is shown above.

To find a notary, try searching online. Some businesses have a notary public on staff, including many mail/shipping services, banks, and real estate offices. Most charge less than $20, and often the price is set by state law. You can usually pay a "mobile" notary more to come to you.

**TIP**
**Notarization is always an option.** Even if we don't suggest you have a form notarized, you may choose to—simply because it adds a measure of legal credibility.

## Spouse's Signature

If you'll be asked to sign a contract that makes you liable for a debt, such as a promissory note, the other person might ask that your spouse sign as well. This is most likely to happen if, for example, you're borrowing money to buy property that both spouses will use, or to help finance a new business venture. For more details, see the discussion of promissory notes, in Chapter 5.

## Resolving Disputes

No matter how airtight your document might be, real life can always creep in, and at some point you might have a legal dispute involving one of the forms or contracts in this book. For example, maybe your partner reneges on an agreement to share property when you split up, or you're upset because your dog sitter acted contrary to the terms of your pet care agreement. One way to resolve a dispute is through a court fight, but lawsuits and trials can be expensive, prolonged, and emotionally draining. It usually makes far more sense to attempt to resolve disputes through other means, including the following.

**Informal negotiation.** The parties to the dispute try to voluntarily work out their differences through open discussions, which often result in each compromising a little to put the matter to rest. It might make sense to have a trusted mutual friend informally negotiate an agreement.

**Mediation.** The parties try to achieve a voluntary settlement with the help of a neutral third party, a mediator. With mediation, the two of you get together to talk face to face about your disagreements, with the mediator working to help you communicate so that you can craft your own solution. No one has the power to impose a solution with mediation—rather, you must work out your own agreement voluntarily. Mediation is inexpensive, quick, confidential, and effective the majority of the time. Depending on your situation, you might want to contact a community mediation agency, which offers free or low-cost mediation, usually by trained community volunteers.

**Arbitration.** If mediation fails to resolve a dispute, arbitration is the next best choice. With arbitration, the parties allow a neutral third party, an arbitrator, to arrive at a binding decision in order to resolve the dispute. Normally, the decision is solely up to the arbitrator, and the parties agree beforehand to abide by the arbitrator's decision. In some situations, however, the parties establish certain rules in advance of the arbitration—for example, a limit on the amount of money that can be awarded. Where limits are set by the parties, the arbitrator is bound by them. Arbitration is almost always speedier and less expensive than litigation.

Ideally, you'd like to be able to settle disputes informally. Unfortunately, however, even when everyone tries in good faith, they don't always reach a compromise. Therefore, a dispute resolution clause (see the one shown below) lets you agree in advance on a framework mandating mediation and arbitration for resolving disputes. This dispute resolution clause is already in several of the forms in this book. If it's not on a particular form and you want to add it, you can find it on this book's online companion page in the file Disputes.rtf. (See Appendix A for details.) To add the dispute clause, simply follow the directions in "Editing the Forms," above, about adding a clause.

This dispute resolution clause allows the parties to make one of three choices:

- **Litigation.** You go to court and let a judge or jury resolve the dispute.
- **Mediation and possible litigation.** You agree to let a mediator help you try to reach a voluntary settlement of the dispute. If mediation doesn't accomplish this goal, either of you can take the dispute to court. You can name the mediator when you prepare the form or agree on one when the need arises.

---

**16. Disputes**

[choose one]:

☐ **Litigation.** If a dispute arises, any party may take the matter to court.

☐ **Mediation and possible litigation.** If a dispute arises, the parties will try in good faith to settle it through mediation conducted by [choose one]:

☐ _____ [name of mediator].

☐ a mediator to be mutually selected.

The parties will share the costs of the mediator equally. If the dispute is not resolved within 30 days after it is referred to the mediator, any party may take the matter to court.

☐ **Mediation and possible arbitration.** If a dispute arises, the parties will try in good faith to settle it through mediation conducted by [choose one]:

☐ _____ [name of mediator].

☐ a mediator to be mutually selected.

The parties will share the costs of the mediator equally. If the dispute is not resolved within 30 days after it is referred to the mediator, it will be arbitrated by [choose one]:

☐ _____ [name of arbitrator].

☐ an arbitrator to be mutually selected.

The arbitrator's decision will be binding and judgment on the arbitration award may be entered in any court that has jurisdiction over the matter. Costs of arbitration, including lawyers' fees, will be allocated by the arbitrator.

- **Mediation and possible arbitration.** You start by submitting the dispute to mediation. If mediation doesn't lead to a settlement, you submit the dispute to arbitration. The arbitrator makes a final decision that will be enforced by a court, if necessary. You can name the arbitrator when you prepare the form or agree on one when the need arises.

RESOURCE
**You'll find lots of information to help you understand common legal issues online at www.nolo.com, including in-depth articles, FAQs, and state laws covering dozens of legal topics.** If you do end up fighting a case in court, read *Represent Yourself in Court,* by Paul Bergman and Sara Berman. If the amount of money at stake in your case is below a certain dollar threshold (in most states the cap is somewhere between $5,000 and $20,000), you might be able to bring it in small claims court. In that case, see *Everybody's Guide to Small Claims Court,* by Cara O'Neill (Nolo).

## Do You Need a Lawyer?

Most of the contracts in this book cover relatively straightforward transactions. Just as you routinely negotiate deals to lend money to a friend or hire someone to paint your kitchen without formal legal help, you can safely complete the basic legal paperwork needed to record what you and the other party have agreed upon.

That said, creating a solid written agreement—especially where a lot of money or property is at stake—could require obtaining the advice of a lawyer. Fortunately, even when you seek a lawyer's help, the forms and information included here will let you keep a tight rein on legal fees. You'll have gotten a running start by learning about the legal issues and perhaps drawing up a rough draft of the needed document, allowing you and your lawyer to focus on the few points that might not be routine.

Ideally, you should find a lawyer who comes highly recommended from personal referrals. In order to minimize legal fees, you might look for someone who's willing to answer a few questions, or possibly to review a completed contract draft, but who respects your ability to prepare the actual paperwork.

---

### Get Forms Online

Remember, all of the forms and contracts found in this book are available for you to download on the book's companion page at www.nolo.com (see Appendix A for access instructions).

CHAPTER 1

# Caring for Children, Pets, and Property

**Form 1: Temporary Guardianship Authorization for Care of Minor** ............................ 12

**Form 2: Authorization for Minor's Medical Treatment** ............................ 13

**Form 3: Authorization for International Travel With Minor** ............................ 13

**Form 4: House-Sitting Instructions** ............................ 14

**Form 5: Children's Carpool Agreement** ............................ 15

**Form 6: Pet Care Agreement** ............................ 15

**Form 7: Authorization to Drive a Motor Vehicle** ............................ 16

**Form 8: Power of Attorney for Finances (Limited Power)** ............................ 17

**Form 9: Power of Attorney for Real Estate** ............................ 20

**Form 10: Notice of Revocation of Power of Attorney** ............................ 25

**Form 11: Request to Begin Special Education Process** ............................ 25

Many of the key decisions we make as adults affect the care of our children, finances, and property. This chapter includes several forms to make sure your family and property are well taken care of, even in your absence, such as a temporary guardianship authorization, a power of attorney for finances, and instructions for the care of your home and pets.

## Form 1: Temporary Guardianship Authorization for Care of Minor

You might find it necessary to leave your child in the care of another adult for a few days, weeks, or months. If so, you should give the caretaker permission to authorize medical care and make other important decisions for your child. These include school-related decisions—for example, if your child needs approval to go on a field trip, or becomes ill and needs to be picked up from school.

When you complete a temporary guardianship authorization, you are establishing what the law calls an "informal guardianship." By contrast, a formal guardianship requires court approval and is used most often when a child will be in a guardian's care for a long period of time—for example, when a young child moves in with grandparents because the parents have died. A formal guardianship permits the guardian to make more extensive decisions for a child, such as moving the child from one school to another.

An informal or temporary guardianship is most often used in these two situations:

- You will be traveling or otherwise unavailable for a relatively short period of time—for example, due to a hospital stay—and will leave your child in another adult's care.
- Your child lives with you and a stepparent who has not legally adopted your child. Because you travel frequently, the stepparent commonly functions as the primary caregiver.

If you have more than one child, you should prepare a separate temporary guardianship authorization for each child.

**RELATED TOPIC**

**Authorizing medical care.** When you make a temporary guardianship authorization, you should also consider making an Authorization for Minor's Medical Treatment, discussed below. Although the temporary guardianship form gives the temporary guardian explicit permission to authorize medical examinations, X-rays, hospital care, and other necessary treatments, the medical treatment authorization form allows you to spell out your child's medical history and needs in more detail. The two forms work well together. Whichever form you complete, you should inform your child's health care providers that the person you name as temporary guardian has your permission to make health care decisions for your child.

### Signing Instructions

You (the parent[s] or guardian[s]) and the temporary guardian must sign the Temporary Guardianship Authorization for Care of Minor before it will be valid. Print out two copies of the form (or enough copies to give each person who will be signing the form). The parent(s) and the temporary guardian should sign and date all copies of the authorization form. Give one of the signed documents to the temporary guardian. Keep the other signed document for your own records and store it in a safe place.

**FORM**

**Notarization is optional.** You can choose to have a form notarized, but it's not required. (See the Introduction for general advice on having a form notarized.) Notarization will add a measure of legal credibility, but it isn't usually necessary. For example, you probably don't need to have your temporary guardianship authorization form notarized if you will be leaving your child with a grandparent for a few days. But if you will be away from your child for a long time—especially if your child stays with a nonrelative—it might be a good idea to visit a notary.

## Form 2: Authorization for Minor's Medical Treatment

You can use a medical care authorization to permit an adult that you name to authorize necessary medical or dental care for your child. This can help you rest easier when your child is participating in sports or other organized activity outside of your supervision. You should provide this authorization to any adult who will be caring for your child when you are away, including babysitters and temporary guardians. This form provides details about your child's doctor, dentist, insurance, allergies, and ongoing medical conditions such as diabetes or asthma, as well as information on how to reach you while your child is in another's care.

If your child is participating in an organized activity, such as a basketball league or dance lessons, the sponsoring organization may require you to complete its own medical authorization for your child. It's fine to use both the organization's form and the one provided by this book as long as the two don't provide conflicting instructions or authorizations.

### Signing Instructions

You (the parent[s] or guardian[s]) must sign the Authorization for Minor's Medical Treatment document for it to be valid. Make two copies and sign and date both. Give one of the signed documents to the person who has permission to authorize medical treatment for your child. Keep the other signed document for your own records and store it in a safe place.

**FORM**

**Notarization is optional.** You can choose to have the authorization for medical treatment form notarized, but it's not required. (See the Introduction for general advice on having a form notarized.) Notarization will add a measure of legal credibility, but it isn't usually necessary.

## Form 3: Authorization for International Travel With Minor

Your child is unlikely to be permitted to travel outside the United States with someone other than a parent or legal guardian unless the travel companion has documentation showing the person's legal authority to travel with your child. If your child will be traveling internationally with someone who is not that child's legal parent or guardian, prepare an Authorization for International Travel With Minor to supply proof that you have given consent for your child to leave the country with another adult. The form also provides information about the child's travel plans and contact information for you (the parents or guardians).

If you have more than one child who will be traveling outside the country with another adult, prepare a separate authorization form for each child.

In planning your child's trip, check travel rules carefully. Start by calling the embassy or consulate for the country to which your child will be traveling. Ask whether the country has any rules or regulations governing adults traveling with an unrelated minor. Chances are good that the country does not, but it's always good to ask. If there are special requirements, you and the child's adult traveling companion can prepare for them in advance.

**RELATED TOPIC**

**Authorizing medical care.** This form does not permit the person traveling with your child to authorize medical care for the minor. To ensure that your child can receive any necessary medical treatment while traveling, you should also complete the Authorization for Minor's Medical Treatment, discussed just above.

### Signing Instructions

You (the parent[s] or guardian[s]) must sign the Authorization for International Travel With Minor for it to be valid. Make at least two copies of the form. You and your child's other parent (if any) should sign and date each copy of the document. If you and your child's other parent are divorced or separated, you must still obtain the signature of the second parent before authorizing your child to leave the country with another adult. This will eliminate the possibility that foreign authorities will detain the travelers, suspecting a violation of child custody laws.

Give one of the signed documents to the person who has permission to travel with your child. You and the other parent keep the other signed document(s) for your own records.

**FORM**

**Your international travel authorization should be notarized.** To have a form notarized, you must go to the notary before signing it. (See the Introduction for general advice on having a form notarized.) The acknowledgment of a notary public will give the form a greater degree of legitimacy, especially in the eyes of a foreign government. This could help if problems arise during the trip.

## Form 4: House-Sitting Instructions

Many people arrange to have a relative, a friend, or even a friend of a friend house-sit while they are away on vacation or for an extended period of time. Even if your house sitter is quite familiar with your home, it's always a good idea to provide written information about its care and maintenance. Use this form to specify details such as what to do about mail, newspapers, garbage, and recycling; gardening and yard maintenance; operation of appliances, locks, and security systems; and where you keep supplies. Write down everything you think the house sitter should know, including the location of emergency gas and water shutoff valves, and any special house rules, such as no smoking. Your house-sitting instructions should also provide details on how to reach you while you're away as well as the names and phone numbers of local contacts who can help with any problems or questions, such as a neighbor who has an extra key, your plumber, and your insurance company. Preparing detailed house-sitting instructions will greatly reduce the chances of problems and give you peace of mind while you're far from home.

**RELATED TOPIC**

**Pets, cars, and kids.** If your house sitter will be taking care of your pet or driving your car, be sure to complete the Pet Care Agreement and the Authorization to Drive a Motor Vehicle. And if your child will be staying at home in this house sitter's care, complete the Temporary Guardianship Authorization for Care of Minor.

## Signing Instructions

There are no signing instructions for the House-Sitting Instructions. Simply fill out the form and leave it with your house sitter. It's probably a good idea to give an extra copy to a friend or neighbor.

## Form 5: Children's Carpool Agreement

Whether it's a trip to school, lessons, clubs, or after-school jobs, carpools make it possible for families to share the burden of transporting children all over town. But as any carpool-savvy parent can tell you, there are good arrangements and there are those that don't work. Our form will help all carpool members get off on the right foot by recording their agreements on issues that should be discussed and settled at the outset. In addition, our form gives you a place to record important information that might come in handy. Think about the following issues and talk them out; then record your conclusions on the form:

- Who will be the drivers, and are you all satisfied that the drivers are qualified to drive and that they'll do so safely? Is each vehicle that will be used adequately insured?
- How long will the carpool driver wait for children who aren't ready when the carpool arrives? What should the driver do in the event that there is no one home at the drop off site?
- Identify two people who can care for your child in an emergency, as you do when asked by your school for your child's records.
- Identify any special considerations, such as a child's dietary restrictions (watch those carpool snacks), items that must be brought along (don't forget to check that the trumpet comes home from the music lesson), and personal quirks (with small children, seating arrangements can assume monumental importance).

## Signing Instructions

After you and the other parents have made your decisions about the issues raised in the Carpool Agreement, record your conclusions in the spaces provided. Then have each parent sign and date the document. Give a copy of the signed agreement to each parent and keep a copy for yourself.

**CAUTION**

**Unlike many of the forms in this book, your Carpool Agreement is not a legally binding document.** If a member doesn't live up to it, your only recourse is to talk it over and come to a consensus about what to do.

## Form 6: Pet Care Agreement

If you're going on a trip or will be otherwise unable to care for your pet for a period of time, you might leave your animal in the care of a neighbor or friend. If you do, it's a good idea to make a written agreement describing the arrangement and setting out clear instructions for your pet's care.

With this form, you can specify your pet's needs (including food, medication, exercise, and grooming), veterinarian contact information, special instructions such as vaccination due dates, how you can be reached, how you will reimburse the caregiver for any expenses involved in caring for your pet, and more. Having an agreement will greatly reduce the chances of a misunderstanding that might hurt your pet—or your relationship with the caregiver.

If you do find yourselves involved in a dispute, this agreement states that you and the pet caregiver will select a mutually agreeable third party to help you mediate the dispute and that you will share equally any costs of mediation. Mediation and other dispute resolution procedures are discussed in the Introduction.

**TIP**

**Payment for pet food and vet bills.** When a friend cares for your pet in their home, you might think it unnecessary to pay for a few dollars' worth of pet food. Think again—you are already asking for a big favor, one that is likely to be extended again only if you are scrupulous about the details. Even if your friend has several animals already and 10 bags of pet food in the garage, bring along more than enough chow to feed your pet while you will be away, plus some cash for unexpected expenses. Also, if your pet is prone to illness or is recovering from an illness or injury, make advance payment arrangements with your vet. Finally, make sure you notify your vet, in writing, that your friend has the authority to make any necessary care decisions while you are away. Your vet might have an authorization form for you to fill out, or might ask you to write a simple letter authorizing the caregiver to make decisions.

### Signing Instructions

You and the caregiver must sign the Pet Care Agreement for it to be valid. Make two copies. You should each sign and date both copies. Give the caregiver one of the signed documents and keep the other one for your own records.

## Form 7: Authorization to Drive a Motor Vehicle

Lending your vehicle to a friend or even a relative isn't always as simple as just handing over the keys. If the person who borrows your car is pulled over by the police or is involved in an accident, it will be important to be able to prove quickly that you agreed to lend out your car. Otherwise, there could be a delay while police investigate whether the vehicle is stolen. Completing this authorization form provides the important legal proof that you've given someone else permission to drive your vehicle.

This form provides a place to list important information, such as your insurance policy number, to help ensure that your guest driver (and car) are taken care of in the event of an accident or other mishap. If you want to set any restrictions on when or where the car may be used—for example, limiting driving to a specific geographic area or for a specific number of miles—you can do so.

This motor vehicle authorization form is designed for a car, but it will work fine for a motorcycle, truck, or other motor vehicle, such as a motorboat.

### Signing Instructions

You (the vehicle owner) must sign your Authorization to Drive a Motor Vehicle form to make it valid. Make two copies of the authorization document. Sign and date both copies. Give one of the signed originals to the person who will be driving your car or other vehicle. Keep the other for your own records.

## Form 8: Power of Attorney for Finances (Limited Power)

A power of attorney is a legal document in which you give another person legal authority to act on your behalf. In legal jargon, you're "the principal," and the person to whom you give this authority is your "attorney-in-fact" or "agent." In this context, "attorney" refers to anyone authorized to act on another's behalf; it's most definitely not restricted to lawyers.

Your attorney-in-fact (including any alternates you choose to name) should be someone you trust completely to act in your best interests—such as a spouse, relative, or close friend—who has enough common sense and experience to carry out the tasks you assign.

A limited power of attorney for finances lets you appoint an attorney-in-fact to help you with one or more specific, clearly defined tasks involving your finances. For example, you might want to name a relative or close friend to monitor certain investments—and sell them, if necessary—while you are on vacation or in the hospital for a short period of time. Or you might need someone to sign business or legal papers for you while you are unavailable.

> **CAUTION**
> **Don't use this power of attorney to give someone control over real estate transactions.** If you need an attorney-in-fact to sell, buy, or manage real property for you, use the Power of Attorney for Real Estate.

> **CAUTION**
> **New York and Pennsylvania have special forms.** If you live in New York or Pennsylvania, don't use Form 8, because your state has unique requirements for powers of attorney. Instead, use Form 8NY or Form 8PA. You can find both of these forms in Appendix B, and they are also available on this book's companion page.

### When the Power of Attorney Begins and Ends

Your power of attorney takes effect on a date you specify in your document. It ends under the circumstances described below.

**The termination date.** When you prepare your document, you can specify the date on which it will expire. You can enter a specific day, such as the day you expect to return from a trip. Or, you can make an open-ended document. If you don't specify an ending date, your attorney-in-fact is legally permitted to act for you until you revoke the power of attorney in writing.

**You revoke the power of attorney.** You can revoke your power of attorney at any time, as long as you are of sound mind. (And if you aren't of sound mind, the document terminates automatically, so you don't have to worry about revoking it.) To revoke your document, all you need to do is fill out a simple form, sign it in front of a notary public, and give copies to the attorney-in-fact and to people or institutions the attorney-in-fact has been dealing with. Form 10 is a revocation form you can use.

**After a divorce.** In a number of states, if your spouse is your attorney-in-fact and you divorce, your ex-spouse's authority is immediately terminated. Regardless of state law, however, if you've named your spouse as attorney-in-fact and you get divorced, you should revoke your power of attorney and make a new one.

**No attorney-in-fact is available.** Your power of attorney will automatically end if your attorney-in-fact dies, resigns, or becomes unable to represent you for any other reason.

**You become incapacitated or die.** Your power of attorney states that it will automatically end if you become incapacitated or die. In most states, however, if the attorney-in-fact doesn't know of your incapacity or death and continues to act on your behalf, these actions are still valid.

To create your limited power of attorney, you'll enter basic information about you (the "principal") and your attorney-in-fact, followed by the exact powers you want to grant—such as selling your car, signing loan papers while you're out of town, or monitoring your investments. Be as specific as possible—for example, if you want someone to sell your car for a minimum of $15,000 cash only, spell this out. Include relevant bank account numbers and complete descriptions of any property the attorney-in-fact may deal with.

The power of attorney form gives your attorney-in-fact the authority to act for you in all matters that you list. The attorney-in-fact, however, has a legal obligation to take only those actions that are in your best interests, and to represent you honestly and carefully.

This power of attorney form includes language designed to reassure third parties that they can accept the document without risk of legal liability. This "indemnification" clause clearly states that a third party may rely on the document without worry—in other words, the third party may conduct business with your attorney-in-fact as you have instructed—unless the person knows that you have revoked the document.

**TIP**

**Financial institutions might have their own power of attorney forms.** If you're giving your attorney-in-fact authority to deal with a bank, brokerage firm, or other financial institution, find out whether it has its own power of attorney form. If it does, you'll probably want to use that form instead of this one. Doing so will reduce hassles for your attorney-in-fact, because a financial institution will know what powers its own form grants and will have no need to quibble with your document.

## Signing Instructions

A Power of Attorney for Finances is a serious document. To make it legally valid and effective, you must observe certain formalities when you sign it. Specifically, you must have your power of attorney form notarized, and, in some states, you'll need to sign your document in front of witnesses. (See "States That Require Witnesses for a Power of Attorney," below.)

### Limited vs. Durable Powers of Attorney

This form is typically referred to as a "limited" or "conventional" power of attorney. As you might know, there is another type of power of attorney, called a durable power of attorney, that remains in effect even if you become incapacitated and can no longer make decisions for yourself. Durable powers of attorney are commonly signed in advance of need by older or ill people who realize that at some point they might require help managing their affairs. In contrast, limited powers of attorney (like this one) are used when you want someone to handle specific transactions for you at a set time. Because state laws vary in this area, if you want a durable power of attorney, you will need more extensive information. One excellent resource is *Quicken WillMaker & Trust* software, with which you can create a valid will, durable power of attorney for finances, health care directive, and final arrangements document using your computer.

In a few states, your attorney-in-fact must sign the power of attorney before taking action under the document. In other states, the attorney-in-fact's signature is not required,

## States That Require Witnesses for a Power of Attorney

Most states don't require a power of attorney to be signed in front of witnesses. The few states that do and the number of witnesses required are listed below. Witness requirements normally consist of the following:

- Witnesses must be present when you sign the document in front of the notary.
- Witnesses must be mentally competent adults.
- The person who will serve as your attorney-in-fact can't be a witness.

Choose witnesses who will be easily available if they are ever needed. It's obviously a good idea to choose witnesses who live nearby and will be easy to contact.

| State | Number of Witnesses | Other Requirements |
|---|---|---|
| Arizona | 1 | Witness may not be your attorney-in-fact, the spouse or child of your attorney-in-fact, or the notary public who acknowledges your document. |
| Connecticut | 2 | Neither witness may be your attorney-in-fact. |
| Delaware | 1 | Witness may not be your attorney-in-fact; be related to you by blood, marriage, or adoption; or be entitled to inherit a portion of your estate under your will or trust. |
| Florida | 2 | Neither witness may be your attorney-in-fact. |
| Georgia | 1 | Your witness may not be your attorney-in-fact or the notary public who acknowledges your document. |
| Illinois | 1 | Witness may not be your attorney-in-fact, or someone related to you or your attorney-in-fact |
| Illinois (continued) | | by blood, marriage, or adoption; a person who provides health services to you; or an owner or operator of a health care facility where you are a resident. |
| Maryland | 2 | Witnesses may not be your attorney-in-fact. |
| New York | 2 | Witnesses should not be your agent, and neither witness should be a person who stands to benefit from your power of attorney document—for example, by receiving gifts you have authorized your agent to make. (Use Forms 8NY and 9NY.) |
| Pennsylvania | 2 | Witnesses may not be your agent or the person who signs your document for you. (Use Forms 8PA and 9PA.) |
| South Carolina | 2 | Neither witness may be your attorney-in-fact. |

but it's a fine idea to include it anyway. The attorney-in-fact's signature acts as assurance that the attorney-in-fact has read and fully understands the document, and is willing to assume the responsibility of acting prudently and honestly on your behalf. For this reason, this power of attorney form includes a blank for the attorney-in-fact to sign. However, your attorney-in-fact doesn't need to sign until it's time to use the document, and that signature doesn't need to be notarized (except in New York).

**FORM**

**A notary public must acknowledge your signature on the power of attorney.** In some states, notarization is required by law to make the power of attorney valid. But even where law doesn't require it, custom does. A power of attorney that isn't notarized might not be accepted by people your attorney-in-fact needs to deal with.

If you will have your form witnessed (see "States That Require Witnesses for a Power of Attorney," above), everyone who has to sign the form must appear together in front of the notary. After watching each of you sign, the notary will complete and attach a certificate of acknowledgment to your document.

For more information on finding and using a notary, see this book's Introduction.

Give the original signed and notarized document to the person you authorized. Your attorney-in-fact will need it as proof of authority to act on your behalf. Make a copy for yourself and store it in a safe place. If you wish, you can give copies of your power of attorney to the people your attorney-in-fact will need to deal with—for example, banks or government offices. If your financial power of attorney is already in their records, it could eliminate hassles for your attorney-in-fact later. Be sure to keep a list of everyone to whom you give a copy.

**CAUTION**

**Revoking a power of attorney.** If you later revoke your power of attorney, you must notify each institution of the revocation. We discuss the Notice of Revocation of Power of Attorney below.

## Form 9: Power of Attorney for Real Estate

A power of attorney for real estate allows you to give someone the authority to buy or sell a piece of real estate for you, or to conduct any other business concerning real estate that you own. A power of attorney for real estate is a "limited" power of attorney, meaning that it automatically expires if you become incapacitated or die. (If you want a document that will stay in effect even if you become incapacitated, you need a "durable" power of attorney—see "Limited vs. Durable Power of Attorney," above.)

A power of attorney for real estate can be useful in a number of situations. Here are a few common ones:

- You will be out of town or otherwise unavailable when important real estate documents need to be signed (particularly if electronic signatures aren't an option).
- You will not be available to look after your real estate for a limited period of time.
- You live far away from property that you own and you want to authorize someone to manage it in your absence.

**EXAMPLE 1:** Alan is purchasing a condominium. Escrow has been opened at a title company, but the closing is delayed for several weeks. Because of the delay, the closing is now scheduled for the middle of Alan's long-planned mountain-climbing expedition, in an area with no internet access. To solve this problem, Alan prepares a power of attorney for real estate, authorizing his sister Jennifer to sign any documents necessary to complete the closing and to withdraw any amounts of money (from an identified bank account) necessary to pay expenses and costs incurred because of the closing. Alan specifies that Jennifer's authority expires on the date he is to return from his trip.

Alan discusses his plans with his bank and the title company before he leaves, to be sure they'll accept the power of attorney and the authority of his attorney-in-fact. Both organizations assure him they'll accept a valid power of attorney for real estate. He has copies of his power of attorney placed in the bank's records and in his file at the title company. He leaves the original document with Jennifer, his attorney-in-fact.

**EXAMPLE 2:** Ann owns a summer cottage. Her friend June lives in the next cottage as her permanent home. Ann and June agree that because June is on the spot she'll take care of renting Ann's cottage, collecting rent, and paying all house bills and costs. Ann prepares a power of attorney for real estate giving June authority to represent Ann for all transactions concerning her property at 20 Heron Lake Road. Ann specifies that the power of attorney will continue indefinitely. She also provides that June has no authority to sell the cottage or to represent her in any transaction that doesn't concern the cottage.

TIP

**Make sure your power of attorney will be accepted.** The most important thing you can do to ensure that financial institutions, such as your mortgage lender or title company, will accept your power of attorney is talk with them in advance. Be sure that they're willing to accept the document and the authority of your attorney-in-fact. Your financial institution might ask you to include certain language in your form or to use its own power of attorney form. If so, you should comply with its wishes.

(If you're working with more than one financial institution, you could end up using more than one form.) Even though you can make a perfectly valid, legal document with this form, your financial institution might balk at accepting any form other than its own. Following your financial institution's recommendations will save time and trouble for you and your attorney-in-fact.

CAUTION

**New York and Pennsylvania have special forms.** If you live in New York or Pennsylvania, don't use Form 9, because your state has unique requirements for powers of attorney. Instead, use Form 9NY or Form 9PA. You can find both of these forms in Appendix B and on this book's companion page.

## Instructions for Preparing Your Power of Attorney for Real Estate

Here are instructions for filling in the Power of Attorney for Real Estate form.

### Step 1. Principal and Attorney-in-Fact

In the first four blanks on the form, fill in your name and the city, county, and state where you live. Enter your name as it appears on official documents such as your driver's license, bank accounts, and real estate deeds. This might or might not be the name on your birth certificate.

**EXAMPLE:** Your birth certificate lists your name as Rose Mary Green. But you've always gone by Mary, and always sign documents as Mary McNee, your married name. You would use Mary McNee on your power of attorney.

Be sure to enter all names in which you hold bank accounts or other property your attorney-in-fact will be dealing with. This will make that person's job far easier. If you're including more than one name, begin by entering your full legal name, followed by "a.k.a." ("also known as"). Then enter your other names.

If during the course of a year you live in more than one state, use the address in the state where you vote, register vehicles, own valuable property, have bank accounts, or run a business. If you've made your will, health care directives, or a living trust, be consistent: Use the address in the state you declared as your residence in those documents.

Next, type in the name of the person who has agreed to serve as your attorney-in-fact. Then enter the city, county, and state where your attorney-in-fact lives.

### Step 2. Description of Your Real Property

There is a large blank space following the first paragraph of the form. In it, type a description of the real estate your power of attorney will govern. Enter the exact street address, if your property has one. Then, attach a copy of the deed to your power of attorney form to avoid the trouble of retyping the lengthy and often confusing legal description contained in the deed.

**SAMPLE INSERT:**

> 9 Lotus Lane, Danville, CA 94558, Contra Costa County, California, as further described in the attached deed.

If you're up for it, you can type in the legal description instead. But be sure to type the entire description, exactly as it appears on the deed.

**SAMPLE INSERT:**

> LOT 195, as shown upon that certain map entitled, "Map of Greenbrae Sub. No. One, Marin Co. Calif.," filed May 2, 1946, in Book 6 of Maps, at Page 7, Marin County Records.

### Step 3. Limiting the Powers Granted to the Attorney-in-Fact

Read through the powers described in the second paragraph of the document. If you don't want to grant one or more of the numbered powers, strike out or delete those that you don't need. If you just want to limit the numbered powers in some way, include your instructions in the blank space following the list of powers. For example, you might want to forbid your attorney-in-fact from selling your property; you can type that limitation in the blank space.

If you don't want to limit the powers in any way, strike out or delete the phrase "However, my attorney-in-fact shall not have the power to".

### Step 4. Additional Powers

In the fourth paragraph of the form, you can authorize your attorney-in-fact to carry out any additional powers related to the real estate powers you've granted. For example, you might want to authorize your attorney-in-fact to withdraw funds from a named bank account to cover any costs that arise in relation to their duties.

**SAMPLE CLAUSE:**

> I further grant to my attorney-in-fact full authority to act in any manner both proper and necessary to the exercise of the foregoing powers, <u>including withdrawing funds from my checking account, #4482 478 880, Anderson Valley Savings and Loan, Boonville, CA</u>, and I ratify every act that my attorney-in-fact may lawfully perform in exercising those powers.

If you don't want to add any powers to the document, strike out or delete the word "including."

### Step 5. Termination Date

In the last paragraph of the form, type in a specific date on which you want the power of attorney to expire. (See "When the Power of Attorney Begins and Ends," in the instructions for Form 8, above.)

If you want the power of attorney to continue indefinitely, strike out or delete "or until _____ , whichever comes first." If you do so, and you later want to terminate the power of attorney, you must revoke it in writing.

### Step 6. Preparation Statement

Insert the name, signature, and address of the person creating the power of attorney document —usually this is the principal. Some states or counties require a preparation statement on documents that will be recorded, but even where the law doesn't require it, tradition often does.

## Signing Instructions

A power of attorney is a serious document, and to make it effective you must observe certain formalities when you sign it. Fortunately, these requirements aren't difficult to meet.

## Notarization

A notary public must acknowledge your signature on your power of attorney document. Go to the notary public with your witnesses (if any), and sign your document in the notary's presence. See the Introduction of this book for more information about notarization.

## Witnesses

Most states don't require the power of attorney to be signed in front of witnesses. (See "States That Require Witnesses for a Power of Attorney," in the instructions for Form 8, above.) Nevertheless, it doesn't hurt to have a witness or two watch you sign, and sign the document themselves. Witnesses' signatures may make the power of attorney more acceptable to lawyers, banks, insurance companies, and other entities the attorney-in-fact may have to deal with.

If you're giving your attorney-in-fact authority to handle real estate in a state other than the state where you live, be sure the document has at least the number of witnesses required by the state where the real property is located. Otherwise, you may not be able to record the power of attorney in that state.

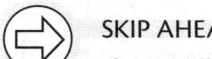

**SKIP AHEAD**
**If you will be using the downloadable forms on this book's online companion page to create your Power of Attorney for Real Estate, you don't need to read the cautionary instructions that follow.** Skip to the section on the attorney-in-fact's signature just below. The form on the companion page contains instructions to help you print the right number of signature lines. (See Appendix A for details on accessing the companion page.)

**CAUTION**
**The Power of Attorney for Real Estate form in the back of the book has multiple last pages that might, at first glance, appear to be duplicates.** Each of these pages is slightly different, however. Choose only the last page that has room for the number of witnesses your state requires—none, one, or two. (See "States That Require Witnesses for a Power of Attorney," in the instructions above, for the appropriate number.) Then, check the page numbers of your document to make sure everything's in proper order and you aren't missing pages or including any extras.

## The Attorney-in-Fact's Signature

In a few states, your attorney-in-fact must sign the power of attorney before taking action under the document. In other states, the attorney-in-fact's signature is not required, but it's a fine idea to include it anyway. The attorney-in-fact's signature acts as assurance that the attorney-in-fact has read and fully understands the document, and is willing to assume the responsibility of acting prudently and honestly on your behalf. For this reason, the form includes a blank for the attorney-in-fact to sign. However, your attorney-in-fact doesn't need to sign until it's time to use the document, and that signature doesn't need to be notarized (except in New York).

### Putting Your Power of Attorney on Public Record

You must put a copy of your power of attorney on file in the county land records office, called the county recorder's or land registry office in most states. This is called "recording" or "registration" in some states. If you don't record the power of attorney, your attorney-in-fact may not be permitted to handle real estate transactions for you.

Recording makes it clear to all interested parties that the attorney-in-fact has power over the property at issue. County land records are checked whenever real estate changes hands or is mortgaged. If, for example, your attorney-in-fact is supposed to sell or mortgage a piece of property for you, there must be something in the public records that proving the authority to do so.

If you put your power of attorney on public record and then later revoke it in writing, you must also record the notice of revocation. You can make a notice of revocation using the Notice of Revocation of Power of Attorney.

### Where to Record Your Power of Attorney

In most states, each county has its own land records office (often called the office of the "county recorder" or "registry of deeds"). Take the power of attorney to the office in the county where the real estate is located. If you are granting your attorney-in-fact authority over more than one parcel of real estate, record the power of attorney in each county where you own property.

### How to Record a Document

You might be able to record your document by mail, but it's safer to go in person. Before you go, check the county's website for details about fees, required forms or coversheets, required margins, and location of the land records office. If you have questions, give the recorder's office a call. When you get there, the clerk will make a copy of your document for the public records. It will be assigned a reference number, often called an "instrument number." The office will charge a fee (often per page) for recording the document.

### What to Do With the Signed Document

Give the original signed, notarized, and recorded document to the attorney-in-fact, who will need it as proof of authority to act on your behalf.

### Making and Distributing Copies

You should give copies of your power of attorney to the people your attorney-in-fact will need to deal with—banks or title companies, for example. If your power of attorney is in their records, it could eliminate hassles for your attorney-in-fact later.

Be sure to keep a list of everyone to whom you give a copy. If you later revoke your power of attorney, notify each institution of the revocation.

### Keeping Your Document Up to Date

If you've made a power of attorney without a specific termination date, you should redo it every year or so. Banks and other financial institutions may be reluctant to accept a power of attorney that's more than a couple of years old, even though the document is still technically valid. You should destroy any copies of the old power of attorney document and notify the people and institutions with copies of the former document that you have revoked your old power of attorney and made a new one.

## Form 10: Notice of Revocation of Power of Attorney

You can use a Notice of Revocation of Power of Attorney form in two situations:
- You want to revoke your power of attorney before the termination date set out in the document.
- Your power of attorney has ended as specified in the document, but you want to be absolutely sure that all institutions (such as banks, stockbrokers, and insurance companies) and people (such as your attorney or accountant) who have received it know that it is no longer in force.

**Signing Instructions**

Sign and date the Notice of Revocation in front of a notary public for your state, as explained in the discussion of the Power of Attorney for Finances (Limited Power).

> **CAUTION**
> **If you recorded your power of attorney, record the Notice of Revocation.** If you put your power of attorney on file in the public records office and it hasn't expired on its own, you should also record your Notice of Revocation. Otherwise, people who don't actually know of your revocation are entitled to continue to deal with your attorney-in-fact on your behalf.

## Form 11: Request to Begin Special Education Process

This form can be used by parents who believe their child is in need of special help from their school district. A federal law—the Individuals with Disabilities Education Act (IDEA)— gives parents and guardians the right to request evaluations (assessments) of their children for physical or psychological disabilities that could affect their ability to learn. Upon your request, the school must present you with an assessment plan, listing all testing to be done on your child. Assessments usually include objective tests of your child's abilities in all areas of suspected disability (for example, reading, memory, motor skills, or vision). In addition to formal tests, assessments often include subjective information relating to your child's educational status, such as comments by teachers, the school psychologist, or a classroom aide.

The IDEA requires the school to provide special services (an Individualized Education Program, or IEP) to a child found to have disabilities. "Special education" is the broad term used to describe the educational system for children who have disabilities, such as intellectual disabilities; autism; specific learning disabilities; hearing, speech, language, orthopedic, or visual impairment; or serious emotional disturbance.

Your child's eligibility for special education will depend on the results of the assessment. This letter starts the formal process by requesting an initial assessment of your child's eligibility for special education, an assessment plan, and general information on the IEP process.

This letter also asks the school district to provide a copy of your child's school file, including all tests, report cards, disciplinary records, and teacher notes about your child, so you can learn everything they already know about your child at school. This information is crucial as you assess your child's difficulties and the need for special education services. You have a legal right to inspect and review any educational record relating to your child. If your child has not yet been found eligible for services under the IDEA, you have the right to a copy of the school's file under the Family Educational Rights and Privacy Act (FERPA; 20 U.S.C. § 1232g). State laws also might give you a right to your child's file. Rules vary in different states, but you should be entitled to obtain the file without unnecessary delay. You may be charged for the copies as long as the fee "does not effectively prevent you from exercising your right to inspect and review the records" (34 C.F.R. § 300.617).

Once you send this letter, the school district is required by federal law to inform you of the regulations, guidelines, and procedures that apply to special education services and to begin the process of evaluation (assessment). Send this Request to Begin Special Education Process to the special education administrator at your child's school. Ask your child's teacher or the school principal for this person's name and address. Be sure to include a brief summary of your child's difficulties at school, such as developmental delays in language or reading problems, that you have noticed or have been told about by teachers, doctors, friends, or anyone who has spent time with your child.

RESOURCE
**For a comprehensive and thorough guide to special education laws and services,** see *The Complete IEP Guide*, by Lawrence Siegel (Nolo).

## Signing Instructions

There are no specific signing instructions for the Request to Begin Special Education Process. Simply sign the form and keep a copy for your records.

---

### Describing Your Child's Special Needs

It is common for parents to recognize that their child has problems with school and simply not know what to do about them. It could be that your child's difficulties can be isolated and addressed very specifically, or the problems might be more wide-ranging. Following are examples of difficulties your child may be experiencing in school that you should mention in your letter to the special education administrator:

- academic problems in reading, spelling, or math
- delays in developmental areas, such as language or fine motor skills
- difficulties processing or retaining information, such as understanding simple instructions or problems with short- or long-term memory
- social or emotional problems
- trouble sleeping, eating, or getting along with family
- sustained difficulties in paying attention or staying focused
- inappropriate or hyperactive behavior, or
- delays in physical milestones, or other physiological difficulties, such as hearing loss, sight problems, difficulties with mobility, or handwriting problems.

Be as specific as possible in describing your child's difficulties, but do not worry about listing everything. Don't get bogged down in things such as special classes or eligibility. Just write down what you have observed about your child's behavior, focusing on specific patterns. Keep in mind that this is just the beginning of the process. Trained professionals and assessments will help determine whether your intuition is correct.

# Chapter 2

# Basic Estate Planning

**Form 12: Property Worksheet** ................................................................. 28

**Form 13: Beneficiary Worksheet** ............................................................. 29

**Forms 14 and 15: Basic Wills** .................................................................. 30

    Form 14: Will for Adult With No Children ........................................... 32

    Form 15: Will for Adult With Child(ren) ............................................... 32

**Form 16: Will Codicil** ............................................................................... 34

Making arrangements for what will happen to your property after you die is called estate planning. Generally, if you die without a will or other legal means for transferring property, your property will be distributed to certain close relatives—your spouse or domestic partner, children, parents, or siblings—under state "intestacy" laws.

Making a will is an important part of estate planning. For many people, a will, coupled with naming beneficiaries for retirement plans, insurance policies, and other investments, is the only estate plan they need. Whether that is true for you or not depends on your circumstances. Broadly speaking, the more wealth you possess, the more you'll want to consider legal issues beyond the scope of a will, such as avoiding probate—the court-supervised process of gathering and distributing a deceased person's assets. And, depending on your situation, you might want to provide for a child with a disability, establish a fund for grandchildren, or make charitable gifts.

This chapter introduces the concept of estate planning and provides some useful worksheets and some basic will forms. Resources listed here explain where to go for more detailed information.

## Form 12: Property Worksheet

Before you write a will or other estate planning document, you might find it helpful to inventory your property, including real estate, cash, securities, cars, household goods, digital assets, and business personal property, such as a company you own or the right to receive royalties. Filling out the Property Worksheet can jog your memory to make sure you don't overlook important items.

Describe each asset on the Property Worksheet under the appropriate section of the "Property" column. If an asset such as a house or car is jointly owned, specify the percentage you own.

Even if you haven't made a will, you might have already named someone to get some of your property at your death. For example, if you have an IRA, 401(k) retirement plan, or insurance policy, you have probably named a beneficiary and alternate beneficiary on a form provided by the account custodian company. If you own real estate, you may hold it in joint tenancy with right of survivorship, meaning that the other joint owner will automatically inherit your share at your death. If you've already named someone to inherit an asset after your death, write down the beneficiary's name on the Property Worksheet under "Name of Any Existing Beneficiary."

The Property Worksheet also prompts you to list your "digital assets," such as your social media accounts, email addresses, apps, or online memberships. Most of these assets won't pass through your estate when you die, but your executor might need to access them in order to wrap up your estate. After using the Property Worksheet to brainstorm about what digital assets you have, consider creating a separate document that includes (1) a list of your digital assets, (2) details on how to access them, and (3) instructions on what to do with those assets after your death. Keep this document in a secure place, and make sure your executor knows how to find it.

### Signing Instructions

You don't need to sign the Property Worksheet. Simply fill it out and use it when preparing your will or other estate planning document.

**RESOURCE**
**Organize your personal information.**
*Get It Together: Organize Your Records So Your Family Won't Have To*, by Melanie Cullen (Nolo), helps you leave survivors a clear record of your important documents and information, including secured places and passwords, retirement accounts, insurance policies, real estate records, and much more. It also provides a road map to the arrangements you have made for after your death.

## Form 13: Beneficiary Worksheet

Like the Property Worksheet, the Beneficiary Worksheet can help you get ready to draft estate planning documents. You'll list each item of property and then the people or organizations to whom you want to leave the property. If you name more than one beneficiary to share a specific gift, state the percentage share each is to receive.

It is also highly advisable to name an alternate beneficiary or beneficiaries for each gift, in case your first choice dies before you do.

You can also list people who owe you money, if you want to forgive these debts at your death. For example, if you loaned your best friend $10,000 and he pays you back with interest $100 a month, it will take him many years to pay off the debt. If he still owes you money when you die, you can forgive or waive the balance due. This means that your heirs cannot go after your friend for the rest.

Finally, list a "residuary" beneficiary or beneficiaries. This is one or more people or organizations who will get everything that's left after your specific gifts are distributed. Do this even if you are sure you have identified all your property and named a beneficiary to receive it; there is always a chance that you'll acquire additional property between the date you make your will and your death.

 **TIP**
**Do you need to use the Beneficiary Worksheet?** If you plan to leave all your property to one or a very few people (for example, "all property to my spouse, or if she predeceases me, to my children in equal shares"), there is no need to complete the Beneficiary Worksheet. You already know who will get your property at your death, and you can turn to the will forms that follow.

## Signing Instructions

You don't need to sign the Beneficiary Worksheet. Simply fill it out and use it when preparing your will or other estate planning documents.

### Common Property That Might Already Have Beneficiaries

You might have already planned the eventual disposition of much of your property before you prepare a will. Here are some examples of property for which you might have already named a beneficiary:

- bank accounts, naming a payable-on-death beneficiary (on a form provided by the bank)
- real estate, either naming a beneficiary on a transfer-on-death deed or holding it with someone else in joint tenancy, in tenancy by the entirety, or (in community property states) as community property with right of survivorship with your spouse
- securities, registering them in transfer-on-death form if your state law allows it
- real estate or vehicles for which you have named transfer-on-death beneficiaries (not available in all states)
- retirement accounts, naming a beneficiary (on a form provided by the account custodian) to take whatever is still in the account at your death, and
- life insurance policies, naming a beneficiary (on a form provided by the company) to receive the proceeds at your death.

> ### Nolo Resources on Estate Planning
>
> Nolo publishes several books and software products containing more sophisticated—but still easy-to-use—information on wills and living trusts. A living trust is the document used most often to avoid probate, the process of distributing a person's property under court supervision. See, for example:
>
> - *Nolo's Guide to Estate Planning*, by Liza Hanks, is a comprehensive guide to estate planning, covering everything from basic estate planning to avoiding probate to using life insurance to help protect your loved ones. If you haven't yet decided how to approach your estate planning tasks, read this thorough overview.
> - *Quicken WillMaker & Trust* lets you make a will online or using interactive software. With *WillMaker*, you can make a more sophisticated will than those offered here. For example, you can choose among three ways to provide property management for children, should you die before they are competent to handle property themselves. In addition, with *WillMaker* you can create a living trust, a health care directive (living will), a durable power of attorney for finances, transfer-on-death deeds, a document that expresses your wishes for your funeral and burial, and more.
> - *8 Ways to Avoid Probate*, by Mary Randolph, explains important and often overlooked ways to avoid probate. It is now possible to avoid probate for many kinds of property without creating a living trust. If you vaguely know you should be paying attention to probate avoidance, but dread thinking about it, start with this small but thorough book.
> - *Special Needs Trusts: Protect Your Child's Financial Future*, by Kevin Urbatsch and Jessica Farinas Jones, explains how you can leave money to a loved one who has a disability, without interfering with eligibility for SSI or Medicaid benefits.

## Forms 14 and 15: Basic Wills

A basic will is easy to make. It's also easy to change or revoke; you won't be stuck with it if you change your mind later. With the will forms in this book, you can:

- leave your property to anyone you wish
- name a guardian to raise young children if you can't, and
- appoint an executor to carry out your will's terms.

This section gives an overview of making a basic will. Next come two bare-bones forms, which can be used by residents of all states except Louisiana.

These wills are a good choice if you have a simple situation. They're also an option if you want to make a will quickly, perhaps on the eve of a long trip. Maybe you plan to draft a more extensive will for the long term. Precisely because these forms are short, simple, and easy to use, they do not include a lot of options. For example, they do not let you create a trust to hold property that may be left to children or young adults.

If you have children, use the Will for Adult With Child(ren). Otherwise, use the Will for Adult With No Children.

Anyone who is of legal age (18 years old in most states) and of sound mind can make a valid will. You have to be very far gone before your will can be invalidated on the grounds that you were mentally incompetent. If you're reading and understanding this book, your mind is sound enough to make a will.

## CAUTION

**Do not just fill in a will form by hand.** A will should not contain a mix of handwritten and machine-printed material. The forms in this book will allow you to sketch out a draft of your document. But then you'll need to use your computer to download, edit, and print a fully typed final version of your will.

**Leaving specific items.** If you want to list specific items of property you're leaving through your will, you'll use the "Specific Gifts" section. When you list items, describe them so that your executor—and anyone else—will know exactly what you meant. There is no need to use formal legal descriptions unless they are really necessary to identify the property. Here are some examples of good property descriptions:

- "my house at 435 76th Avenue, Chicago, Illinois"
- "all household furnishings and possessions in my house at 435 76th Avenue, Chicago, Illinois," and
- "$10,000 from my savings account, No. 44444, at First National Bank, Chicago, Illinois."

Then you'll need to say what you want to happen to the rest of your property, which is called your "residuary." For example, say you make a few small specific gifts and want everything else to go to your three children. You would use the "Specific Gifts" section to make your specific gifts and the "Residuary Estate" clause to leave everything else to your children.

## CAUTION

**Don't use broad categories or descriptions of people.** You might be tempted to refer to beneficiaries with phrases like "all my children," "my surviving children," "my lawful heirs," or "my issue." Don't do it. Name each beneficiary individually to avoid any confusion later.

**Leaving everything.** If you want to leave everything to just one beneficiary, or a group of them—your spouse or your three children, for example—don't use the "Specific Gifts" part of the will. Instead, use the "Residuary Estate" clause. Because "residuary" simply refers to the rest of your estate and you have made no specific gifts, everything will go to the person(s) you name as your residuary beneficiary(ies).

**Property with debt.** When you leave property, any encumbrances on it—for example, a mortgage—pass with the property. In other words, the beneficiary takes the debt as well as the property.

**Naming your executor.** In your will, you must name someone to be in charge of winding up your affairs after your death. This person is called your executor (the term "personal representative" is used in some states). The executor must shepherd your property through probate—the court process of distributing the property of a deceased person—if it's necessary, and must see that your property is distributed according to the wishes expressed in your will.

Many people name their spouse or a grown child as executor. The executor usually doesn't need special financial or legal expertise. The important thing is that the person you choose is completely trustworthy, reasonably organized, and the type to deal fairly with other beneficiaries.

**Preparing your will.** Use the forms in this book to make a rough draft of your will. For this initial draft, you can fill in the blanks by hand, cross out clauses you don't need, and renumber the remaining clauses. Then, either retype the entire will, or download, edit, and print a will form from this book's companion page. (See Appendix A.)

When you're done, read your will carefully to make sure you understand and agree with every word. If you do not agree with something in the will, do not reword the will language yourself, or you'll risk your will's validity. Instead, you might need to use a more complex will that can be more carefully tailored to your situation. (See "Nolo Resources on Estate Planning," above.)

**Signing Instructions**

Your signature on your will must be witnessed. When you are ready to sign it, gather together two adults who aren't beneficiaries of your will. Your witnesses do not need to read your will. You simply tell them, "This is my will." Then you sign and date your will while the witnesses watch. Finally, each witness signs while the other witness watches. You do not need to have your will notarized. Be sure to store your will in a safe place.

> CAUTION
> **If you're married or in a registered domestic partnership, your spouse may be able to claim a share of your estate.** In most states (all except Arizona, California, Idaho, Louisiana, Nevada, New Mexico, Texas, Washington, and Wisconsin, which follow the community property system), a surviving spouse has the right to reject what the will says and instead claim a share of the deceased spouse's entire estate. In many states, that share is about one-third of the estate. The details get tricky fast. As long as you plan to leave your spouse or partner at least half of your property, you don't need to worry about it. But if you plan to leave less than half of your property to your spouse or partner, see a lawyer and don't try to use the forms in this book.

## Form 14: Will for Adult With No Children

This is the will to use if you don't have children. Remember, these forms can be used by residents of all states except Louisiana.

Read the introduction to basic wills (above) for brief but important instructions on filling out the form correctly, so that you will create a legally valid will that accomplishes what you want.

## Form 15: Will for Adult With Child(ren)

To begin, read the material on basic wills, above, for brief but important instructions on filling out the form correctly, so that you will create a legally valid will that accomplishes what you want. Because you have children, you have some special issues to consider before you make your will.

**Heading off claims.** You should mention each of your children in your will, even if you don't use your will to leave one or more of them any property. That's because, although children are not usually entitled to claim any property from a parent's estate, they do have certain rights if it appears that they were unintentionally overlooked. By listing all of your children, including those you have legally adopted, you head off any argument that you forgot any of them.

**Custody of minor children.** If you have children younger than age 18, use Clause 8 to name the person you want to raise the children if you die and if the other parent is unavailable to raise them. This person is called their "personal guardian." It is also wise to nominate an alternate personal guardian, in case the first choice can't serve.

If a guardian is ever needed, a judge will review your choice. If no one objects, the person you name will most likely be appointed. But in an unusual situation, a judge who is convinced that naming a different personal guardian is in the best interests of the child has the authority to do so.

> **CAUTION**
>
> **With this will form, you cannot name different guardians for different kids.** This form requires that you name the same personal guardian for all of your minor children. If you want to name different people as guardians for different children, use *Quicken WillMaker & Trust*.

**Property left to minor children.** When a minor owns anything more than a small amount of property (usually a few thousand dollars' worth, depending on the state), an adult must be legally responsible for managing it. So if your children or other minors might inherit property through your will—even if they're only alternate beneficiaries—you should arrange for an adult to supervise it. You can do this easily in your will.

Form 14 gives you two ways to provide for adult supervision for gifts to minors:

- **Name a custodian for each young person who might receive property through your will.** The custodian will manage any property slated for the child until the child turns a specific age, usually between 18 and 30. The age depends on your state's law. A custodian is authorized under your state's Uniform Transfers to Minors Act (UTMA; see below and see Clause 10 of the will).
- **Name a property guardian for each of your own minor children.** You should always name a property guardian and successor property guardian in your will, even if you appoint a custodian under UTMA. The property guardian will be formally appointed by a court and will manage any property not left through your will (and so not covered by the UTMA custodianship)—for example, property the minor gets from someone else.

---

### Other Property Management Options

The Will for Adult With Child(ren) does not offer two other fairly common—but legally more complicated—ways to arrange for a minor's property to be managed by an adult:

- **A family pot trust.** This will hold property left to all your minor children, allowing the trustee you name to spend it as needed. For example, if one child had an expensive medical problem, the trustee could spend more for that child and less for others.
- **A trust for each child.** This option is primarily of value for people with larger estates who do not want adult children to take control of money outright until they are in their middle or late 20s. It gets around the fact that in most states a custodianship under the terms of the Uniform Transfers to Minors Act ends at age 18 or 21.

These options are available in *Quicken WillMaker & Trust*.

---

**Uniform Transfers to Minors Act.** All states have now adopted the UTMA. This law authorizes you to appoint an adult custodian and successor custodian in your will to supervise property you leave to a minor.

The custodianship ends, any remaining property must be turned over to the child outright, at the age the UTMA specifies. In many states, this is 21, but a growing number of others allow you to choose age 21 or 25. Our form sets the ending age at the oldest age allowed in your state. To find out the UTMA ages in your state, try searching online for your state name and "UTMA age of termination."

Under UTMA, the custodian has almost complete discretion over management of the property. It's therefore essential that you name someone who is totally honest and has good financial management skills. The custodian also has a legal duty to act prudently in the best interests of the child. Normally, no court supervision is required.

Complete a separate UTMA clause for each young beneficiary.

## Form 16: Will Codicil

A codicil is sort of a legal "P.S." to a will. In a codicil, you can revoke a clause in your will and then substitute a new clause. Or you can simply add a new provision, such as a new gift of an item of property.

A codicil must be signed and witnessed just like a will. The form must be retyped or computer printed (start with "First Codicil to the Will of _____ ," leaving off our title), then dated and signed by you in front of two witnesses. You don't have to use the same witnesses who signed your will, but in many states the witnesses cannot be people named as beneficiaries in your will or codicil.

Today, codicils are less commonly used than they were in the days when wills were laboriously copied by hand or typed on a typewriter. With almost universal access to computers, it's usually easier—and less likely to confuse—to prepare a whole new will, revoking the previous one. Nevertheless, codicils can still be sensibly used to make limited changes to a will—for example, when you want to change who receives one item.

CHAPTER 3

# Things to Do After a Death: Documents for Executors

**Form 17: Notice to Creditor of Death** ............................................................. 36

**Form 18: Executor's Checklist** ......................................................................... 37

**Form 19: General Notice of Death** .................................................................. 37

**Form 20: Obituary Information Fact Sheet** ..................................................... 38

**Form 21: Notice to Deceased's Homeowners' Insurance Company** ............... 38

**Form 22: Notice to Deceased's Vehicle Insurance Company** ......................... 39

After a death, someone must step in and wind up the deceased person's affairs. An executor—sometimes called a "personal representative" or "administrator"—is the person named in the will, or appointed by the probate court, who has legal responsibility for safeguarding and handling the deceased person's property, seeing that debts and taxes are paid, and distributing what is left to beneficiaries as directed by the will. Here are a number of simple forms and letters you can use if you are named as someone's executor, as well as a checklist to help you be sure you are taking care of all that needs to be done.

**RESOURCE**

**Nolo has books that can help you.** *How to Probate an Estate in California: A Step-by-Step Guide*, by Lisa Fialco, provides step-by-step instructions for handling probate procedures in California. *The Executor's Guide: Settling a Loved One's Estate or Trust*, by Mary Randolph, covers the legal and financial matters that crop up after a death, helping the surviving family through what is often a difficult and confusing time.

**CAUTION**

**These forms are not applicable in all situations.** The forms in this chapter cannot be used to claim benefits under an insurance policy or retirement plan. You will need to contact the appropriate companies and complete their forms.

Note that as you wrap up the deceased person's estate, you'll need certified copies of the death certificate, as proof of death. (For example, you'll need to attach a certified copy of the death certificate to some of the forms discussed below.) A mortuary or funeral home will usually arrange for you to receive copies, but if you need to order them yourself, you can do so by contacting your state or county vital records office. You might also be able to submit a request form on its website. You'll typically need at least 10 certified death certificates over the course of winding up the deceased person's affairs.

## Form 17: Notice to Creditor of Death

After someone dies, the executor needs to notify creditors of the death and close the deceased person's credit accounts. That's the purpose of this form. You can send it to credit card issuers, department stores, banks, mortgage companies, and other businesses that extended credit to the deceased person.

You will need to put the date of death and the appropriate account number on this notice. You might also need to attach a document showing your appointment as executor or administrator.

**CAUTION**

**If a formal probate court proceeding is conducted, you'll also have to follow special rules for notifying creditors,** for example, mailing a notice to creditors you know about and publishing a notice in a local newspaper to alert those you're not aware of. Check with the lawyer who is handling the probate proceedings, or, if handling probate on your own, ask the probate clerk at the county courthouse for the rules.

### Signing Instructions

Sign the notice and mail two copies to each of the deceased's creditors. The creditor who receives this notice should sign and date it—and mail a copy to you in the stamped, self-addressed envelope you enclose. Keep the completed copy you receive for your records.

You might later need it as proof that you notified the creditor of the death.

**TIP**
**Reconcile the deceased person's records.** This notice asks the creditor to forward information to you about any remaining balance owed by the deceased. Once you hear back from the creditor, check the information sent by the creditor against the deceased person's records.

## Form 18: Executor's Checklist

The executor of an estate has many small and large jobs. The Executor's Checklist lists those that an executor must typically complete when winding up the affairs of someone who has died. Keep in mind, however, that an executor's specific duties depend on the needs of the estate and the requirements of state law. These vary based on the size of the estate, the kind of assets in the estate, and personal factors, such as the needs and expectations of the family. Use the Executor's Checklist as a guide, tailoring it to your situation.

### Signing Instructions

There's no need to sign or fill in any part of the Executor's Checklist. Simply use it as a guide to ensure that you are taking care of the tasks required of you.

## Form 19: General Notice of Death

You might want to notify businesses and organizations that aren't creditors—that is, they aren't owed any money—of the death. For example, you could send a simple notice communicating the fact that someone has died to charities to which the deceased person has donated regularly, magazine publishers, and mail-order businesses that frequently send catalogs.

You can also send this notice to individuals who need to be notified of the death—unless they are friends or relatives who merit a personal call or note.

**CAUTION**
**Do not use this general notice of death form for creditors and government agencies.** Many need specific information about the deceased, such as the accounts owing or type of benefits received. To notify creditors, use the Notice to Creditor of Death, above. For other government agencies, it's a good idea to call and find out what type of notice they require.

**TIP**
**How to stop Social Security payments after a death.** If a deceased person was receiving Social Security benefits, the executor or personal representative must notify the Social Security Administration (SSA) of the death. To stop payments, call the SSA at 800-772-1213 or 800-325-0778 (TTY).

### Signing Instructions

If sending your General Notice of Death by mail, sign it, then send it to the business or organization you wish to notify. If emailing this information to a business or organization, simply copy and paste the body of the form into your email, leaving out the signature line. At the bottom of the email, type your name, relationship to the deceased, and contact information.

It's wise to keep a record of everyone on your mailing list so you can track the organizations and people that you've already informed of the death.

## Form 20: Obituary Information Fact Sheet

When a family member or friend dies, it's a challenge to focus on the many details that need your attention. This form will help you with one of those tasks: organizing information for your loved one's obituary.

An obituary can take many different forms. It might be published in print or on an online memorial site, or simply distributed by email or social media.

For newspaper obituaries, families typically submit information directly to the newspaper, and the cost can vary widely depending on the paper (metropolitan versus small-town, for example) and the length of the obituary. Most commonly, families publish a brief death notice; that is, a small-print listing containing the date of death, names of survivors, the location of any memorial services, and some memories of the deceased (depending on how much they're willing to pay for print space). If your loved one was particularly well known in the community or in a field of work, a staff writer on a newspaper, magazine, or newsletter might request information to write a lengthier obituary. Unlike a paid-for death notice, this type of obituary is a news item that runs in standard type and contains a headline—for example, "Former Local School Principal Dies."

In addition to or in place of a print obituary, people frequently use online obituaries, which are less limited by space and can include photos, videos, and music. Importantly, they are also accessible worldwide and provide a place for family and friends to leave a note or memory. Some mortuaries or funeral homes provide online obituaries as part of their service, and many newspapers also print their death notices online. However, families can create their own online memorials through websites like www.forevermissed.com. Or they might simply write a tribute and share it on social media.

Whether you're writing an obituary or collecting information for one, you can use the Obituary Information Fact Sheet form to gather the most relevant information. Be sure to spell all names accurately, and include any business or personal information of interest. For example, "He founded the Carverville Barbershop Quartet" or "She was widely traveled and a frequent visitor to Nairobi and the Serengeti." When listing survivors, include surviving spouses and children of previous marriages.

### Signing Instructions

You don't need to sign the Obituary Information Fact Sheet form. Simply fill it out and use the collected information to write an obituary or have ready for a publication or another writer to use. The mortuary will have a list of contacts for local obituary columns.

## Form 21: Notice to Deceased's Homeowners' Insurance Company

Use this form if the deceased person owned a home and insured it. The form notifies the insurance company of the death and asks that you, the executor, be added as a "named insured" to the homeowners' insurance policy.

 **CAUTION**

**If you are a co-owner of the home, do not use this form.** Instead, call the insurance company to report the death.

As the executor, you will want to be added as a named insured to that policy as soon as possible. This status will give you all the protections and rights that the deceased person had under the policy. This means that you will be covered if you or anyone is injured on the premises due to your carelessness. And you will be able to make claims for property damage, if necessary. As a named insured, you also have the right to increase coverage or change policy limitations. For example, if you discover that the home and its contents are underinsured, you can purchase additional coverage. Finally, if the insurance company makes a payment after a claim has been made under the policy—for example, paying for repairs to a wind-damaged roof—you will be a copayee on the check. This is important because these payments are part of the estate, and you will need to receive and account for them.

After you are added as a named insured, discuss with the insurance agent or broker how best to continue insurance coverage for the deceased's home. You might want to add coverage or increase coverage limits, particularly if you discover that the home was underinsured. You might also want to add riders for jewelry or other special items.

To complete this form, you will need the following information:
- the deceased person's full name (if it is different on the insurance policy, be sure to note that)
- the date of death
- the name of the insurance company that issued the policy and the complete address of its home office
- the homeowners' policy number, and
- a certified copy of the death certificate.

You'll also need to provide documentation that you are, in fact, the executor for the deceased's estate. It's possible that the insurance company will accept informal proof—like a declaration you sign under oath. But if it wants official documents from the court (usually called "letters"), you won't be able to use this form until you have that documentation. Consider calling the company to ask what it requires, and get help from a probate attorney, if needed.

### Signing Instructions

Sign and date the Notice to Deceased's Homeowners' Insurance Company. Make two copies of the signed notice. Mail the original and one copy to the insurance company office, along with a stamped, self-addressed envelope and a certified copy of the death certificate. Keep the second copy of the notice for your records.

## Form 22: Notice to Deceased's Vehicle Insurance Company

Use this form if the deceased person owned and insured any automobiles, trucks, motorcycles, motor homes, or trailers. The notice informs the insurance company of the death of the insured person and asks them to add you, the executor, to the insurance policy.

You will want to be added as a "named insured" so you will have all the protections and rights that the deceased person had under the policy. Most important, you will be permitted to add or delete coverage or adjust policy limits, if appropriate. Also, you will be named as a copayee (along with others insured under the policy) in any payment from the company. Because these payments are part of the estate, you must receive and account for them.

Many people own more than one vehicle, and they might be insured under separate policies. Even if the deceased person used the same company for multiple policies, you should send a separate notice for each policy.

After you are added as a named insured, talk to the insurance agent or broker about how best to continue insurance coverage for the deceased's vehicles. You might want to add coverage or increase coverage limits; if the deceased was rated a poor risk, you might even want to ask for a reduction in premiums.

Even if you do not expect that the vehicle will be used, you must insure it in case of a fire or other calamity. A parked car in a home garage, for example, will not be covered by the homeowners' policy if there is a fire—you need an auto policy or other insurance coverage. When the vehicle is distributed or sold and is no longer part of the estate, you can easily cancel the insurance you have purchased.

To complete this form, you will need the following information:

- the deceased person's full name (if it is different on the insurance policy, be sure to note that)
- the date of death (if you don't know it, look on the death certificate)
- vehicle year, make, and model
- the name of the insurance company that issued the policy and the complete address of its home office
- the vehicle insurance policy number
- the latest billing statement from the insurance company
- a certified death certificate for the person who has died, and
- in some cases, a certified copy of your driving record (available from your state's department of motor vehicles).

As with the Notice to Deceased's Homeowners' Insurance Company, you'll need to provide proof that you are the executor. Consider calling the company to ask what proof it requires.

**Signing Instructions**

Sign and date the Notice to Deceased's Vehicle Insurance Company. Make two copies of the signed notice. Mail the original and one copy to the insurance company office, along with a stamped, self-addressed envelope. Enclose a certified copy of the death certificate. Keep the second copy of the notice for your records.

# Chapter 4

# Renting a Place to Live

Form 23: Rental Application ................................................................................................................ 43

Form 24: Tenant References ............................................................................................................... 43

Form 25: Landlord-Tenant Checklist ................................................................................................. 44

Form 26: Move-In Letter ...................................................................................................................... 45

Form 27: Resident's Maintenance/Repair Request ....................................................................... 46

Form 28: Semiannual Safety and Maintenance Update .............................................................. 47

Form 29: Landlord-Tenant Agreement to Terminate Lease ........................................................ 47

Form 30: Consent to Assignment of Lease ..................................................................................... 48

Form 31: Month-to-Month Tenant's Notice of Intent to Move Out ......................................... 49

Form 32: Demand for Return of Security Deposit ........................................................................ 49

Whether you rent or own property, you probably understand just how bad a failed landlord-tenant relationship can be. But there is an excellent way to get any landlord-tenant relationship off to a good start and minimize the possibility of future misunderstandings and legal problems: Put all agreements in writing. This chapter includes a rental application, a move-in letter, a repair request, and other forms that will help you start—and keep—the tenancy on good terms all the way through move-out.

RESOURCE

**To learn more about landlord-tenant law, see the following Nolo books and forms.**

**From the landlord's point of view:**

- *Every Landlord's Legal Guide*, by Ann O'Connell and Janet Portman. This 50-state book provides extensive legal and practical information on leases, tenant screening, rent, security deposits, privacy, repairs, property managers, discrimination, roommates, liability, and tenancy termination, and includes 50-state law charts on important rules affecting landlords. It includes more than 30 legal forms and agreements, all available for download on Nolo's website.

Nolo also publishes two books for California landlords: *The California Landlord's Law Book: Rights & Responsibilities*, and *The California Landlord's Law Book: Evictions*, as well as other national books for landlords, such as *First-Time Landlord: Your Guide to Renting Out a Single-Family Home*, *Every Landlord's Tax Deduction Guide*, and *Every Landlord's Guide to Managing Property*.

In addition to books, Nolo offers dozens of state-specific leases and other forms for landlords at www.nolo.com. And for hundreds of free articles of interest to landlords, see the Landlords & Rental Property section on the Nolo website.

**From the tenant's point of view:**

- *Every Tenant's Legal Guide*, by Ann O'Connell and Janet Portman. This book gives tenants in all 50 states the legal and practical information they need to deal with their landlords and protect their rights when things go wrong. It covers all important issues of renting, including signing a lease, getting a landlord to make needed repairs, fighting illegal discrimination, protecting privacy rights, dealing with roommates, getting the security deposit returned fairly, moving out, and much more.

For dozens of free article of interest to tenants, see the Renters' & Tenants' Rights section of www.nolo.com.

---

**State Landlord-Tenant Laws Regulate Many Aspects of Renting**

State laws vary from state to state and regulate things such as the maximum dollar amount allowed for a security deposit and the deadline for returning it; the amount of notice required to change or end a month-to-month tenancy; tenants' privacy rights; late rent charges (and rent limits in states and localities with rent control); a tenant's right to install locks; disclosures regarding the condition of property; tenant options, such as rent withholding, if a landlord fails to make repairs; eviction rules and procedures; antidiscrimination laws; and much more. (For details, see the Nolo resources listed above.)

## Form 23: Rental Application

Many landlords use rental applications to screen potential tenants. They use the information they collect to select tenants who are likely to pay the rent on time, keep the unit in good condition, and not cause problems. This Rental Application calls for a wide variety of information, including a list of personal references as well as the applicant's rental, employment, and credit history.

Ask all serious applicants to fill out and sign an application, not just those whom you think need special scrutiny. Getting the applicant's signature is key—it authorizes you to verify information, call references, and run a credit check. Also, use the "Notes" section at the end of the application to write down your legal reasons for refusing an applicant—for example, negative credit history, insufficient income, or your inability to verify information. Landlords will want this kind of record in order to survive a fair housing challenge if a disappointed applicant files a discrimination complaint.

If you're a renter, complete the application in advance of apartment hunting. You can either give it to prospective landlords or use the information to more easily complete the landlord's application.

**CAUTION**
**Make sure you understand how discrimination laws work.** Many types of discrimination are illegal, including discrimination based on race, religion, national origin, sex (including gender identity and sexual orientation), familial status, and disability. Some states and localities prohibit additional forms of discrimination, such as marital status, military status, or source of income. For more information on legal and illegal reasons to reject a tenant, see the resources listed at the beginning of this chapter. The Landlords & Rental Property section of www.nolo.com has several useful articles.

### Signing Instructions

Before giving prospective tenants this Rental Application, landlords should complete the box at the top of the form, filling in the property address, rental term, first month's rent, and any deposit or credit check fee tenants must pay before moving in. Any credit check fee should be reasonably related to the actual cost of the credit check. Check your state law for any limits on this fee.

If you're a landlord, give a copy to each tenant applying for your rental property. Note the date and time you received it at the top of the form. Check that the tenant has filled out the application completely and signed it before you call references or order a credit check.

## Form 24: Tenant References

If a prospective tenant's Rental Application looks good on its face, conscientious landlords will want to verify the information provided. Landlords should contact the applicant's current and previous landlords, checking to see whether the applicant paid rent on time or caused any problems, such as damaging the rental unit or bothering neighbors. Other key parts of the screening process include verifying the applicant's income and length of employment and obtaining a credit report to see how responsibly the applicant manages money.

Applicants need to authorize the landlord to contact landlords, employers, and other references and run a credit report. The Rental Application, discussed above, includes a section at the end providing this authorization.

A landlord talking with the applicant's previous landlords, employers, and other references, should ask the questions listed on the Tenant References form and take notes of all conversations about the applicant's rental history and behavior. Also ask about problems with any pets (and try to meet the dog or cat, to make sure it's well groomed and well behaved).

You should also verify the applicant's employment and see if the employer will comment on the person's suitability as a tenant (most employers will only verify dates of employment). Many landlords don't check with personal references, except in the case of college students or others who have never rented before, but it's a good idea to do so if you need additional references. All landlords should check credit and financial information and make a general comment on the Tenant References form, such as "Credit report fine— see attached."

If you'll be rejecting an applicant, note on the Tenant References form your reasons for doing so—for example, negative credit information, bad references from a previous landlord, or your inability to verify information on the Rental Application. You want a record of this information so that you can survive a fair housing challenge if a disappointed applicant files a discrimination complaint against you.

Carefully consider whether to inquire about criminal history or placement on a sex offender database. Our rental application and tenant references forms do not have a place for you to ask about and record this information. Although landlords have asked about criminal history for years, laws in some states make the practice illegal at worst, and could expose you to legal challenges at best. If you carefully confirm the other information provided in the application, chances are you will learn enough about an applicant to be able to conclude whether they are a good risk.

See the articles in the "Rental Applications" and "How to Screen Tenants" subsections (located under "Finding Good Tenants") in the Landlords & Rental Property section of www.nolo.com for more on the subject.

**Signing Instructions**

Fill in the name of the applicant and the address of the rental unit that the applicant wants to rent at the top of the Tenant References form. Then, fill in the references' contact information provided by the applicant. (If you're a tenant, you have probably provided your references as part of the landlord's Rental Application, as is the case with the rental application included in this book. If not, it's a good idea to have your references available for the landlord early on.)

Landlords should then write down all the information collected from calling references and checking credit reports of prospective tenants on the Tenant References form, including reasons for rejecting a particular tenant.

# Form 25: Landlord-Tenant Checklist

Legal disputes between tenants and landlords have the potential to get nasty. The most common dispute arises when a landlord keeps all or part of a tenant's security deposit, claiming the place was left excessively dirty or damaged.

Using the Landlord-Tenant Checklist can help minimize deposit-related disputes. At the start of the tenancy, the landlord and tenant should inspect the rental unit and fill out the Checklist together. Then, at the end of the tenancy, the inspection should be repeated, filling out the Checklist again. This type of inspection is a legal requirement in some states, and a good practice in all.

The point of the Checklist is to identify damage, dirt, mildew, and obvious wear and tear before the tenant moves in (use column 1, Move-In Condition), in both the General Condition of Rental Unit and Premises section of the form and the Furnished Property section.

Your comments should be as specific as possible. Mark "OK" next to items that are in satisfactory condition—basically, clean, safe, sanitary, and in good working order.

You will then inspect the unit again just before the tenant moves out (ideally landlord and tenant will do this together) and fill out column 2 (Move-Out Condition).

In some states, landlords must offer tenants a "pre–move out inspection," which happens close to the end of the tenancy. Landlords alert tenants to needed repairs and cleaning, giving tenants a chance to perform them and avoid deductions. If you do a pre–move out inspection, use the column for the final inspection, and just note your findings in the first half of the space provided.

Tenants should read and check the boxes regarding smoke detectors and carbon monoxide detectors on the bottom of the last page of the General Condition of Rental Unit and Premises section of the form.

In the "additional explanation" section at the end of the Landlord-Tenant Checklist form, note any areas of disagreement between the landlord and the tenant. (Incidentally, to avoid a court battle over security deposit deductions, many wise landlords and tenants try to resolve any disputed damage claims when doing the final inspection.)

### Signing Instructions

After completing the Landlord-Tenant Checklist at move-in time, make two copies. The landlord and tenant should sign and date both originals and each keep one original.

Review the Checklist again at move-out time, fill in the appropriate columns as noted above, and sign and date both originals.

**TIP**
**Take photos or videos at move-in and move-out to avoid disputes.** Having photos lets you compare "before" and "after" images, rather than deal with differing memories of the condition of the property. In fact, your state law might require such actions: As of July 1, 2025, California landlords must take photos of the unit at the beginning of the tenancy. (Cal. Civ. Code § 1950.5 (2025).) If you end up in court fighting over the security deposit, photos will be invaluable visual proof. Tenants should consider bringing a friend to the move-in and move-out inspections—someone who will be available to testify in court about the rental's condition if necessary.

## Form 26: Move-In Letter

A clear, written lease or rental agreement is the key to starting a tenancy. But smart landlords often go further and prepare a move-in letter for new tenants that dovetails with the lease or rental agreement. The letter summarizes key clauses, such as rules on rent, roommates (ideally, your lease specifies that any new roommates must be screened and preapproved by you), and deposits, and clearly spells out tenants' rights and responsibilities. This Move-In Letter provides a template for this purpose.

The Move-In Letter is also a useful place for landlords to provide basic information tenants need to know, such as the manager's phone number and email address; rules that are too detailed to include in the lease or rental agreement, such as the location and use of laundry rooms, pickup day for garbage and recycling, and maintenance dos and don'ts; and anything else that is important or unique to the specific rental.

**Signing Instructions**

After tailoring this Move-In Letter for the specific rental, you should date and sign it and deliver to the tenant. Also, make a copy of your signed letter for tenants to sign, indicating that they have read the letter. Update your Move-In Letter from time to time as necessary.

## Form 27: Resident's Maintenance/Repair Request

Landlords are legally required to provide tenants livable premises, and to maintain the rental property in decent condition throughout the rental term. Most states' laws refer to this obligation as the landlord's legal duty to fulfill the "implied warranty of habitability."

Even when tenants knowingly move into a place that's clearly substandard (below reasonable habitability standards), landlords are required to provide habitable premises. Or, put another way, all courts have rejected the sleazy argument that tenants waive the right to a livable place when they accept a substandard rental unit. The implied warranty of habitability is not waivable.

Tenants who have a problem with the physical condition of their rental unit will want to notify their landlord or manager as soon as possible. The best approach is to put every repair and maintenance request in writing, using the Resident's Maintenance/Repair Request, and to keep a copy for yourself. Then email, hand deliver, or mail your repair request. You might find it easier to call your landlord first, particularly in urgent cases, but be sure to follow up with a written repair request.

Be as specific as possible regarding the problem—whether it's plumbing, heating, security, weatherproofing, or other defects. Note how the problem affects you, what you want done, and when. For example, if the thermostat on your heater is always finicky and sometimes doesn't function at all, explain how long you've been without heat and how low the temperature has dipped—don't simply say "the heater needs to be fixed." If the problem poses a health or safety threat, such as a broken front door lock, point out the specific danger to the landlord and ask for it to be fixed immediately.

Note the best time to make repairs, the date of the request, and (in "Other comments") how many requests, if any, have preceded this one. Keep records of all repair requests and details on how and when the landlord responded. Your records will serve as potential evidence in case you need to prove that serious problems with your unit were the subject of repeated repair requests.

If you're a landlord, it's a good idea to give tenants copies of the Resident's Maintenance/Repair Request form and encourage them to immediately report any defects or safety problems. Landlords should note details as to how and when the problem was fixed, including reasons for any delay, on the bottom of the form. Keep copies of all completed forms in the tenant files.

**Signing Instructions**

Landlords should give tenants blank copies of the Resident's Maintenance/Repair Request form. If you're a tenant and your landlord hasn't provided you with a form like this, go ahead and use it on your own. Tenants should simply fill in and sign the document and keep a copy for their records. If your landlord has an on-site office or a resident manager, deliver the repair request personally. If you mail it, consider sending it certified mail (return receipt requested) or use a delivery service that will provide you with proof of delivery. Besides keeping a copy of every written repair request (including emails), keep notes of oral communications with your landlord, too.

Do not use text messaging as your means of communication, because should you need to prove that you alerted the landlord to a problem, it can be complicated and possibly expensive to convert phone and text records into a form that's acceptable to most courts.

> **TIP**
> **If your landlord ignores your requests and your rental is unlivable, consider taking stronger measures.** These might include calling state or local building or health inspectors, moving out, withholding the rent, or repairing the problem yourself. These remedies, available only in certain situations according to your state's laws, are thoroughly discussed in the Nolo books listed at the beginning of this chapter. Tenants will also find useful information in the "Repairs and Maintenance" section under Renters' & Tenants' Rights on www.nolo.com.

# Form 28: Semiannual Safety and Maintenance Update

The best way to avoid disputes about repair and maintenance problems is for landlords to establish and communicate clear procedures for tenants to ask for repairs, document all complaints, and respond quickly to tenants' complaints. Begin by clearly setting out tenant responsibilities for repair and maintenance in the lease and rental agreement and again in the Move-In Letter. Landlords should also use the Landlord-Tenant Checklist before tenants move in, and encourage tenants to immediately report plumbing, heating, security, and other problems, using the Resident's Maintenance/Repair Request.

In addition, landlords should give tenants a form on which to report any potential safety hazards or maintenance problems that might have arisen since move-in, such as low water pressure in the shower, a sticky front door lock, or security problems in the neighborhood. That's the purpose of the Semiannual Safety and Maintenance Update.

**Signing Instructions**

The Semiannual Safety and Maintenance Update has no signing instructions. Landlords should give tenants a blank copy of this form twice a year. Tenants who have not been given one can go ahead and use the form on their own. Tenants should simply sign and date the document and keep a copy for their records.

Landlords should note how they handled the problems on the bottom of this form and keep a copy for their records.

# Form 29: Landlord-Tenant Agreement to Terminate Lease

If you're a tenant with a long-term lease, ideally it will cover just the amount of time you need the rental. Sometimes, though, despite your best efforts to plan ahead, you might want to move before your lease is up.

Surprisingly, many landlords will agree to let tenants out of the lease early, if they've been good tenants, or (ironically) because they've been difficult and the landlord is happy to see them go. Or, the tenant's departure might give the landlord a chance to raise the rent earlier than expected. So, a simple request should be your first consideration. (If the landlord initially balks at canceling the lease, you might prevail by offering to pay an extra month's rent in exchange.)

Use the Landlord-Tenant Agreement to Terminate Lease for this purpose. When you and the landlord both sign and date this form, your obligations for rent beyond the termination date end. (You're still responsible for unpaid back rent and any damage you've caused beyond normal wear and tear.)

In some states, landlords must allow early termination of a lease under certain conditions, such as a tenant needing to move when their employer has relocated the tenant's job, or upon suffering a disabling illness or accident. Some states allow tenants who are victims of domestic violence to terminate a lease early. In all states, federal law allows military and other personnel to terminate a lease early when called to active duty or if they're active duty personnel being transferred. If you have a good reason for a sudden move, check your state's law. See the Nolo resources listed at the beginning of this chapter for details.

A tenant might be able to move out without providing proper notice if the landlord has violated an important lease provision or state law and has refused to fix the problem—for example, by failing to maintain the rental unit in accordance with health and safety codes.

 **TIP**
**Check your lease for a clause titled "Early termination."** In some states, you and the landlord may agree that you will pay a certain amount, called a "termination fee," if you leave early. This provision means that you will not be subject to the default rule that you're responsible for rent for the remainder of the term if the landlord hasn't been able to re-rent the unit. (Most states require landlords to try to re-rent; when a new tenant takes over, your responsibility for rent ends.)

If you can't get the landlord to cancel the lease outright, your best approach is probably to find a new tenant who will be ready to move in as soon as you leave and who will sign a new lease at the same or higher rent. You should owe nothing additional, because the landlord won't be able to argue that a suitable replacement tenant couldn't be found.

 **TIP**
**What to do if the landlord won't accept the tenant you find.** Keep careful records of all prospective tenants you find, especially their credit histories—you can use the Rental Application. If the landlord sues you for back rent, present these records to the judge as proof the landlord failed to limit (mitigate) damages by refusing to accept a suitable replacement tenant.

If the landlord accepts the new tenant, you and the landlord complete the Agreement to Terminate Lease. The landlord and the new tenant can sign their own lease, and you will no longer be in the picture.

### Signing Instructions

Print two copies of the Landlord-Tenant Agreement to Terminate Lease—one for the landlord and one for the tenant(s). The landlord and every tenant should sign and date both originals. The landlord should keep one signed original and the tenant(s) the other. (Cotenants, if any, may make their own copies of the tenants' signed document.)

## Form 30: Consent to Assignment of Lease

If you are a tenant who wants to move out permanently, but the landlord won't cancel your lease or sign a new lease with a tenant you find, your next best option might be to "assign" your lease to a new tenant (called an "assignee") who is acceptable to the landlord. With an assignment, you turn over the remainder of your lease to someone else. You can do this with the Consent to Assignment of Lease. Unless the landlord agrees otherwise, you remain in the picture as a guarantor of rent payments in case the new occupant (the assignee) fails to pay. Having a second source for the rent is one reason a savvy landlord might agree to an assignment but not a cancellation.

Landlords can voluntarily waive their rights to look to you as the guarantor of the assignee's rent, something that's not uncommon when the new tenant has excellent credit. Clause 4 of this form releases you from this worrisome obligation, essentially putting you in the position of someone who has terminated the lease. If the landlord understands that normally you would remain responsible for your assignee's unpaid rent and balks at the release, and you're reasonably sure of your replacement's ability to pay the rent, you might not be risking much if you cross out Clause 4 and remain theoretically responsible for the rent (you and the landlord should initial the cross-out).

### Signing Instructions

Print out three copies of the Consent to Assignment of Lease form—one for the landlord, one for the tenant, and one for the assignee. Each person should sign and date all originals in the spaces indicated. The landlord should keep one signed original and the tenant and assignee the others.

## Form 31: Month-to-Month Tenant's Notice of Intent to Move Out

If you have a month-to-month tenancy, in most states and for most rentals you must provide 30 days' notice to your landlord if you want to move out. In some states, if you pay rent weekly or twice a month, you can give written notice to terminate that matches your rent payment interval. For example, if you pay rent every 2 weeks, you might need to give only 14 days' notice.

In most states, you can give notice at any time during the month. For example, if you pay rent on the 1st of the month but give notice on the 10th, you will be obliged to pay for only 10 days' rent for the next month, even if you move out earlier. To calculate the amount, prorate the monthly rent using 30 days.

Check the Nolo resources listed at the beginning of the chapter for requirements as to how and when to give notice. The Leases & Rental Agreements section under "Landlords & Tenants" on www.nolo.com includes useful information on the subject.

### Signing Instructions

Tenants should sign and date the Tenant's Notice of Intent to Move Out form and give it to the landlord. Be sure to check your state rules to make sure you are meeting the state's notice requirements.

**TIP**

**If you give oral notice, follow up in writing with this form.** If you know your landlord or manager well, you might wish to convey your moving plans in a face-to-face or phone conversation. That's fine, but immediately follow up with written confirmation. The law almost always requires written notice. You can use Form 31 for this purpose.

## Form 32: Demand for Return of Security Deposit

Getting cleaning and security deposits returned can be a problem for tenants. To avoid trouble, or to successfully deal with a landlord who unfairly retains your deposit, use the Landlord-Tenant Checklist to make a written and photographic record of what the place looks like when you move in and when you move out. Be sure you leave the rental in good condition, give proper notice, and are paid up in rent when you leave. And don't forget to give the landlord your new address.

Depending on the law of your state, you should receive your deposit back within 14 to 30 days of moving out, minus any legitimate deductions for unpaid rent and damage beyond wear and tear. If you don't get the refund, send a written request using the Demand for Return of Security Deposit. If this doesn't work, you might need to sue the landlord in small claims court. (Some state security deposit statutes require tenants to make a written request; in some states, small claims court rules require you to send a demand letter before you can sue.) You can find your state security deposit rules in the "Security Deposits" section under Renters' & Tenants' Rights on www.nolo.com.

Your demand letter should state the date you moved out of the rental and lay out the reasons your landlord owes you deposit money. Refer to any statutory deadlines and tangible evidence supporting your demand, such as photos or a before-and-after Landlord-Tenant Checklist. In the Demand for Return of Security Deposit, you make it clear that if the landlord does not promptly return your deposit by a specified date (we suggest 7 to 10 days), you plan to go to small claims court.

In many states, if a landlord withholds a deposit without giving the tenant a good written reason for doing so within the required time (for example, withholding to cover specific damage or unpaid rent), the tenant has some powerful options. Tenants might be able to sue for the amount of the wrongly withheld deposit, plus an extra amount for punitive damages if the landlord intentionally failed to return the deposit on time. Check your state law for specifics and refer to it in any correspondence with your landlord. For example, California landlords have 21 days to return the security deposit with an itemized statement of deductions and copies of receipts or invoices for needed cleaning or repairs. (Cal. Civ. Code § 1950.5 (2025).)

## Signing Instructions

Sign your Demand for Return of Security Deposit letter and send it certified mail (return receipt requested) to the landlord, or use a delivery service that will give you proof of delivery. Keep a copy of your letter and all related correspondence. You'll need this if you end up in a court dispute over your security deposit.

### Going to Small Claims Court

Hopefully, your Demand for Return of Security Deposit letter will spur action on the landlord's part and you'll get your deposit back. If it doesn't, you might need to file a lawsuit in small claims court. These courts will handle disputes worth up to a certain amount—typical limits are between $5,000 and $20,000 (each state sets its own limit, and a few fall outside this range). Most security deposit disputes will fit within the court's limit. You can sue your landlord for your security deposit and for interest (if it's required in your state or city). In many states, you can also sue for extra, punitive damages if the landlord intentionally failed to return the deposit on time.

It is inexpensive (usually less than $50) to file a case in small claims court, you don't need a lawyer, and disputes usually go before a judge (no juries) within 30 to 60 days. Small claims courts are informal places, intended to be used by regular folks presenting their own cases.

 **RESOURCE**

**For detailed advice on filing (or defending) a case in small claims court,** see *Everybody's Guide to Small Claims Court,* by Cara O'Neill (Nolo). Also, check out the "Small Claims Court & Lawsuits" section on www.nolo.com (click "Explore Your Legal Issue" and scroll down to "Small Claims Court & Law Suits") for useful articles including state laws and dollar limits.

# CHAPTER 5

# Borrowing and Lending Money

**Form 33: Loan Comparison Worksheet** ........................................................................................... 52

**Form 34: Authorization to Check Credit and Employment References** ........................ 52

**Form 35: Monthly Payment Record** ................................................................................................ 54

**Forms 36–40: Promissory Notes** ...................................................................................................... 54

    Form 36: Promissory Note—Installment Payments With Interest ............................... 56

    Form 37: Promissory Note—Installment Payments With Interest and
    Balloon Payment ............................................................................................................................ 57

    Form 38: Promissory Note—Installment Payments Without Interest ....................... 58

    Form 39: Promissory Note—Lump-Sum Payment With Interest ................................. 58

    Form 40: Promissory Note—Lump-Sum Payment Without Interest ......................... 59

**Form 41: Cosigner Provision** .............................................................................................................. 59

**Forms 42–45: Security Agreements** ................................................................................................ 59

    Form 42: Security Agreement Provision for Promissory Note ...................................... 60

    Form 43: Security Agreement for Borrowing Money ......................................................... 61

    Form 44: U.C.C. Financing Statement ..................................................................................... 61

    Form 45: Release of U.C.C. Financing Statement ............................................................... 62

**Form 46: Agreement to Modify Promissory Note** .................................................................... 62

**Form 47: Overdue Payment Demand** ............................................................................................ 62

**Form 48: Demand to Make Good on Bad Check** ...................................................................... 63

This chapter contains several promissory notes you can use to borrow money from or lend money to a friend, relative, or someone else who isn't a commercial customer. (Banks and other institutional lenders follow many legal rules and must use forms with far more fine print.) This chapter also includes a Loan Comparison Worksheet to keep track of information you collect on different loans (whether from a personal or commercial lender), a form to authorize a lender to check the borrower's credit, and "demand" letters to use when trying to collect an overdue payment or bad check.

## Form 33: Loan Comparison Worksheet

A good consumer shops around before making a significant purchase. There is no reason to do otherwise when looking to borrow money. A loan from one bank might come with very different terms than a loan from a credit union or finance company—or even from a different bank across town. And a loan from your former college roommate or your Aunt Charlotte could be very different still.

The cost of a loan doesn't depend only on how much interest you pay. Long-term loans carry a higher rate of interest than short-term loans (the lender runs the risk that inflation will erode the real value of the interest it receives for a longer period, so it passes some of this risk on to you in the form of a higher interest rate). But short-term loans aren't necessarily cheaper. You need to consider application fees and other up-front fees, which can vary considerably from one lender to the next, when computing the cost of a loan. Fortunately, this isn't true of all short-term loans, so be sure to shop around. When you apply for a commercial loan, the lender must tell you the annual cost of the loan. This cost is stated as the annual percentage rate, or APR. You can use that figure to compare the annual cost of different loans.

APR isn't the entire story, especially for adjustable-rate loans or loans with a balloon payment or other features. For a full comparison of loans you're considering, use this worksheet to record the terms. (See "Basic Loan Terms Explained," below, before you start collecting information on different loans.)

Because mortgage loans involve far more considerations than the loans discussed in this chapter, use the Mortgage Rates and Terms Worksheet in Chapter 6 when shopping around for a mortgage.

### Signing Instructions

There are no signing instructions for the Loan Comparison Worksheet. Simply fill one out each time you start collecting information on different loans.

## Form 34: Authorization to Check Credit and Employment References

Commercial lenders—banks, credit unions, and finance companies—will always check a loan applicant's credit before agreeing to lend money. If you're thinking of lending someone money, it makes good sense to check their credit and employment references. You'll need the borrower's signed authorization to do this. Most employers, financial institutions, and credit sources require this kind of signed authorization before providing information on the borrower. That's the purpose of this Authorization to Check Credit and Employment References. The borrower should complete all sections, including details on employment and credit history.

## Basic Loan Terms Explained

To understand your loan agreement, you'll need to know the meaning of a few terms.

**Adjustable rate.** An interest rate that changes over time. It is set initially by the lender, usually fairly low, and then fluctuates (usually meaning it increases) every several months.

**Balloon payment.** A lump-sum payment made at the end of a loan to cover the remaining balance. For example, you borrow $10,000 for 5 years at 6% interest. The monthly payments are $193.33. You can afford to pay only about half that amount, so the lender lets you pay $100 a month. At the end of 5 years, however, you owe a balloon payment of $6,511.53. Balloon payments are usually bad deals. Borrowers often get into trouble by focusing on the low monthly payments rather than the large and often unaffordable sum due at the end of the loan term.

**Cap.** On an adjustable-rate loan, the cap refers to both the maximum amount the interest rate can increase each year and the ultimate maximum an interest rate can reach. For example, an adjustable-rate loan that begins at 4% might have an annual cap of 0.5% and a lifetime cap of 7%. This means that at the beginning of the second year, the rate will be 4.5%. If the loan continues to increase 0.5% each year, it will reach its lifetime cap of 7% in six years.

**Collateral.** Property a borrower pledges as security for repayment of a loan. Sometimes it's the item being purchased, such as a car. Other times the collateral is property the borrower already owns. If the borrower defaults, a lender can usually take the collateral without first suing the borrower and obtaining a judgment.

**Cosigner.** A creditworthy person who agrees to be fully liable for repayment of a loan if the borrower defaults.

**Credit check.** A lender getting a copy of the borrower's credit report from a credit reporting agency to verify the borrower's creditworthiness.

**Credit insurance.** Insurance coverage offered by some lenders to ensure payment of a loan in the event the borrower becomes disabled or dies. Most consumer advocates say credit card insurance is a waste of money.

**Fixed rate.** An interest rate that is established by the lender at the outset and will never change.

**Grace period.** The number of days a borrower has after a loan payment is due to make the payment without being charged a late fee. For example, if your loan payments are due on the 1st of the month, you might have a grace period until the 10th, meaning that the lender will accept your payment until that date without penalizing you.

**Late fee.** The fee a lender charges when a borrower pays late. (See "Grace period.")

**Loan application fee.** Fees charged by lenders for the work involved in lending money. These include credit checks, appraisals on collateral, and loan processing fees.

**Loan discounts.** Incentives offered by a lender that reduce a loan's interest rate. For example, you might be offered a 0.5% discount if you set up direct payment from your checking account or if you maintain a checking account with the lender with a minimum balance requirement.

**Points.** Real estate loans usually come with points, an amount of money equal to a percentage of your loan. This money is paid to the lender simply for the privilege of borrowing money or to reduce the interest rate.

**Prepayment penalty.** A penalty imposed on a borrower for paying off a loan early. It's usually expressed as a flat fee or a percentage of the interest the lender lost as a result of your prepaying.

Doing a credit and reference check will give you an idea whether the borrower is likely to repay you in full and on time, and put you in a good position to say "no" to someone with poor credit. Checking credit references and saying "no" is likely to put a strain on a personal relationship, but making a loan to someone who can't handle the payments is more likely to cause long-term problems.

### Signing Instructions

The person borrowing money should sign and date the Authorization to Check Credit and Employment References. The lender should keep the original and give the borrower a copy. The lender should also send copies of the signed authorization form to the credit and employment references that will be checked. It might be helpful to enclose a stamped, self-addressed envelope.

## Form 35: Monthly Payment Record

If a loan will be repaid over many months or years, it's easy to forget whether and when every payment has been made. This is especially likely if the debtor misses several payments because of an emergency and then makes them up a little at a time. In this case, the amounts will be different each month. Use the Monthly Payment Record to keep track of payments made under installment notes, such as the promissory notes included in this chapter.

### Signing Instructions

There are no signing instructions for the Monthly Payment Record. The lender simply records payments due and made every month.

## Forms 36–40: Promissory Notes

A "promissory note" is a written agreement to pay money to someone. As with all legal documents, promissory notes often contain legalese. Because the notes in this chapter are designed to be used primarily between family and friends, we prefer to keep the language simple.

The primary function of a promissory note is to document the amount of a debt and the terms under which it will be repaid, including the interest rate (if any). A promissory note is typically signed when a person borrows money or buys something on credit. Here are several important reasons why all promissory notes should be put in writing:

- You are assured that the borrower and lender have agreed to the same terms, including the repayment schedule and interest rate.
- You specify exactly what those terms are.
- Both parties have a written document to refresh their memories.

This chapter contains five promissory notes, each designed to deal with a somewhat different repayment scenario:

- Form 36: Promissory Note—Installment Payments With Interest
- Form 37: Promissory Note—Installment Payments With Interest and Balloon Payment
- Form 38: Promissory Note—Installment Payments Without Interest
- Form 39: Promissory Note—Lump-Sum Payment With Interest, and
- Form 40: Promissory Note—Lump-Sum Payment Without Interest.

All of these notes are for unsecured loans—meaning that the borrower doesn't pledge any property, such as a car, as collateral to guarantee repayment. So, if the borrower doesn't repay the loan, the lender must sue in court to get a judgment, which then makes the lender eligible to use wage garnishment or property attachments to collect on the note. A lender can add a security provision to the note using Form 42, which gives the lender the right to force the sale of personal property pledged as collateral if the borrower doesn't repay. Form 43 is the actual security agreement used when property is pledged.

## Signing Instructions for Promissory Notes

The borrower(s) must sign the promissory note for it to be valid. (There may be two borrowers—for example, if spouses are jointly borrowing money. See "Does a Borrower's Spouse Need to Sign a Promissory Note?," below.) Print out one copy of the form. The borrower(s) should sign and date only one copy of the document in the space provided. This signed original should be given to the lender. The borrower(s) should keep a copy of the signed document for their own records.

**FORM**

**Using a notary public.** You might want to have the borrower sign the promissory note in front of a notary public. This step might be required in some states; even if it is not, notarization adds a measure of legal credibility to your promissory note. (See "Signing the Forms," in the Introduction, for general advice on having a form notarized.) If you do get the promissory note notarized, attach the notary certificate where indicated on the form.

**TIP**

**If the borrower's credit is questionable, consider requiring a cosigner.** You can add a cosigner clause to your promissory note by using the Cosigner Provision explained below.

### Does a Borrower's Spouse Need to Sign a Promissory Note?

A "promissory note" is a contract that makes a borrower liable for a debt. The lender may ask that the borrower's spouse sign as well. This requirement is likely, for example, if someone is borrowing money to buy property that both spouses will use or to help finance a new business venture. Keep in mind that a lender might not require a borrower's spouse to sign if the borrower is the only one applying for the loan and no jointly held or community property is involved.

By having the borrower's spouse sign, a second person becomes legally liable for repaying the debt. Normally, if only the borrower signed the contract and didn't repay it, the other party to the agreement could get a judgment against the borrower but not the borrower's spouse. This means that the creditor would be able to seize property that the borrower owns as sole owner, but not property that the borrower and a spouse own in both of their names or that the spouse owns solely, unless the borrower lives in a community property state such as California. (See "Who Pays the Debts in Community Property States?," below for more details.) But if the borrower and spouse both sign a contract and then default, the other party can sue and get a judgment against both. That judgment can be enforced by seizing the couple's joint bank account, putting a lien on jointly owned real estate, seizing property in the borrower's name alone, and seizing property in the spouse's name alone.

> ### Who Pays the Debts in Community Property States?
>
> Arizona, California, Idaho, Louisiana, Nevada, New Mexico, Texas, Washington, and Wisconsin follow the community property system. (In some other states, a couple can choose to have their property treated as community property by preparing a written agreement.) In these states, property acquired during a marriage is generally considered community (joint) regardless of whose name it's in or who paid for it. In addition, all debts incurred during the marriage—even if only one spouse signed the loan papers—are considered community (joint) debts unless a creditor was explicitly told that only one spouse would be liable for the debt.
>
> In most situations, the rights of creditors to seize property after getting a judgment for nonpayment of a debt depend on whether the property is considered community or separate.
>
> - **Community property.** Usually, property earned or acquired by either spouse during the marriage—except property acquired by gift or inheritance or defined as separate under a premarital agreement—is considered community property. A creditor can go after all community property to pay for either a community debt or a separate debt of one spouse incurred during the marriage.
> - **Separate property.** This is property a spouse owned before getting married, acquired during the marriage by gift or inheritance, or agreed in writing to be kept separate. It's also property acquired using separate assets. For example, if a woman owned a house when she got married, then sold it and used the proceeds to buy stock held in her name, the stock is clearly her separate property. For community debts, a creditor can seek reimbursement from either spouse's separate property. For example, for debt the wife accumulates while married, a creditor can go after her separate property, all community property (including her spouse's share), and her spouse's separate property.

## Form 36: Promissory Note— Installment Payments With Interest

This form allows the borrower to repay the note in installments rather than all at once, and charges interest. Charging a friend or family member interest strikes some people as being ungenerous. In our opinion, this view is based on a misconception about the function of interest, which is to compensate the lender for the use of the money. Think of it this way. Suppose Jenn lends Harry $5,000 for a year, interest free. If Jenn had put the money in a certificate of deposit (CD), she would have earned the going rate of interest. By giving Harry the money interest free, Jenn ends up paying for the privilege of lending the money to Harry.

Interest charged on money lent to friends and relatives tends to run between 5% and 10%. If you wish to charge a higher rate of interest, check your state law to see if the rate is legal; it might constitute the crime of usury. How much interest is appropriate? In an effort to be generous to a relative or friend, many lenders charge interest at somewhat less than the market rate, sometimes as little as—or just slightly more than—they would receive if they purchased a bank CD for the same period. This is a great deal for the borrower; after all, even if Harry qualified to borrow from a bank or other commercial lender, he would have to pay a much higher rate of interest than Jenn would receive if she put the money in a CD.

Charging interest does add a level of complication when it comes to figuring out the amount of the monthly payments. For this, you will need an amortization calculator (available online) or a software program. You plug in the loan amount, interest rate, and number of months the borrower will take to repay the loan. The calculator gives you the monthly payment amount.

If the borrower decides to pay off part of the principal sooner than the promissory note calls for under the installment plan, you will have to recalculate the payments based on the new outstanding balance. This is easy to do with an amortization calculator.

**TIP**

**What is a "buyer in due course"?** Forms 36–40 all contain a phrase that says that "the term Lender refers to any person who legally holds this note, including a buyer in due course." This phrase refers to any person who buys goods from another person. In the context of these forms, it refers to anyone who might purchase the promissory note from the original lender, and says that such a purchaser would hold the same rights as the original lender to collect the money from the borrower.

## Form 37: Promissory Note—Installment Payments With Interest and Balloon Payment

Form 37 is similar to Form 36 in that the loan must be repaid in installments with interest. But it has an additional twist: Individual payments are lower than they otherwise would be, with the shortfall made up by one large balloon

### Legal Terminology of Promissory Notes

Here we translate some legal terms into plain English.

**Acceleration.** Our promissory notes accelerate the borrower's responsibility to make all necessary loan payments, meaning that if the borrower misses one or more regularly scheduled payments, the entire loan amount is immediately due. You specify the number of days—typically 30 or 60—the borrower has to pay before you exercise this option. Without this provision you can't sue for loan installments not yet due, even though the borrower has missed several payments and obviously has no plans to repay.

**Attorneys' fees.** Our promissory notes include a clause providing that the borrower has to pay the lender's attorneys' fees and court costs in a legal dispute if the lender wins. Under the laws of some states, this type of clause will be read by a court to go both ways. This means that if the borrower wins, the borrower will be entitled to attorneys' fees and court costs, even if the loan papers don't specifically say so.

**Buyer in due course.** This is a person who buys or otherwise legally receives a promissory note from a lender. The borrower's obligation to repay the note doesn't change just because the lender sells the note to someone else.

**Joint and several liability.** This means that if there is more than one borrower, they're all liable for repaying 100% of the loan. If Chuck and Laura borrow $5,000 from Miguel and then default, Miguel can go after either Chuck or Laura for the full $5,000. They can't claim that each person is liable for only $2,500.

payment at the end of the loan term. Let's say you lend a friend $10,000 at 7% interest and want the money paid back in three years. Using an amortization calculator, you discover that your friend would have to pay you $308.78 each month to pay it back over that time.

Your friend can't afford to pay that amount each month now, but expects to receive some money in about three years when a trust matures. So you propose the following: Your friend can borrow $10,000 from you at 7% and repay it over 3 years. But to make the payments affordable now, you agree to amortize the loan as though it were to be paid off in 10 years, meaning your friend's monthly payments are only $116.11, far less than $308.78. You agree to take these low payments for 36 months and at the end, your friend will make you one large payment, called a "balloon payment," of the remaining principal. That amount is $7,693.

## Form 38: Promissory Note— Installment Payments Without Interest

Use this form if the borrower will repay you in installments, but you won't charge interest. When the parties involved in the transaction are family members or close friends, the amount borrowed is relatively small, and the probability of repayment is high, lenders sometimes prefer to use an interest-free installment note.

Be aware that if the IRS learns of an interest-free loan, it can impute interest. This means that the lender will be assumed to have earned interest and will be required to report that interest as income on that year's tax return. For most personal loans, this won't be a problem because uncharged interest can be treated as a tax-free gift, as long as the total amount given and imputed to the borrower in a calendar year is $19,000 (2025 and 2026) or less. (This figure is adjusted for inflation and changes periodically.)

## Form 39: Promissory Note— Lump-Sum Payment With Interest

This note is normally used when the borrower won't be able to repay the loan for a period of months or years. For example, you might borrow money from a friend to help you open a small business. You aren't likely to have the cash flow for at least six months or a year to repay the loan. In such a situation, your friend might agree to be repaid in a lump sum in two years.

The easiest way to determine the amount of annual interest that will be due on the loan is to use simple, not compound, interest. Multiply the amount of the loan by the annual interest rate. For instance, if the loan is for $4,000 and your annual interest rate is 10%, the annual amount of interest on the loan is $400. To determine the total amount of interest due, multiply the annual interest amount by the time period of the loan. In our example, if the loan is for two years, the interest due would be $800.

If you need to compute the interest for a period of months rather than years, compute the interest for one year, divide by 12, and then multiply the result by the number of months. For example, assume the $4,000 loan is for an 18-month period. Take the annual interest amount ($400), divide by 12 ($33.33), and multiply by 18 ($600).

If the loan is paid back before it is due, Clause 2 gives the lender two choices:

- Charge the full interest. This is not unreasonable, given that you committed yourself to being without the amount of the entire loan for the time indicated.
- Prorate the interest to correspond to the actual period of time the loan was outstanding. Returning to the $4,000 loan example, if you originally figured interest at 10% for two years ($800), but the loan was paid back in 18 months, simply charge the 18-month figure ($600) instead.

## Form 40: Promissory Note—Lump-Sum Payment Without Interest

This promissory note, which calls for a lump-sum loan repayment and no interest, is about as basic as you can get. This sort of note is normally used by people with a close personal relationship when the person lending the money is primarily interested in helping out the borrower and expects nothing in return except, eventually, the amount borrowed.

If the IRS learns of the loan, it can impute interest. This means that the lender will be assumed to have earned interest and will be required to report that interest as income on that year's tax return. For most personal loans, this won't be a problem because uncharged interest can be treated as a tax-free gift, as long as the total given to the borrower by the lender and imputed by the IRS is $19,000 (2025 and 2026) or less in a calendar year.

## Form 41: Cosigner Provision

A "cosigner" is someone who promises to repay a loan if the primary debtor defaults. If you'll be lending money to someone with a questionable (or no) credit history or a background of sporadic employment, you might require one or more cosigners, such as a parent or friend. (Each cosigner is 100% liable to repay the note if the borrower fails to.)

Federal law requires that commercial lenders give cosigners a notice of their potential liability when they agree to cosign a debt. Although this notice isn't required for personal loans between friends and relatives, we believe full disclosure of the risks of cosigning is a good idea, so we incorporate much of that notice language in this form.

### Signing Instructions

After filling in the top of the Cosigner Provision, staple it to your promissory note and then have the cosigner complete, sign, and date it. The lender should keep the original and give each cosigner a copy, along with a copy of the promissory note.

## Forms 42–45: Security Agreements

If you lend money to someone who doesn't repay it, your only recourse usually is to sue the person, get a court judgment, and then take money or property that can legally be seized to satisfy a debt.

There is an easier way: You can attach a security agreement to the promissory note. In a security agreement, you specify certain property belonging to the borrower, such as a car or computer, as collateral for repayment of the loan. It's best to use the purchased property as collateral, called a "purchase money security," because a nonpurchase money security agreement using certain household goods likely won't be upheld. If the borrower doesn't repay the loan, you can take the property, sell it, and use the proceeds to satisfy what you are owed. You don't have to go to court. However, you do have to follow proper procedures when you take back (repossess) the property.

Sometimes, a dishonest borrower will try to use the same piece of collateral to secure more than one debt. If that happens and the unscrupulous borrower later defaults on these secured loans, the lenders will find themselves competing to sell the collateral and use the proceeds to satisfy all their debts. How can secured creditors protect themselves? It's very simple: They must be the first to file evidence of their claim with the correct recording agency.

This chapter includes four different forms relating to security interests:

- Form 42: Security Agreement Provision for Promissory Note
- Form 43: Security Agreement for Borrowing Money
- Form 44: Uniform Commercial Code (U.C.C.) Financing Statement, and
- Form 45: Release of U.C.C. Financing Statement

> ### Using Your House as Collateral
>
> Think twice before you pledge real estate, and especially your home, as collateral for a loan. If you are unable to make loan payments, you could lose a large investment, not to mention a roof over your head.
>
> When you pledge your home or other real estate as security for a loan, a security agreement isn't adequate to protect the lender. The borrower generally needs to sign a mortgage or a deed of trust, which can then be recorded (filed) at a county office to establish the lender's security interest in the real estate. Then, if the borrower defaults, the lender has the right to sell the property to recover the amount due under the promissory note. This sort of transaction is complicated—you should seek the advice of a real estate lawyer before signing a mortgage or deed of trust.

Creating a security interest is a multistep process. First, you must add Form 42 to your promissory note. Second, you must complete a Security Agreement (Form 43) and attach it to your promissory note. Third, if the collateral is personal property, such as manufacturing equipment or vats of wine, a U.C.C. Financing Statement (Form 44) will usually need to be filed with the appropriate state agency (the lender typically takes care of this filing). This step "perfects your lien," meaning it gives you priority over creditors filing after you. (See the box above to learn how to perfect a real estate lien.)

Note that the forms in this book are intended to be used only when the borrower is securing a loan with tangible personal property, such as a computer or car. If you are considering using real property, such as a house, as collateral for a loan, you should seek the assistance of a real estate lawyer. Title to real estate is a highly technical matter beyond the scope of this book. Similarly, if you are considering using intangible personal property (bank accounts, stock in a corporation) or intellectual property (copyright, trademark, patent) as collateral for the loan, you should consult an attorney.

## Form 42: Security Agreement Provision for Promissory Note

You can use this form to identify the security interest, such as a car or valuable personal property, as a part of your contract. Choose the sample language on the form that is most appropriate for your situation and delete the others.

### Signing Instructions

There are two ways to use the Security Agreement Provision. Either you can copy the security language that's appropriate into your promissory note itself, or you can complete the security agreement form and staple it to your promissory note. If you use the form separately, the borrower (owner of the collateral) should sign and date the form. The lender should keep the original and give the borrower a copy, along with a copy of the promissory note. Otherwise, if the security provision becomes part of the note, the signing instructions for the note apply.

## Form 43: Security Agreement for Borrowing Money

Use the Security Agreement to state the terms of the lender's security interest in the property that will be used as collateral for the loan, and to describe the property.

> **! CAUTION**
> **Do not use this agreement if the collateral is real property, such as a house.** In that case, you will need to file a mortgage or deed of trust with the county land records office. See a real estate lawyer for assistance with this transaction.

When describing the property that will be used as collateral, be sure that you describe it in enough detail that the property can be easily identified. For example, you would describe a vehicle as a "2025 Toyota Tacoma, license plate number 9876543, Vehicle Identification Number ABC1234567" instead of simply "my red truck."

In Paragraph 1 of the agreement, you'll need to insert information from the promissory note (the date, amount, and annual percentage rate). In Paragraphs 5 and 9, insert the state where the property is located and the state whose laws will govern the agreement—usually the state where the parties live.

The agreement states that the lender will file a U.C.C. Financing Statement explained below and that the borrower will sign any additional documents needed to protect the lender's security interest. Signing additional documents might be necessary in some situations, such as when the secured property includes certain kinds of assets (particularly cars and boats) that might require the lender to be added to the asset's certificate of title instead of filing a Financing Statement.

Be sure that you read and understand the entire agreement—it contains many important clauses, including requiring the borrower to take care of the secured property, stating when the borrower will be considered in default, and describing what the lender can do if the borrower defaults.

### Signing Instructions

After completing the Security Agreement, both parties should sign and date the last page. The lender will keep the original and will attach it to the original promissory note. Because the Security Agreement is an important part of the promissory note, be sure to also attach a copy of the signed agreement to the borrower's copy of the promissory note.

## Form 44: U.C.C. Financing Statement

Use the U.C.C. Financing Statement to record your security interest in personal property.

Once you have completed the Security Agreement, contact the appropriate state agency to find out your state's rules for documenting the lender's security interest in the property. If the collateral is a car, boat, or similar vehicle, you will most likely need to contact the motor vehicles department. Some kinds of assets (often those that are licensed by the state, such as cars and boats) require the lender to take a security interest in the property by listing its name on the certificate of title instead of filing a financing statement. For most other property, such as electronics equipment or a computer system, contact the secretary of state's office. Ask for a copy of your state's rules for filing a U.C.C. Financing Statement, and find out whether your state has any special form you must use. If it does, use the state form (not this one).

## Signing Instructions

The borrower(s) should sign and date the U.C.C. Financing Statement. The lender should keep the original and give the borrower a copy. The lender should attach the promissory note and the Security Agreement to the U.C.C. Financing Statement and file these with the appropriate state office, such as the secretary of state. Leave the section at the bottom of the form blank; the filing officer will complete this.

Before using this form, make sure your state doesn't have special U.C.C. form requirements.

## Form 45: Release of U.C.C. Financing Statement

Once a loan is paid off, the borrower will want the public record to reflect that the property is no longer encumbered (being used as collateral) in favor of the lender. To do this, you will need to file this release with the public agency, such as the secretary of state's office, where you filed the U.C.C. Financing Statement. That will let prospective lawyers, creditors, and credit rating agencies know that the lender no longer claims an interest in the borrower's collateral.

This form should correspond to your original U.C.C. Financing Statement. So, make sure the description of property listed as collateral is identical and the other information makes clear which U.C.C. Financing Statement is being released. Again, find out whether your state has any special form you must use. If it does, use the state form (not this one).

## Signing Instructions

The borrower(s) should sign and date the Release of U.C.C. Financing Statement. The lender should keep the original and give the borrower a copy. The lender should file this release with the appropriate state office, such as the secretary of state. Leave the section at the bottom of the form blank; the filing officer will complete this.

**Note:** Before using this form, make sure your state doesn't have special U.C.C. form requirements.

## Form 46: Agreement to Modify Promissory Note

If someone who borrows money from you falls behind on repayment, contact that person to find out what's wrong. Offer whatever help you can to get the borrower back on track. Sometimes this will require no more than being willing to extend the repayment period for a few months. In other instances, you might take interest-only payments or rewrite the loan at a lower interest rate. Whatever you agree on, you must put it in writing. You can use this agreement for that purpose.

## Signing Instructions

The borrower(s) who signed the promissory note should sign and date the Agreement to Modify Promissory Note, and indicate the location (city or county) where this agreement is being signed. The lender should keep the original signed document and give a copy to the borrower(s).

## Form 47: Overdue Payment Demand

If someone who owes you money under a promissory note falls behind on repayment despite your efforts to work out a new repayment plan, your next step is to send the borrower a formal demand letter. You can use this form in such a situation. It serves as a formal notice to the borrower that you are demanding repayment. It states that if you do not hear from the borrower within 15 days, you will enforce your rights under the promissory note, including possibly filing a lawsuit to collect the debt.

> **CAUTION**
> **Be careful not to make any threats that you don't intend to follow up.** Although the federal and state fair debt laws probably don't apply to you, it's still a good idea to be fair, yet firm, in trying to persuade the borrower to pay you back.

### Signing Instructions

Sign the Overdue Payment Demand and send it to all borrowers and all cosigners by certified mail (return receipt requested). Keep a copy for your records. You might later need this copy if you end up suing the borrower to collect the money owed.

> **RELATED TOPIC**
> **If you are writing to request the return of a security deposit on rental property,** use the Demand for Return of Security Deposit in Chapter 4.

## Form 48: Demand to Make Good on Bad Check

This form is similar to the Overdue Payment Demand in that it's used when someone who owes you money isn't meeting the obligation to pay you and has ignored all your efforts to resolve the problem informally. The difference is that this form is used when the person who owes you money writes you a bad check, a slightly more complicated legal situation. Use this form to make a formal written demand for payment on a bad check.

Although writing a bad check is a crime in every state, prosecutions for writing bad checks are rare. Even in the unlikely event that a district attorney is willing to bring charges, there's a good chance the person would avoid a trial by agreeing to attend a diversion program for bad-check writers and making restitution—that is, paying up.

In most states, you'll want to deal with a bad check through civil, not criminal, remedies. The person who receives a bad check can usually sue for extra damages (above and beyond the amount of the check) if not paid within 30 days of making a formal written demand for payment.

A clause is included in the Demand to Make Good on Bad Check stating that if you sue over the bad check, you may ask for the maximum monetary damages allowed under state law. This amount is often two or three times the amount of the check. To find out what the maximum damages are in your state, check your state's laws.

### Signing Instructions

Sign the Demand to Make Good on Bad Check form and deliver it personally to the person who wrote you the bad check. Have the person acknowledge receipt by signing and dating an extra copy. Alternatively, send the form by certified mail (return receipt requested) or use a delivery service that will give you a receipt establishing delivery. Some states (California, for example) require that the demand be sent by certified mail (return receipt requested) for the lender to recover statutory damages. Keep copies of the demand and the return receipt. You might later need this evidence if you end up filing a lawsuit to collect payment.

CHAPTER 6

# Buying a House

**Form 49: Ideal House Profile** ........................................................................ 66

**Form 50: House Priorities Worksheet** ........................................................... 67

**Form 51: House Comparison Worksheet** ...................................................... 67

**Form 52: Family Financial Statement** ........................................................... 68

**Form 53: Monthly Carrying Costs Worksheet** ............................................... 70

**Form 54: Mortgage Rates and Terms Worksheet** ......................................... 71

**Form 55: Moving Checklist** ............................................................................ 74

**N**o doubt about it—a house is one of the most important investments you'll ever make. Careful planning and organization are key to getting the best house for your money. The forms in this chapter help you:

- identify house features most important to you and keep a record of relevant information about each house you visit (Forms 49 to 51)
- determine how much you're able to spend on the down payment and monthly mortgage payments (Forms 52 and 53), and
- keep track of information you collect on different loans and compare features such as interest rates and loan costs (Form 54).

This chapter also includes a handy checklist (Form 55) to help plan your move.

---

### Real Estate on Nolo.com

You can find a range of house-buying resources in the "Real Estate" section of Nolo's website (www.nolo.com), which has information on:
- screening houses that meet your financial and other needs
- checking sales prices of comparable properties to make a realistic offer
- arranging home inspections
- finding a real estate agent, home inspector, or other professional, and
- closing the deal.

---

**RESOURCE**

**For an excellent resource,** check out *Nolo's Essential Guide to Buying Your First Home,* by Ilona Bray and Ann O'Connell. It covers the entire process, from deciding whether you're ready to buy to settling into your new home.

## Form 49: Ideal House Profile

When looking for a house, it's easy to become overwhelmed by the variety of choices, from size to style to floor plan. Then there's the issue of location—houses come in all sorts of neighborhoods, school districts, and potential hazard zones (fire, earthquake, and flood, to name a few). Price and purchase terms are also crucial considerations. To cope with all the variables, and the fact that your search could take longer than expected, it's essential to establish your priorities in advance.

The Ideal House Profile lists all major house features, such as upper price limit, number and type of rooms, and location. Use it to identify the essential characteristics you're looking for.

Price is an obvious consideration for most people. For example, under "Upper price limit," you might note $800,000, with a maximum down payment of $80,000. And if you have two kids, you might note that three bedrooms and excellent public schools are "Must haves."

In most cases, it will be obvious where to note your priorities. For example, if quiet is important (you don't want to be near a freeway off-ramp) or you want walking access to a park, list these under "Desired neighborhood features." If you're not sure where to list a particular "Must have" such as a hot and dry climate, ocean view, or garage parking, put it in the "Other desired features" category on the Ideal House Profile.

Once you've compiled your list of "Must haves," jot down features that you'd like but that aren't crucial to your purchase decision. For example, under "Type of yard and grounds," you might note "patio and flat backyard" in the "Hope to have" column. Or under "Number and type of rooms," you might list "a finished basement."

Be sure to list your "Absolute no ways" (you won't buy a house that has any of these features) at the bottom of the form. Avoiding things you'll always hate, such as location in a flood zone or in a poor school district, or too far from where you work, can be even more important than finding a house that otherwise has everything you wanted.

If buying with another person, prepare your list of priorities together, so that each person's strong likes and dislikes are respected.

 **TIP**

**Can any of your priority items be added after you move in?** A new kitchen, deck, patio, and sometimes even an extra room can be added a few years down the road. Of course, replacing a small dark yard with a large sunny one can't be done.

 **TIP**

**Get more neighborhood information.** If you're moving to a new area, you might not have a good sense of what particular cities and neighborhoods are like. For example, if under your "Must have" column you've written "excellent public schools," you need in-depth information about the school system in each community you are considering. It's fine to ask a real estate agent. There's also a wealth of community and neighborhood information online. Or, take the time to talk to people in the area whose kids currently attend its schools.

## Form 50: House Priorities Worksheet

Now it's time to use the information collected in your Ideal House Profile to create a House Priorities Worksheet, which will help you see how each house you visit stacks up.

To start, copy your "Must haves," "Hope to haves," and "Absolute no ways" onto a master copy of this worksheet. Then, make several copies. Take one worksheet copy with you each time you visit a house, and fill in the top. Enter the address, asking price, name and contact information for the listing agent (or seller if it's for sale by owner), and the date you saw the house.

As you walk around each house and talk to the owner or agent, enter a check mark if the house has a desirable or undesirable feature. Also make notes next to a particular feature if it can be changed to meet your needs (an okay kitchen could be modernized for around $30,000). Add comments at the bottom, such as "potential undeveloped lot next door" or "neighbors seem friendly." If you look at a lot of houses, these notes will ensure you don't forget important information.

You should seriously consider only those houses with all or most of your "Must haves" and none of your "Absolute no ways."

 **TIP**

**Set up a good filing system or database.** To begin, copy your "Must haves," "Hope to haves," and "Absolute no ways" onto a master version of this Worksheet. Then, create separate copies for each time you visit a house, and fill in the top. Enter the address, asking price, name and contact information for the listing agent (or seller if it's for sale by owner) and the date you saw the place.

## Form 51: House Comparison Worksheet

If, like many people, you look at numerous houses over an extended period of time, you could soon have trouble distinguishing or comparing their features. That's where the House Comparison Worksheet comes in.

Across the top of the form, list the addresses of the three or four houses you like best. In the left column, fill in your list of priorities and "Absolute no ways" from your Ideal House Profile and House Priorities Worksheet. Then put a check mark on the line under each house that has that feature, to allow for a quick comparison.

## Form 52: Family Financial Statement

When planning to buy a house, one of your most important tasks is to determine how much you can realistically afford to pay. Begin by preparing a thorough family financial statement that includes:
- your monthly income
- your monthly expenses, and
- your net worth (your assets minus your debts or liabilities).

We use the word "family" as shorthand for the economic unit that will buy a house. For these purposes, an unmarried couple or a single person is just as much a family as is a married couple with three kids.

Preparing a family financial statement begins the process of learning how much house you can afford—in terms of both the down payment and monthly mortgage payments.

**CAUTION**

**This statement is for you, not your lender.** No matter how much debt a lender ultimately says you can handle, the purpose of this statement is to help you develop your own realistic picture of what this debt will mean for your monthly cash flow. The information you collect will help you fill out your loan application, but you won't give this statement directly to the lender. So if you exaggerate your income or underestimate your expenses, you'll only be fooling yourself.

### Directions for Completing the Family Financial Statement

**Top.** Indicate the name(s), address(es), email address(es), phone number(s), employer's name(s) and address(es), and work phone number(s) for yourself and any coborrower. A coborrower includes anyone with whom you are purchasing the house.

#### Worksheet 1: Income and Expenses

This worksheet shows you how much disposable income you have each month, a key fact in determining how much you can afford to spend on a house. In the first two columns, you and any coborrower each list your monthly income and expenses. Total them in the third column.

IA. **Monthly gross income.** List your monthly gross income from all sources. Gross income means total income before amounts such as taxes, Social Security, or retirement contributions are withheld.

1. **Employment.** This is your base salary or wages plus any bonuses, tips, commissions, or overtime you regularly receive. If your income is irregular, take the average of the past 24 months. If you have more than one job, include your combined total.

2. **Public benefits.** Include income from Social Security, disability insurance, Temporary Assistance for Needy Families (TANF), Supplemental Security Income (SSI), and other public programs.

3. **Dividends.** Include all dividends from stocks, bonds, and similar investments.

4. **Royalties.** If you have continuing income from the sale (licensing) of books, music, software, inventions, or the like, list it here.

5. **Interest and other investment income.** Include interest received on savings or money market accounts, or as payments on rental property. If the source of the income has costs associated with it (such

as the costs of owning rental property), include the net monthly profit received.

6. **Other.** Include payments from pensions, child or spousal support, or separate private maintenance income. Specify the source.

**IB. Total monthly gross income.** Total up items 1–6. (This is the figure that lenders use to qualify you for mortgages.)

**IIA. Monthly nonhousing expenses.** List what you spend each month on items such as child care and clothing. Here are some notes clarifying specific items. (Also, see Form 66, Daily Expenses, for advice on computing average monthly expenses.)

1. **Child care.** Self-explanatory
2. **Clothing.** Self-explanatory
3. **Food.** Include eating at restaurants, as well as at home.
4. **Insurance.** List the monthly cost of your auto, life, and medical and dental insurance. If you pay any of these costs yearly, divide the annual amount by 12 and include here.
5. **Other medical.** List uninsured medical expenses.
6. **Personal.** Include costs for both personal care (haircuts, shoe repairs, and toiletries) and personal fun (attending movies and buying lottery tickets, subscribing to newspapers). Also, include any regular personal loan payments.
7. **Education.** Include monthly payments for education loans here, plus educational payments, such as your child's private school tuition.
8. **Taxes.** Take your annual average income tax bill and divide by 12.
9. **Phone, cable, streaming, Wi-Fi services.** Enter your monthly payments for all such electronic services.
10. **Transportation.** Include costs for both motor vehicles (including monthly car loan payments, but excluding insurance, which you've already listed) and public transit. Include monthly upkeep for a vehicle and a reasonable amount for repairs.
11. **Other.** Specify such expenses as regular monthly credit card payments, charitable, political, or religious donations, savings deposits, and child or spousal support payments.

**IIB. Current housing expenses.** If you currently own a home, list the monthly mortgage payments, taxes, insurance, and utilities (including gas, electricity, water, sewage, garbage, telephone, and cable service). If you rent, include your monthly rent and renter's insurance (if any).

**IIC. Total monthly expenses.** Here, total your nonhousing and housing expenses. Then subtract line C from line B to see how much disposable income you have available to put toward a monthly mortgage payment. Of course, you can also add in whatever amount you currently spend on your mortgage payment or rent.

## Worksheet 2: Assets and Liabilities

I. **Assets.** In the first two columns, you and any coborrower write down the cash or market value of the assets listed. Total them up in the third column.

A. **Cash and cash equivalents.** List your cash and items easily converted into cash. Deposits include checking accounts, savings accounts, money market accounts, and certificates of deposit (even if there is a withdrawal penalty).

B. **Marketable securities.** Here you list items like stocks and bonds that are regularly traded and that you can turn into cash fairly readily. List the cash surrender value of any life insurance policy. Include items such as a short-term loan you made to a friend under the category "Other."

C. **Total cash and marketable securities.** Add up items A and B.
D. **Nonliquid assets.** These are items not easily converted into cash.
   1. **Real estate.** List the market value—the amount the property would sell for.
   2. **Retirement funds.** Include public or private pensions and self-directed accounts (IRAs, Keoghs, or 401(k) plans). List the amount vested in the plan.
   3. **Business.** If you own a business, list your equity in it (market value less the debts of the business). Many small businesses are difficult to sell, and therefore difficult to value, but do your best.
   4. **Motor vehicles.** List the current market value of any car, truck, recreational vehicle (RV), or motorcycle, even if you're still making payments. Check used car guides for the information; you can check the *Kelley Blue Book* at www.kbb.com.
   5. **Other.** Include nontangible assets such as copyrights, patents, and trademarks. Yes, it's hard to value these, but it can be done, especially if you've been receiving income that promises to continue. Depending on your field, professional organizations that serve authors, inventors, musicians, or software writers might be able to help. In the "Other" category, also include the current value of long-term loans you've made to others, and any really valuable personal property such as expensive jewelry, cameras, or electronic gear.
E. **Total nonliquid assets.** Total up items D1–5.

F. **Total all assets.** Total up items IC and IE.

IIA. **Liabilities—*debts*.** In the first two columns, you and any coborrower write the total balances remaining for your outstanding loans under their respective categories.

Under "Other," don't include monthly insurance payments or medical (noninsurance) payments; these go on Worksheet 1, Section IIA, Monthly Expenses—Nonhousing. Do include stock pledges, lawyers' and accountants' bills, and so on.

IIB. **Total liabilities.** Total the monthly payments and balances remaining for items 1–7.

III. **Net worth.** Total of all assets minus total liabilities.

Now that you understand what assets you have available, you can estimate how much money you'll have to put toward a down payment.

## Form 53: Monthly Carrying Costs Worksheet

Your next step is to understand how much money a lender will allow you to borrow. This will be based on your income, your debts, and the monthly expenses—called "carrying costs"—associated with buying your home. To make this calculation, complete the Monthly Carrying Costs Worksheet. You will need to provide the following information.

**Line 1: Estimated purchase price.** State how much money you'll likely need to spend on a house that has at least most of the "Must have" features listed on your Ideal House Profile.

**Line 2: Down payment.** Enter the down payment you plan to make (ideally 20% of the purchase price).

**3: Loan amount.** Subtract your anticipated down payment (line 2) from your estimated purchase price (line 1). The result is the amount you'll need to borrow.

**Line 4: Interest rate.** Estimate the mortgage interest rate you'll pay based on the rates listed online at sites such as bankrate.com. (You'll get a more exact idea of what rate you'll need to pay when you start shopping for a mortgage, using the Mortgage Rates and Terms Worksheet.)

**Line 5: Monthly mortgage payment.** Calculate your monthly mortgage payments by using a calculator on a website such as bankrate.com.

**Line 6: Homeowners' insurance.** You can get exact quotes in advance from insurance agents. Expect to spend several hundred dollars per year on insurance, depending on your home's size, features, and location.

**Line 7: Property taxes.** These vary tremendously depending on where you live. Get an estimate from a local tax assessor's office.

**Line 8: Total monthly housing costs.** Now add up your mortgage payment (line 5), insurance (line 6), and taxes (line 7). This is your monthly carrying cost (also called PITI—principal, interest, taxes, and insurance).

**Line 9: Other monthly debts.** These are items such as monthly payments on a car or student loan. Exclude any debts that will be paid off within 10 months.

**Line 10: Private mortgage insurance (PMI).** Your lender may require you to purchase this if you're making a down payment of less than 20%. PMI premiums are often about 0.5% of the loan.

**Line 11: Homeowners' association fee.** You might have to pay this monthly fee if you're looking to buy a condo, townhome, or a house in a planned unit development.

**Line 12: Total monthly housing costs and other debts.** Add lines 8–11 for the sum of your total monthly carrying costs and long-term debts.

**Line 13: Lender qualifying ratio.** Lenders normally want you to pay the house's monthly carrying costs (mortgage payment, property taxes, and homeowners' insurance) with no more than 28%–36% of your monthly gross income. Whether you qualify at the bottom or top of this range depends on the amount of your down payment, the interest rate on the type of mortgage you want, your credit score (which reflects how you've managed credit in the past), and the level of your other long-term debts.

**Line 14: Monthly gross income to qualify.** Divide line 12 by line 13 to determine the monthly income needed to qualify.

**Line 15: Yearly gross income to qualify.** Multiply line 14 by 12 (which represents months in a year) to calculate the yearly income to qualify.

# Form 54: Mortgage Rates and Terms Worksheet

As with any consumer product, you can save money by carefully shopping for a mortgage. But because of the variety of mortgages on the market and the fact that fine-print terms can significantly influence how much you'll really have to pay, it's essential that you carefully compare the total cost of different deals.

Use the Mortgage Rates and Terms Worksheet to keep track of information you collect on different loans. It is helpful whether you'll be working with a loan broker (who specializes in matching house buyers and appropriate mortgage lenders) or loan shopping on your own.

This form is helpful for three primary reasons:
- Filling it out all but requires you to understand the fine-print details of every loan you consider.
- Having this information will aid your memory later when trying to recall what you've been offered.
- Assuming you get information about more than one loan, you can efficiently compare features.

## Instructions for Completing the Mortgage Rates and Terms Worksheet

### Heading

At the top of the table, enter the lender's name (such as Bank of Richmond), the name of the loan agent you met or spoke with, the agent's phone number, email, and any other contact information, and the date of your meeting or conversation.

### Section 1: General Information

Enter the type of loan: fixed or adjustable; the rate, if it's a fixed mortgage; whether it qualifies for government financing (if that's a need you have); the minimum down payment; whether PMI is required and, if so, whether you'll need to set up an impound account; the term (number of years of the loan); whether it's assumable (currently possible only with Federal Housing Administration (FHA) or Department of Veterans Affairs (VA) loans); and whether it lets you (and for how much) lock in at a certain interest rate. (See the box below for a brief description of key mortgage terms.)

### Section 2: Debt-to-Income Ratio Information

Indicate the percentage of your income each lender allows for the monthly carrying costs to obtain the mortgage and for monthly carrying costs plus monthly payments on other long-term debts. Then, based on these debt-to-income ratios, enter the maximum loan each lender will make.

### Section 3: Loan Costs

If possible, enter the costs associated with getting the loan—the number of points and their cost, PMI, additional loan fee, credit report, application fee, appraisal fee, and other miscellaneous costs. Then total them up. Your estimate will have to be rough, because most lenders won't estimate closing costs until they start processing your loan.

### Section 4: Time Limits

You want to know how long it will take for the lender to process your loan application and, if it's approved, come up with the money (called "funding the loan"), thus enabling you to close the deal. Enter this information in the fourth section. Pay attention to the following items:
- the date each month your payment will be due (the 1st of the month is standard, although some portfolio lenders set the 15th or allow you to choose a date)
- how many "grace" days you have (after which the payment is considered late—15 days is standard), and
- the fee for late mortgage payments.

### Section 5: Other Features

If the loan has any special features, such as discounted points if you have a savings account with the bank, indicate them.

### Section 6: Fixed-Rate Two-Step Loans

If you look at any fixed-rate loans that step up to a higher rate after several years, indicate the initial annual percentage rate, and for how many years it stays in effect.

### Section 7: Fixed-Rate Balloon Payment Loans

If you're considering a fixed-rate loan for a short period (often three, five, or seven years) that ends with one large balloon payment, indicate the interest rate and monthly payment, the term of the loan, and the amount of the balloon payment.

## Key Mortgage Terms

Here's help deciphering some of the mortgage jargon you might encounter.

**Fixed-rate mortgage.** The interest rate and the amount you pay each month remain the same over the entire mortgage term, which is traditionally 30 years, or in some cases 15 years.

**Adjustable-rate mortgage (ARM).** The interest rate fluctuates according to interest rates in the economy. Initial, discounted interest rates are typically offered for a set period (sometimes as short as one month). This rate is lower than the going rate for fixed-rate mortgages. When the initial discount period ends, the interest rate adjusts according to current market rates. The amount of the adjustment is tied to a market-sensitive number called the "index." A "margin" is the factor or percentage a lender adds to the index to arrive at the interest rate you pay over the market rate. Though your interest rate can increase based on the index plus the margin, there's usually a maximum limit, called the "life-of-the-loan cap" (usually, five or six percentage points above the initial rate). A periodic cap limits the amount your interest rate can go up or down at each adjustment period, such as going up 2% annually, with your payments increasing accordingly.

**PMI and impound account.** Lenders may require PMI if you're making a down payment of less than 20%. PMI insures the lender if you don't pay the mortgage. Some lenders require that you set up an impound account at the time you close the house purchase, where you deposit up to a year's payments of PMI. In addition, you make monthly payments into the impound account for property taxes and homeowners' insurance, which in turn are paid by the lender or company that services the loan.

**Assumable loan.** A loan that a creditworthy buyer can take over (assume) from a seller. Most fixed-rate loans are not assumable unless they're FHA or VA loans.

**Rate lock-in.** A lender's guarantee to make a loan at a particular interest rate, even if the market changes before the closing. The lock-in is usually for a specific time period, such as three to six weeks.

**Debt-to-income ratio.** The ratio of your monthly mortgage payments (including insurance and property taxes) plus long-term debts to your income; also called lender qualification.

**Monthly carrying costs.** The sum of your monthly payments for your mortgage principal and interest, homeowners' insurance, and property taxes.

**Points and loan costs.** The fees associated with getting a mortgage, which usually add up to 2%–5% of its cost. Points make up the largest part of lender fees, with one point equaling 1% of the loan principal. Not all loans come with points; they're a way for you to buy down the interest rate. If you will own a house for many years, paying relatively high points is usually a good idea—their cost is more than paid for by the reduction in interest payments over the life of the loan. But the reverse is also true—if you move in three to five years or less, it's better to pay as few points as possible, even if you pay a little higher interest. It takes several years for the monthly interest savings to offset the initial high cost of points.

### Section 8: Adjustable-Rate Mortgages (ARMs)

First, enter the adjustable loan criteria—what index it's tied to and the amount of the margin.

Second, write down interest rate information—the initial rate, how long it lasts, the periodic interest rate cap, the adjustment period, and the life-of-the-loan cap.

Third and finally, enter the payment information—the initial payment, cap, and payment cap period. Also calculate your worst-case scenario: the highest interest rate and monthly payments possible with the adjustable-rate loan offered for different time periods.

### Section 9: Hybrid Loans

If you're interested in an ARM that has a fixed rate for the first few years and then becomes adjustable, enter the information here. Pay particular attention to how much the interest rate can jump at the first adjustment period.

## Form 55: Moving Checklist

Congratulations! If you're looking at this form, chances are you've found a good house, closed escrow, and are getting ready to move in. Use the Moving Checklist to help you plan your move.

CHAPTER 7

# Buying or Selling a Car, Dog, or Personal Property

**Form 56: Motor Vehicle Bill of Sale** ........................................................................................................... 76

**Form 57: Boat Bill of Sale** ............................................................................................................................ 78

**Form 58: General Bill of Sale** ...................................................................................................................... 78

**Form 59: Bill of Sale for Dog** ...................................................................................................................... 78

This chapter contains forms for use when buying or selling used personal property, such as a car, boat, appliance, or furniture. It also includes a bill of sale for a dog. Use these simple agreements to record the terms of sale of all types of property (with the exception of real estate and securities, which are closely regulated by law).

A "bill of sale" is a written document that, at a minimum, sets forth:
- the names of the seller(s) and buyer(s) (there may be two sellers—for example, if the goods are co-owned as joint property)
- a statement that a sale has taken place
- a description of the item(s) sold
- the amount paid, and
- the signature of the person selling the property and the date of the signing.

In addition, the bills of sale in this chapter often contain:
- a promise that the seller owns or otherwise has the right to sell the item, and details of any liens or encumbrances giving someone else an ownership stake in the goods being sold
- a written warranty or guarantee that the item is in good condition and will be repaired or replaced if it fails within a certain set period
- disclosures of any major defects known to the seller, and
- if appropriate, a statement that the item has been inspected by an expert and that the expert's report is attached.

**TIP**

**A well-drafted bill of sale can head off future legal trouble.** When used cars, boats, and other items of property are sold without a written bill of sale, the chances of future legal problems—maybe even a court battle—go way up. Far better to define in advance all key terms of the sale, including the condition of the goods being sold and whether the sale includes any seller's warranty (for example, 30 days on parts and labor) or is made "as is."

In some states, a bill of sale must have a notary clause. Although this isn't common, we've included a Certificate of Acknowledgment of Notary Public on each bill of sale form in this chapter. If your state doesn't require notarization, you don't need to use it—but it can't hurt. (See the Introduction to this book for more about notarization.)

## Form 56: Motor Vehicle Bill of Sale

Use this bill of sale when you buy or sell a vehicle that must be registered with your state's motor vehicles department. This typically includes cars, trucks, motorcycles, recreational vehicles, and motor homes. It does not include stationary nonregistered mobile homes that are designed to be used semipermanently at a fixed location, such as a mobile home park. Such homes are commonly treated as real property—just as if they were houses—and are covered by special transfer, financing, and recording rules not discussed here. This category of motor vehicle also doesn't include off-road farm machinery—for that, use the General Bill of Sale—unless it can be registered in your state as a motor vehicle.

Describe the vehicle in detail on the bill of sale, including the vehicle identification number, or VIN (typically found on the driver's side of the dashboard, close to the windshield), and indicate the price paid. (Your state motor vehicles department needs the price to compute the sales tax.) List any personal property included in the sale, such as a bicycle rack.

> **CAUTION**
> **Double-check ownership interest in the vehicle.** If you are buying a motor vehicle and you don't know much about the seller, check with the motor vehicles department where the vehicle is registered to be sure that the seller is the owner, and that no one else claims an ownership interest (lien) in the vehicle. (If the seller hadn't yet repaid a purchase loan, for example, the lender might have an ownership claim). You can get additional useful information about the vehicle's ownership history from services such as Carfax Vehicle Reports (carfax.com) or AutoCheck (autocheck.com) if you have the VIN. For example, you can learn whether the car was ever severely damaged and "salvaged" or whether the odometer has been rolled back.

Clauses 8 and 9 relate to inspections and condition of the vehicle. These provisions will help the seller avoid future legal problems. If the vehicle is inspected by a mechanic who prepares a written report that is given to the buyer, and the seller conscientiously discloses all known defects, it's highly unlikely that a dissatisfied buyer can later get a judge to agree that the seller misrepresented the car's condition.

Be sure to contact your state motor vehicles department for any special requirements when selling a motor vehicle. For example, the vehicle might have to qualify for a smog certificate. If there are other requirements, include them in Clause 10.

Also, find out whether your state provides a special form for you to use. If it does, use the state form (not this one).

If the seller hasn't fully repaid a loan on the vehicle, the seller should ask the lender if its permission is required to sell the vehicle. If the vehicle is leased, the seller should ask the lessor what it requires before the vehicle can be transferred or sold.

### Signing Instructions

The buyer(s) and seller(s) must sign the Motor Vehicle Bill of Sale for it to be valid. Print out two copies of the form (or enough for everyone who signs the form to have a separate copy). Each person should sign and date all copies of the form and keep a signed document with all original signatures.

Be sure to check with your state motor vehicles department regarding any official signing requirements that must be met. For example, the seller's signature on the vehicle's title might need to be notarized. And in some states, the bill of sale itself needs to be notarized. (If so, see the instructions about notarization in the Introduction to this book.)

In addition, the seller might need to file an official form to avoid liability if the buyer hits someone with the vehicle after the sale, and the buyer might have to file an official form to register the vehicle in the buyer's name.

## Form 57: Boat Bill of Sale

This form is similar in content to the Motor Vehicle Bill of Sale, but it covers boats of all kinds. The form contains details about the boat, as well as any engines, electronics, and other equipment that are to be sold along with it.

Carefully read the discussion that accompanies the Motor Vehicle Bill of Sale, especially the advice about arranging for an inspection by a third party and having the seller list (disclose) all defects. These provisions make it difficult for a lawyer to claim later that the seller misrepresented the condition of the boat.

This bill of sale includes a number of entries unique to boat sales. Fill in the details key to your sale, such as a thorough list of all personal property items included in the sale or the maintenance history of the boat.

Also, find out whether your state provides a special form for you to use. If it does, use the state form (not this one).

If the seller hasn't fully repaid a purchase loan on the boat, the seller should ask the lender whether its permission is required in order to sell the boat.

### Signing Instructions

The buyer(s) and seller(s) must sign the Boat Bill of Sale for it to be valid. Print out two copies of the form (or enough for each person signing the form to have a separate copy). Each person should sign and date all copies of the form and keep a signed document with all original signatures.

Be sure to check with your state motor vehicles department (or the department in your state that registers boats) regarding any official signing requirements that must be met. For example, the seller's signature on the boat's title might need to be notarized. In addition, the seller might need to file an official form to avoid liability if the buyer hits someone with the boat after the sale, and the buyer might have to file an official form to register the boat in the buyer's name.

## Form 58: General Bill of Sale

The General Bill of Sale should be used for the sale of personal property such as jewelry, artwork, sports equipment, rare books, furniture, collections, appliances, tools, photographic equipment, and electronic items. Don't use this form if you are selling a car or other motor vehicle, or a boat. (These categories are specifically covered above.) Before using this form, read the brief discussion that precedes the Motor Vehicle Bill of Sale, which discusses key clauses in a bill of sale.

### Signing Instructions

The buyer(s) and seller(s) must sign the General Bill of Sale for it to be valid. Print out two copies of the form (or enough for each person signing the form to have a separate copy). Each person should sign and date all copies of the form and keep a signed document with all original signatures.

## Form 59: Bill of Sale for Dog

Use this bill of sale when you buy or sell a dog in a transaction with a private party or a breeder. It spells out exactly what terms the seller is promising, including price, how and when the dog will be turned over to the buyer, and who will pay shipping costs (if any). This form provides basic information on the dog, including birth date, medication information such as vaccination history, health, name of breeder, special training (if any), and registration with the American Kennel Club or other entity. Most of the form is self-explanatory. You can add any items of special concern—for example, if the seller wants the buyer to have the dog spayed or neutered.

Clause 6 gives the buyer two options if a veterinarian certifies, in writing, that the dog has a disease or a congenital defect that was present when the buyer bought the dog. Within 14 days, the buyer may either return the dog to the seller and be reimbursed for the purchase price and for reasonable veterinary bills already paid, or keep the dog and also receive reimbursement for reasonable veterinary bills, up to the amount of the purchase price.

**If you're buying a dog from a pet store.** You might have other legal rights in addition to those set out in this bill of sale. Because consumers have had so many problems with dogs bought in pet stores, many states impose special requirements on pet retailers (rules that don't apply to breeders who raise and sell dogs themselves.) You could be entitled to a disclosure sheet stating where the animal came from (it might have been shipped across the country at a young age) and its health and vaccination history. You might also have a right to return or exchange an unhealthy dog, or get reimbursement for veterinary bills.

> **Consider Dog Adoption**
>
> According to the ASPCA, approximately 607,000 animals were euthanized in shelters last year. By adopting a dog, you are saving a life. Not only do you rescue the pet you adopt, but you also help create space and resources in the shelter for another animal in need. Additionally, adopting a dog is usually much less expensive than buying one from a breeder. If you're looking for a specific breed, many dogs in shelters are purebred. Many nonprofit dog rescues also have purebred dogs available for adoption.

## Signing Instructions

The buyer(s) and seller(s) must sign this Bill of Sale for Dog for it to be valid. Print out two copies of the form (or enough for each person signing the form to have a separate copy). Each person should sign and date all copies of the form and keep a signed document with all original signatures.

CHAPTER 8

# Renting Personal Property and Storing Goods

**Form 60: Personal Property Rental Agreement** ........................................................................... 82

**Form 61: Notice of Termination of Personal Property Rental Agreement** ........................... 83

**Form 62: Storage Contract** ................................................................................................................. 83

People frequently rent tools, equipment, and other personal property. While equipment is often rented from commercial companies that have their own forms, it is also not uncommon to rent briefly needed items from a neighbor or friend, perhaps a rototiller and weight drum to lay sod or a power saw and sander to do a small remodeling job. Or, you might rent property for a recreational purpose—for example, if you're assigned to bring a volleyball net and badminton set to the family reunion.

This chapter includes a form for renting personal property. You can tailor the form based on the type of property you're renting, its value, and how long you need it for. The chapter also includes a notice to end this type of rental agreement.

In addition to borrowing or renting tools, equipment, and other items, people often turn to friends or neighbors to store their personal property, such as furniture, for an extended period of time. This chapter includes a storage contract for use in these situations.

Whether a rental or storage fee is paid, it makes sense to write down your understanding of key issues, such as the length of the rental or storage period and who will be responsible if the rented or stored property is damaged. Having a written agreement is especially important if valuable property is to be rented or stored for an extended period. If any problem comes up, having a simple written contract will help you arrive at a fair settlement and preserve relations between the parties.

## Form 60: Personal Property Rental Agreement

You can use this form for a short-term rental (30 days or less) of personal (non–real estate) property. It is primarily geared toward renting relatively inexpensive personal property from a neighbor or friend. It isn't intended to be used for rental of a motor vehicle, motorcycle, ATV, boat, personal watercraft, or the like. Because not much is at stake, this rental agreement doesn't deal with the many potentially complex issues that can arise when expensive property is rented for an extended period. But this Personal Property Rental Agreement covers all the basics, including the names of the parties (owner and renter), a description of the property and its condition, the rental dollar amount, the length of the rental period, and delivery arrangements. It includes a dispute resolution clause that provides for negotiation, mediation, and/or arbitration as a means for the parties to resolve any disputes that might arise over the agreement. (See the Introduction for more on dispute resolution procedures.)

**TIP**
**Use this agreement even if no rent is being paid.** Simply put a zero (0) on the dollar amount lines in Clauses 3, 4, 5, and 6. Fill in all the other sections. And depending on the particular personal property, the renter should consider giving the owner a small thank-you gift, such as movie tickets.

### Signing Instructions

The owner and the renter must both sign this Personal Property Rental Agreement for it to be valid. Print out two copies of the form (or enough for each person who will be signing the form to have a separate copy). Each person should sign and date all copies of the form and keep a signed document with all original signatures.

## Form 61: Notice of Termination of Personal Property Rental Agreement

This form can be used by either the owner or the renter to end any personal property rental agreement that isn't made for a specific period. You don't need to give a reason (unless this is required by your rental agreement).

 **CAUTION**
**Do not use this termination notice if you have rented personal property for a specific rental period.** In that case, you can't terminate the agreement unless both parties agree.

### Signing Instructions

Simply sign the Notice of Termination of Personal Property Rental Agreement and give it to the other party. Keep a copy for your records, and note on your copy the date and time you delivered the notice.

## Form 62: Storage Contract

It is common to store property with friends and relatives—everything from bikes, beds, and books to washing machines, weights, and walking sticks. Sometimes this situation amounts to nothing more than leaving a few small objects for a short time. On other occasions, however, it means storing a household- or garage-full of goods for a year or more. In many situations involving friends and family, money isn't charged for storage, although payment certainly can be appropriate when bulky or valuable objects are stored for a considerable period of time. This is especially true when the goods are stored in a place (for example, a garage or spare room) that might otherwise be rented or used.

This form covers the basics of storing personal property, including the names of the parties (we call them "property owner" and "property custodian"); a description of the property being stored and its condition and value; storage location, term, and payment; who's responsible for theft of or damage to property during the rental period; and how the custodian will deal with abandoned property never reclaimed by the owner. This storage contract includes a dispute resolution clause that provides for negotiation, mediation, and/or arbitration as a means for the parties to resolve any disputes that might arise over the agreement. (See the Introduction for more on dispute resolution procedures.)

It is especially important that you carefully identify property and its value and condition. One common dispute involves the property owner claiming that a valuable item is missing, while the custodian says it was never present in the first place. The best way to prevent this is to make a thorough list of the items to be stored, and take pictures and attach them to the contract. In Clause 1, you should identify each item as thoroughly as possible, including (as appropriate) the make, model, year, and color (you'll spell out the condition in Clause 12). Also, when you state the value of the property (Clause 11), be sure to specify whether you mean the replacement value or the fair market value of the property. (You'll be asked to make a choice.) Replacement value is how much it would cost for you to buy another of this item, such as the cost of a new TV. Fair market value is how much you would get for an item, such as a TV, if you sold it—for example, online or at a garage sale. Whichever you choose, specify the value of each item you store, to reduce the chance of a misunderstanding if any items are damaged or missing. Use Clause 12 to spell out any defects or damage in the property being stored (such as a stain on a sofa).

Clause 13 requires the property custodian to use reasonable care while storing the property, but the custodian will not be responsible for damage due to inherent flaws or the property's inherent defective condition. The optional part of the clause specifies that the property will be insured by the owner, and that the custodian will also cover the property subject to the limits and limitations of the owner's own homeowners' or other insurance policy. Homeowners' policies will generally cover damage or loss to another's property up to a certain amount, and typically will not cover automobiles.

Use Clause 18 to describe any special terms of the storage—for example, if you want the custodian to start the car at least once a week while it's in storage.

## Signing Instructions

Both parties must sign this Storage Contract for it to be valid. Print out two copies of the form (or enough for each person who will be signing the form to have a separate copy). Each person should sign and date all copies of the form and keep a signed document with all original signatures.

CHAPTER 9

# Home Repairs and Maintenance

**Form 63: Home Maintenance Agreement** ........................................................... 87
**Form 64: Home Repairs Agreement** ................................................................... 88
**Form 65: Contractor Mid-Job Worksheet** .......................................................... 88

This chapter contains three agreements that cover home maintenance and repairs, as well as other work you plan to have done at your residence, such as painting or yard work. To get the job done right, your most important task is to find a contractor who has done excellent work for other people in your community. (Our forms use the term "contractor" for someone who does home repairs or maintenance.)

But even with a highly recommended person, serious misunderstandings can easily arise if the key job specifications, payment details, and work schedule haven't been carefully worked out and written down before the work begins. That's the purpose of these forms. They'll help you get the work done right, on time, and within your budget.

> **CAUTION**
> **The first two forms in this chapter are not suitable for complicated jobs.** You'll need a more detailed contract if you're planning on remodeling a kitchen, adding a room, putting on a new roof, painting the complete exterior or interior, or doing any other similarly large project. A large firm doing major home repairs and remodeling will usually present you with its own contract. The forms in this chapter can help you analyze an agreement proposed by a contractor and make sure the basics are covered.

## State Licensing and Registration Requirements for Home Repair Work

Almost all states have licensing requirements for certain categories of highly skilled home improvement and construction work. For example, most states license people who do residential electrical and plumbing work or who build new structures. By contrast, there is less uniformity among the states as to whether licensing is required for contractors who do general repair and remodeling work, such as framing, drywall installation, paneling, deck construction, siding, and painting.

License and registration requirements are often tied to the following factors:

- **Size of the project**—a license might be required for work on any job over a specified amount, such as $5,000.
- **Type of job**—some states require a license for plumbing or electrical work but not for painting, for example.
- **Location of contractor**—most states regulate contracting work of any type that is done by out-of-state contractors.

Most states that require a license for general repair and remodeling tasks require some experience and skills training, as well as some evidence of financial responsibility or effective customer recourse policy. For details, contact your state's consumer protection office or visit its website to find out whether your state regulates the type of contractor you are hiring, and if so, the name of the agency that does the regulating, such as the Contractors State License Board. Many let you check online whether a contractor's license is current and in good standing. Also, many state agencies publish and distribute free consumer information on home repair work, with useful advice on finding and working with a home repair contractor and the legal requirements that apply in your state.

> **CAUTION**
> **Beware of unlicensed contractors.** Even where licenses are required, you can always find someone unlicensed who will do the work, usually promising a cheap price. Be wary—unlicensed contractors are not bonded, meaning that their work isn't insured, and your homeowners' insurance might refuse to cover their injuries, leaving you open to personal liability. And, of course, an unlicensed contractor is almost sure to work without getting a building permit, which could cause problems later.

Some states require people who do home repair and remodeling work to register with a particular government agency. Registration usually doesn't require demonstrated experience or training. It's primarily designed to keep track of people offering contractor services so that homeowners can locate them if something goes wrong during or after the job.

### Local Permits and Approvals for Home Repair Work

In addition to state licensing and registration rules, homeowners often must obtain a permit from a city or county agency for jobs that involve structural alterations, additions, substantial remodeling, or new electrical wiring or plumbing installations. Permits \are usually not required for casual carpentry, minor plumbing and electrical repairs, or replacing a window or door.

In addition to a local permit, if the house is part of a condominium complex or planned unit development, a homeowners' association or "architectural review committee" will likely insist on formal approval of the work, especially if the work affects the home's exterior appearance. Homeowners' association approval is usually necessary for new windows, exterior painting, roofing, and room additions.

Either the homeowner or the contractor must be responsible for getting information about necessary permits. If the job requires a permit or approval but no one obtains it, the homeowner might have to redo some or all of the work if a later inspection reveals deficiencies. Also, the resale value of the home could be adversely affected if or when the buyer learns of the nonpermitted work.

### Independent Contractor vs. Employee

Our contracts (Clause 4 in each) assume that the person who will work on your house is an independent contractor, not your employee. As long as the contractor is doing one job or occasional work, this is legal. If a person will work for you regularly (an everyday gardener, for example), the law probably requires that you treat them as an employee, for whom you are legally required to pay income taxes, Social Security, and other benefits.

**RESOURCE**
**For more information on the difference between an independent contractor and an employee,** see IRS Form SS-8, available on the IRS website at www.irs.gov.

### Dispute Resolution Clause

The first two forms in this chapter do not include a dispute resolution clause mandating mediation and arbitration to resolve disputes before going to court. But you can add one. See the Introduction to this book, where this option is explained.

## Form 63: Home Maintenance Agreement

This form is intended for hiring unskilled labor on a one-time job that isn't expected to last for more than a day or two and doesn't need a significant amount of materials.

Typical jobs that fall into this category are hauling trash, cleaning a garage or house, washing windows, and gardening and other yard work. Such jobs are usually performed by one person, who supplies the required tools.

This form is easy to complete. Simply spell out the details of the work and the amount, form, and schedule of payment, and any additional terms that are relevant, such as who will pay the fee for hauling refuse to the dump, or who will be responsible for obtaining and paying for any necessary permits.

### Signing Instructions

You (the homeowner) and the contractor must sign this Home Maintenance Agreement for it to be valid. Print out two copies of the form and have each party sign and date both. Give the contractor one of the signed documents and keep the other for your own records.

## Form 64: Home Repairs Agreement

This form covers home repairs done by skilled laborers for a job that isn't expected to take more than a few days, such as installing new locks or windows, nonstructural carpentry repairs, touch-up painting, masonry work, or roofing repairs. Use it to spell out the who (names of the homeowner and contractor), what and how (specific details of the job, such as painting the kitchen or installing new bathroom flooring), how much (the dollar amount and details of payment), and when (beginning and ending dates) of the work, plus any additional terms, such as who will be paying for and picking up materials and supplies, such as paint.

**TIP**

**Don't pay too much up front—just enough to let the contractor purchase the materials needed to get started.** It's usually best to agree to make periodic payments that are tied to measurable, easy-to-define completed tasks. Clause 2 is the place to spell out the details of your payment arrangement. For example, you might decide to pay one lump sum at the end of the work, pay in increments (such as half at the beginning of work and half at the end), or pay an hourly rate for work done.

Simple home repairs probably won't require a contractor's license or permit, but if they do, Clauses 4 and 5 of the Home Repairs Agreement allow you to spell out the details. If you don't need them, follow the instructions in the Introduction for deleting unnecessary contract clauses.

Clause 6 specifies that the contractor must carry insurance and accept responsibility for injuries that occur during the course of the work.

### Signing Instructions

You (the homeowner) and the contractor must sign this Home Repairs Agreement for it to be valid. Print out two copies. Have each party sign and date both. Give the contractor one of the signed documents and keep the other for your records.

## Form 65: Contractor Mid-Job Worksheet

If you've hired a contractor to perform home or business repair or maintenance, you probably have a good idea of what work will be done and what it's going to cost. For extensive jobs, you might have a full-blown contract, which you've accepted by signing it, or you might have a written bid that you've orally agreed to. Or, you might have only an oral bid and acceptance—basically, you and the contractor had a conversation and came to an understanding of the work and the cost. All of these methods for recording the scope of the work and the cost are legal and enforceable—although, of course, a written understanding is always preferable.

However, events might not turn out as planned. In fact, anyone who has done even modest remodeling will tell you that surprises are inevitable as work progresses. Questions might pop up as you arrive home at night to survey the day's work or, more likely, as you lie in bed at night. You'll be wondering, "Will it look like this when it's done?" "Is this the final color?" "Can I change the placement of that fixture?" "Should we do this other upgrade while we're at it?" and so on. Most importantly, if the scope of the work changes or the time needed to do it increases, you'll want to know how, if at all, these changes will affect the cost of the job.

It's important that you and your contractor have continuing, clear communication about the progress of your repair or remodeling job. Don't let important questions go unanswered during the brief exchange you typically have with your contractor each morning. Write questions down as they occur to you and go over the list with your contractor on a daily basis. Even the busiest contractor will pause as you approach with clipboard in hand, and will take a few minutes to go over your questions.

Our Contractor Mid-Job Worksheet, which you'll date as of the day of your discussion, provides a place for you to list your issues and gives you room to record the answer and, possibly, the plan. You'll be able to note whether the intended resolution will alter the bid and, if so, by how much. (To be extra careful, after deciding whether the bid will be affected, ask your contractor to initial or sign the form.) You'll also be able to record whether the work or variation was actually done and whether it's satisfactory.

This worksheet is valuable primarily as a way to preserve and present your questions, but it has other uses, as well. If uncertainty develops later about what you agreed to—and whether it should cost more—you'll have a record of the discussion and the plan. If worst come to worst and you and the contractor get into a legal squabble, your notes will be valuable evidence as well.

Use our Contractor Mid-Job Worksheet on a daily basis if your project is multifaceted and moving quickly, or use it weekly if progress is slow.

Keep all worksheets in a safe place (in a folder or binder, along with the original contract), and keep all documents for at least 10 years (the typical time period in which a homeowner can sue for construction defects).

## Signing Instructions

For each issue you discuss with your contractor, fill in a row on the Contractor Mid-Job Worksheet. Once you reach agreement on a given issue, have your contractor initial the last column, and place your initials next to the contractor's.

CHAPTER 10

# Handling Personal Finances

Form 66: Daily Expenses ............................................................................................. 92

Form 67: Monthly Income ......................................................................................... 93

Form 68: Monthly Budget ......................................................................................... 93

Form 69: Statement of Assets and Liabilities ........................................................... 94

Form 70: Assignment of Rights ................................................................................. 94

Form 71: Notice to Terminate Joint Account ........................................................... 96

Form 72: Notice to Stop Payment of Check ............................................................. 96

Form 73: Request for Credit Report .......................................................................... 97

Form 74: Request Reinvestigation of Credit Report Entry ...................................... 98

Form 75: Dispute Credit Card Charge ..................................................................... 100

Form 76: Demand Collection Agency Cease Contact ............................................ 101

You might not think too much about monthly budgets, credit reports, or stopping payment on a check unless you are having financial problems. But by being proactive—reviewing your finances in advance and knowing your legal rights—you can often avoid legal and money problems. The forms in this chapter are designed to help you get a handle on your personal finances—budgeting, dealing with debts and debt collectors, and reviewing your credit report—whether you're trying to avoid problems or are in the midst of a crisis.

> **RESOURCE**
> **Detailed information and forms on dealing with debts, planning a budget, rebuilding your credit, and other similar topics** can be found in *Solve Your Money Troubles: Strategies to Get Out of Debt and Stay That Way* and *Credit Repair: Make a Plan, Improve Your Credit, Avoid Scams*, both by Amy Loftsgordon and Cara O'Neill (Nolo).

## Form 66: Daily Expenses

Creating a budget—comparing your average monthly expenses to your total monthly income—is the most effective way to start putting your financial house in order. Although it's not hard to do, budgeting is a three-step process. Step one is to get a clear picture of how you spend your money. You can do that using this form (Daily Expenses), on which you record everything you spend over the course of a week. Step two is to total up your income using the Monthly Income form. The final step is comparing the two and figuring out where you might need to make some changes. For that, you can use the Monthly Budget form.

Here's how to use the Daily Expenses form:
1. Make 10 copies of the Daily Expenses form or print a new copy each week. Keep in mind that you don't have to use a paper version of this form. For some people, it will be easier to use a spreadsheet on a smartphone, tablet, or laptop.
2. Begin recording your expenses on the first of the month; record that date in the blank at the top of one copy of the form.
3. Record every expense you pay by cash or cash equivalent—check, ATM, debit card, or automatic bank withdrawal—on that week's form. Include deposits into savings accounts, certificates of deposit, or money market accounts, and purchases of investments. Do not record credit card charges. When you make a payment on a credit card bill, however, list the amount of your payment and the items it covers.
4. At the end of the week, total your weekly expenses. Put away the completed Daily Expenses form, take out another copy, and fill it out according to Step 3. Repeat until you have two full months of expenses recorded.
5. At the end of the 2 months, take out the 10th sheet. Anywhere on it, list seasonal, annual, semiannual, or quarterly expenses that you incur each year but that did not come due during your two-month recording period. Common examples are property taxes, car registration, charitable gifts, tax preparation fees, and auto and homeowners' or rental insurance payments. Divide the annual cost of these items by 12 to figure out the monthly amount.

6. Total up all expenses for the two months you tracked, including two months' worth of the expenses described in Step 5. Divide the total by two to calculate your average monthly expenses.

### Signing Instructions

There are no signing instructions for this form. Simply fill it out and use it to evaluate your spending patterns and prepare a budget.

## Form 67: Monthly Income

Use this form together with the Daily Expenses form to help you create a budget. On this form, total up your monthly income. Be sure to include income information for both people if you and another adult share finances.

Part A is for jobs for which you receive a salary or wages. Part B is for self-employment income, including sales commissions. Part C is for investment income, and Part D is for other sources of income, such as bonus pay, alimony or child support, pension or retirement income, and public assistance.

After listing all sources of income, add them all up for your total monthly income. If your income varies each month, repeat this process for two or three months to determine your average monthly income.

**TIP**

**Don't include income that is automatically reinvested.** As you list your income, you might be inclined to include interest and dividends that are automatically reinvested, such as retirement plan income and stock dividends, to get a true sense of your earnings. But the purpose of creating a budget is to keep track of your actual expenses and the income you have available to pay those expenses. By listing income you don't actually receive, you will be left with the impression that you have more to spend each month than you actually do.

### Signing Instructions

There are no signing instructions for the Monthly Income form. Simply fill it out and use it to prepare a monthly budget.

## Form 68: Monthly Budget

After you've kept track of your expenses and income for a couple of months, you're ready to create a budget using this form. Follow these steps:

1. Using your actual expenses, project your monthly expenses for the categories relevant to you on this Monthly Budget form. Be sure to include the monthly equivalent of any seasonal, quarterly, semiannual, or annual expenses that you noted on your 10th sheet of the Daily Expenses form.

2. Enter your projected monthly expenses into the projected (Proj.) column on this Monthly Budget. Remember, this is just an estimate based on two months of record keeping. Enter the total at the end of the form, near the bottom of the column.

3. Enter your projected monthly income (bottom line of your Monthly Income form) below your total projected expenses on this Monthly Budget.

4. Figure out the difference. If your expenses exceed your income, you might have to cut your projected expenses or increase your income to make ends meet.

5. During each month, write down your actual expenses in each category. Do this as accurately as possible—remember, creating a budget is really designed to help you adopt a sound spending plan, not to fill in the "correct" numbers. Check your actual monthly expenditures periodically to help you keep an eye on how you're doing. Are you keeping close to your projected figures? If you are not, you will need to change the projected amount for those categories.

**TIP**

**When a large payment comes due.** While you have included one-twelfth of your quarterly, semiannual, and annual expenses in each month's projection, those expenses and other unanticipated ones don't arise every month. Ideally, your budget provides for a monthly cushion—that is, your income exceeds your expenses—so you'll be able to handle the large payments when they come due by using that month's cushion or the savings you've built up. If you don't have the cash on hand to pay the large payment, you will have to cut back in other expense categories.

### Signing Instructions

There are no signing instructions for this Monthly Budget form. Simply fill it out and use it to balance your income and expenses.

## Form 69: Statement of Assets and Liabilities

Subtracting what you owe (liabilities) from what you own (assets) reveals your net worth. A net worth statement can help you and a lender analyze your eligibility for a loan.

To find your net worth, use this Statement of Assets and Liabilities form. Fill in as much information as you can. Don't worry about listing every asset or debt; the information on this form changes daily as your assets change value and the balances on your debts rise or fall. You can estimate the date of purchase, or write "N/A" in this column if you don't know.

What values should you use for your assets? As best you can, you will want to include an asset's current market value—the amount you could get if you sold the item on the open market. This means you are not looking at what you could get in a forced sale—such as a house foreclosure, or if you had to sell all your personal belongings at a garage sale. Instead, you're looking at what your home could bring in under normal selling conditions, how much you could get for your car by selling it through the paper or to a dealer, and how much your household goods are worth, considering they generally depreciate about 20% a year.

**RELATED TOPIC**

**For a related form, specifically geared toward determining eligibility for a home loan,** see the Family Financial Statement in Chapter 6.

### Signing Instructions

There are no signing instructions for this Statement of Assets and Liabilities. Simply fill this form out and update it from time to time. Use it to determine your net worth, information that will be useful should you apply for a loan.

## Form 70: Assignment of Rights

You can use this form to transfer property or money that you are entitled to receive (for example, under a contract or promissory note) to another person. This is called "assigning" your right to receive the property or money. In legal terms, you are the "assignor": the person transferring a right to property or money to another person, who is the "assignee." For example, if Bette signed a promissory note owing you money and you owe Roger money, you might assign your right to Bette's money to Roger. You are the assignor and Roger is the assignee. Or, you might assign your right to receive income from a book contract to your teenage son so that the money would be taxed in his bracket, not yours. (See a tax adviser before you do this, though.)

This Assignment of Rights form provides for one or two assignors and one or two assignees. There could be situations in which two people have the right to receive money or property and jointly transfer that right, or in which two people are granted the right to receive money or property. This typically, but not exclusively, arises when spouses jointly have the right to money or property or are jointly granted such a right. (Chapter 5 includes a discussion of marital property.)

Often the assignment covers a set period, especially when you assign the right to receive payments. This form (Clauses 3 and 4) allows you to specify the beginning and ending dates of the assignment; if you don't have an exact end date in mind, you can simply say that the assignment will end when a specific event occurs or you revoke the assignment.

Here are some questions to ask when considering an assignment:

- **If you are assigning rights based on a previously existing contract, does the contract allow the assignment?** Be sure to read the contract carefully and make sure you can assign your rights under it. For example, leases and installment purchase contracts for motor vehicles typically prohibit assignment without the lessor's or lender's advance written consent. Mortgages and deeds of trust also typically cannot be assigned.
- **Are there tax implications of the assignment?** If you assign money to another person and receive something of equal value in return, there should be no tax implications. If, however, you assign your right to receive money to another person as a gift and the IRS learns of the assignment, the IRS will treat the assignment as a taxable transaction. For many assignments, this won't be a problem because you can make a tax-free gift of up to $19,000 per individual per year (2025 and 2026). But if you are assigning more than that, you should get tax advice.
- **Does the assignment substantially change the obligations of the person with whom you signed a contract?** If the contractual obligations will become more onerous, you may not be allowed to make the assignment. For example, if you have signed a contract with Happy Housekeepers to clean your house once a week for $150, you may not assign this obligation to a neighbor whose house would require a lot more time and effort to clean.

## Signing Instructions

You must sign the Assignment of Rights form for it to be valid. Print out two copies of the form (or enough for each person who will be signing the form to have a separate copy). Each person (assignor and assignee) should sign and date all copies of the form and keep a signed document with all original signatures.

## Form 71: Notice to Terminate Joint Account

If you are separating from or divorcing a spouse or partner, you will want to close any joint credit cards or accounts immediately. This involves notifying all creditors of your request to close joint accounts so that no new charges can be made. You should send this notice to every creditor, including credit card issuers, banks, department stores, and other retailers, with whom you and your spouse or partner hold a joint credit account. Send it to the customer service address on the back of a billing statement, not to the address where you send payments. You must complete a separate Notice to Terminate Joint Account for each credit card account you want to close. Be sure you enter the full names of the joint account holders exactly as they appear on the account, and include the correct account number.

The only way to make sure that an account is truly closed is to insist, as this notice does, that the creditor do a "hard close," so that no new charges can be made. (You can close your account even if you haven't paid off the balance. In that case, the account will remain active only for the purpose of paying off the balance.) This notice states that if a "hard close" isn't done, you won't be responsible for any charges made on the account. While such a letter might not fully protect you, it is better than doing nothing and puts the burden on the creditor to show why the account wasn't closed as you requested.

If time is of the essence, call the creditor and request a hard close. Follow up by sending a signed copy of this form, along with a cover letter referring to your earlier phone call. You might also be able to close accounts on the card issuer's website.

### Signing Instructions

Print out a copy of the Notice to Terminate Joint Account form and sign it in the space provided. Make two copies of the signed form and mail the original and one of the copies to the creditor you want to notify of the joint account termination. Include a stamped, self-addressed envelope. The creditor will sign the copy and return it to you in the self-addressed envelope as a receipt.

Send the form by certified mail, return receipt requested, and keep a copy of the form and receipt for your records. You might later need it as proof that you properly notified the creditor of your intent to close the joint account.

**TIP**

**Don't overlook home equity lines of credit.** You and your ex might have applied for a home equity line of credit a while ago and forgotten about it. Because the risk of leaving an equity line of credit open is so great (you could lose your home if your ex is irresponsible with the funds), we recommend closing it in person. Pay a visit to your banker to request that the account be closed or frozen. Get a written record that the bank has closed the account.

## Form 72: Notice to Stop Payment of Check

It's not unusual to write a check, hand it over or mail it to the recipient, and then change your mind and want to stop payment. For example, you might not notice that delivered goods were defective until after the delivery person was paid and left.

The initial thing to do is call the bank, savings and loan, credit union, or other financial institution where your account is located to make an oral request to stop payment. Ask how much the charge is, if any, for this service. Then immediately send or, better yet, drop off a written confirmation of your stop payment notice (this form). Include payment for any required charge with your notice.

In many situations, the stop payment notice lasts only six months or a year. If you fear the person to whom you wrote the check will try to cash it much later, you might need to renew your stop payment notice. Banks, savings and loans, credit unions, and other financial institutions have the option of rejecting checks they deem too old, often six months or older, but they usually don't exercise this right. In fact, most people who work in a bank or other financial institution never look at the date of the check. They simply post it to the account. If the money is there to cover it, the check is paid.

### Signing Instructions

Print out three copies of the Notice to Stop Payment of Check form. Sign the copies and mail or give two of them to the appropriate bank or financial institution along with a stamped, self-addressed envelope. As requested in this form, the financial institution should then sign and return one of the copies, acknowledging receipt of your letter. Keep a copy for your records.

## Form 73: Request for Credit Report

If you want to repair your credit, establish credit, or apply for a loan, your beginning step is to get a copy of your credit reports. A "credit report" is a file maintained by credit reporting agencies that sell information to banks, lenders, landlords, and others who routinely evaluate customers' creditworthiness. Credit reports contain personal information about you, including your current and past use of credit cards; loans (home, car, student, and the like); any defaults on bills, such as utility payments or doctor's bills; public records, such as lawsuits; and inquiries by creditors.

The federal Fair Credit Reporting Act (FCRA) requires each major national credit reporting agency—Equifax, Experian, and TransUnion—to provide you one free copy of your credit report each year.

You can request your free report by one of these means:
- telephone—877-322-8228
- internet—www.annualcreditreport.com, or
- mail—Annual Credit Report Request Service, P.O. Box 105281, Atlanta, GA 30348-5281.

You must provide your name, address, Social Security number, and date of birth when you order. You also might be required to provide information that only you would know, such as the amount of your monthly mortgage payment.

You can also get free weekly online credit reports from www.annualcreditreport.com. And through 2026, you can get six free reports from Equifax as part of a legal settlement.

With all the free ways to get your reports, you shouldn't ever need to pay for them. But if you already received your limit of free reports from the nationwide reporting agencies, use this form (Request for Credit Report) to get an additional copy and send it to one or all of the three major national credit bureaus:
- Equifax, 866-349-5191; www.equifax.com
- Experian, 888-397-3742; www.experian.com, and
- TransUnion, 800-888-4213; www.transunion.com.

Additional copies of your credit report usually cost less than $20 (and are free in some more cases, listed below), but check first for the exact amount.

You are also entitled to an additional copy of your credit report at no charge or at a reduced fee if:

- One of the following happened because of information in your credit file: You were denied credit; you were granted credit, but not nearly the amount or on the terms you requested; your credit account was terminated; the creditor made unfavorable changes to your account (but did not change the terms of all, or substantially all, other consumers' accounts of the same type); or the creditor took an action or made a determination in connection with an application or transaction you initiated that is adverse to your interests. The creditor must tell you the name and address of the credit reporting agency reporting the information that led to the denial of credit or other adverse action. You must request your report from that particular credit reporting agency within 60 days from the denial of credit or adverse action.
- You are unemployed and planning to apply for a job within 60 days following your request for your credit report. It's a good idea to include documents verifying your unemployment (such as a recent unemployment check or layoff notice). You must also provide a statement swearing that the information is true. You are entitled to one free report in a 12-month period.
- You receive public assistance. Enclose a statement swearing that this is true and provide a copy of your most recent public assistance check as verification. You are entitled to one free report in any 12-month period.
- You reasonably believe your credit file contains errors due to someone's fraud, such as using your credit card, name, or Social Security number. Here, too, you will need to enclose a statement swearing that this is true. You are entitled to one free report in any 12-month period.
- You are a victim of identity theft or fraud, or think that you might be. The FCRA gives consumers the right to request free credit reports in connection with fraud alerts.
  - If you suspect in good faith that you are, or could be, a victim of identity theft or another fraud, you can instruct the major bureaus to add a "fraud alert" to your file. You can request a free copy of your report from each bureau once it places the fraud alert in your file.
  - If you are a victim of identity theft, you can send the major bureaus an identity theft report and instruct them to add an extended fraud alert to your file. You can request two free copies of your credit report from each bureau during the next 12 months once it places the extended fraud alert in your file.

## Signing Instructions

Sign your Request for Credit Report and mail it certified mail, return receipt requested, to the credit bureau. Keep a copy of the letter for your files. Include payment and any supporting documentation required, as noted above.

## Form 74: Request Reinvestigation of Credit Report Entry

Under the FCRA, you have the right to dispute all incorrect or incomplete information in your credit file, such as an incorrect name, employer, account, or tax history; a lawsuit older than 7 years or one you weren't involved in; or a bankruptcy older than 10 years for Chapter 7 and 7 years for Chapter 13. You can use this form to request a reinvestigation of an item you dispute ("reinvestigation" is what the credit reporting agencies call this process).

Once the credit reporting agency receives your letter, it must either reinvestigate the items you dispute or delete them from your credit report within three business days after receiving your dispute.

If the agency doesn't delete the information within 3 business days, it must:

- complete its investigation within 45 days if you disputed the information after receiving your free annual credit report (otherwise it has only 30 days, which can be extended up to 45 days if you send the agency additional relevant information during the 30-day period)
- contact the creditor reporting the information you dispute within 5 business days of receiving your dispute
- review and consider all relevant information you submit and forward this information to the creditor that provided the information, and
- provide you with the results of its reinvestigation within five business days of completion, including a revised credit report if any changes were made.

If the credit reporting agency can't verify that the disputed information is correct (or agrees that it is incorrect), in addition to either removing it or correcting it, the agency must notify the creditor that furnished the information that it has been deleted or modified. This lets the creditor know that it must correct the information in its records as well.

If you let an agency know that you're trying to obtain a mortgage or car loan, it can often do a "rush" reinvestigation. Requesting a reinvestigation won't cost you anything.

The credit reporting agency isn't required to investigate any dispute that it determines to be frivolous or irrelevant. It might make this determination if, for example, you don't provide enough information to investigate the dispute, or your dispute appears to be a blanket dispute of almost everything in your credit file either generated by a credit repair company service or prepared by you using a credit repair service's forms. Once the agency determines that the dispute is frivolous, it has five business days to notify you of the decision and its reasons for the decision.

To make sure your dispute isn't dismissed as frivolous, dispute only those items in your report that you believe are incorrect or incomplete, explain your reasoning, and if you have documentation, include it. When using this form, be sure to delete any paragraphs that don't apply to you. For more information, see *Credit Repair: Make a Plan, Improve Your Credit, Avoid Scams*, by Amy Loftsgordon and Cara O'Neill (Nolo).

You can also dispute inaccurate or incomplete items of information online by going to the credit report agency's website (contact information appears in the instructions for the Request for Credit Report). Look for the button or link for submitting disputes online.

## Signing Instructions

Sign your Request Reinvestigation of Credit Report Entry form and send it by certified mail, return receipt requested, to the credit bureau that prepared the report you are disputing. Include copies of any documents supporting your claim. Keep a copy of the letter for your files.

## Form 75: Dispute Credit Card Charge

If you use a credit or charge card but don't receive the product you purchased, or you received a defective item, you can legally refuse to pay using what's called a "claims and defenses" process if you meet certain criteria:

- **Dispute concerning a purchase made with a credit card issued by the seller, such as a department store or gas station.** You can legally refuse to pay if you first attempt in good faith to resolve the dispute with the merchant who refuses to replace, repair, or otherwise correct the problem.
- **Dispute concerning a purchase made with a credit card, such as Visa or MasterCard, not issued by the seller.** You can legally refuse to pay if you first attempt in good faith to resolve the dispute with the merchant who refuses to replace, repair, or otherwise correct the problem. But, you can withhold payment only if the purchase was for more than $50 and was made within the state in which you live or was within 100 miles of your home.

You may withhold only the balance on the disputed item or service that is unpaid when you first notify the seller or card issuer of the problem. (To cover yourself as fully as possible, make sure that the card issuer receives your dispute within 60 days after the date of the first credit card statement showing the disputed purchase.)

If you are entitled to withhold payment, complete and mail this form to the credit card company at the address for disputed charges (not the billing address) and explain why you aren't paying. Explain how you tried to resolve the problem with the merchant. Attach a copy of the credit card bill showing the disputed item, along with any additional documentation of your attempt to resolve the dispute, such as a letter you sent to a merchant regarding a defective item.

The card issuer can't tell a credit reporting agency that the amount you withheld is delinquent until the dispute has been settled, provided that you don't withhold more than you are entitled. Nor can the issuer "freeze" or place a hold on any funds that you might have on deposit with it. However, the issuer can tell a credit reporting agency that your failure to pay is "disputed," so it's important not to abuse this right.

For more information on credit card problems, check the Federal Trade Commission website at www.ftc.gov.

> **TIP**
> **Do not use this form if the problem is unauthorized use of your credit card**—for example, charges made by someone who stole your card. In this situation, promptly report your loss to the police and the credit card issuer to limit your liability for unauthorized charges. Then call the three major credit reporting agencies to report fraud (contact information appears in the instructions for the Request for Credit Report form).

### Signing Instructions

Sign your Dispute Credit Card Charge letter and mail it to the credit card issuer, along with copies of any documents supporting your claim. Keep a copy of the letter and your original supporting documentation for your files.

## Form 76: Demand Collection Agency Cease Contact

If you owe money and your debt has been passed along to a collection agency, you will no doubt be contacted by a collector working for the agency. Many people don't understand that they have the legal right under federal law (the Fair Debt Collection Practices Act (FDCPA), 15 U.S.C. §§ 1692 and following) to tell a bill collector who works for a collection agency to leave them alone. (This doesn't apply to in-house collectors—for example, at a bank, department store, or hospital—unless your state has enacted a similar restriction on in-house collectors.)

Under amendments to the FDCPA, you can also stop communications through a particular medium, subject to some exceptions. For example, if you tell a debt collector to "stop calling," this statement means you've requested that the debt collector not use telephone calls to communicate with you. Or you may request that a debt collector not use a specific address or phone number. You don't have to put this kind of request in writing; you can just tell the collector to stop contacting you in a specific way.

But if you want all communication to stop, put your demand in writing (that's the purpose of this form) and send it to the collection agency. By law, once you put your request in writing, all collectors from the agency must then cease all phone calls, letters, and other communications with you, unless they are contacting you to notify you that:
- collection efforts against you have ended, or
- the collection agency or the creditor will invoke a specific remedy against you, such as suing you.

Alternatively, you can inform the collector that you are represented by an attorney and instruct that all communications be directed to the attorney (you must provide the attorney's name and address).

**TIP**
**It's usually best not to ignore the debt or try to hide from the collector.** The longer you put off resolving the issue, the worse the situation and consequences might become. Whether you negotiate directly with the collector or obtain a lawyer's assistance, many counselors feel the best strategy almost always is to engage the collector, at least initially.

**Signing Instructions**

Sign your Demand Collection Agency Cease Contact letter and mail it to the collection agency, along with copies of any documents supporting your demand. It's best to send this letter by certified mail and request a return receipt. Keep a copy of the letter and your original documents for your files.

CHAPTER 11

# Hiring Child Care, Elder Care, or Household Help

**Form 77: Child Care Agreement** ...........................................................................................................106

**Form 78: Child Care Instructions** ..........................................................................................................108

**Form 79: Elder Care Agreement** ............................................................................................................109

**Form 80: Housekeeping Services Agreement** ....................................................................................109

Many people hire others to work regularly in their homes—for example, to take care of children while they work, care for elderly parents, or clean the house. These relationships are often set up informally, with no written agreement. But informal arrangements can lead to serious disputes—perhaps serious enough that someone bitterly backs out of the arrangement. Far better to draft a clear written understanding of what the job entails in advance.

The agreements in this chapter are for hiring care providers and other household workers who are employees, not independent contractors. This distinction is crucial for tax and legal purposes: When you hire an employee, you set the hours, responsibilities, and pay rate of the worker. Legally, most babysitters and household workers who work for you on a regular basis are considered employees for whom you are required to pay taxes, Social Security, and other benefits described below. In contrast, independent contractors typically own their own businesses and work for you only occasionally.

This chapter also includes a Child Care Instructions form you can use for either a full-time child care provider or an occasional babysitter.

**RESOURCE**

**For more information on hiring non-employees,** see *Consultant & Independent Contractor Agreements,* by Stephen Fishman (Nolo).

## Legal Obligations for Employees

Assuming your child care worker, elder care worker, or house cleaner is your employee, you have legal obligations to that person, which come with a certain amount of paperwork and record keeping. You do not have to put this information in your child care, elder care, or housekeeping agreement, but you need to be aware of your responsibilities.

**Social Security and income taxes.** If you pay a child care or elder care worker $2,800 or more in a calendar year (2025 figure), you must make Social Security (FICA) payments on those wages and withhold the employee's share of FICA taxes. You do not have to deduct income taxes from wages paid to an employee for working in your home unless the employee requests it and you agree to do so. You make these payments by attaching Schedule H, *Household Employment Taxes,* to your annual Form 1040.

Your state government may also impose separate tax withholding requirements. Contact your state taxing authority, or ask your payroll service (if you use one).

**Unemployment compensation.** If you pay a household employee $1,000 or more in a 3-month period (a "calendar quarter"; 2025 figure), you must pay quarterly taxes under the Federal Unemployment Tax Act (FUTA), using IRS Form 940 or 940-EZ. As with FICA taxes, you pay this amount by attaching Schedule H, *Household Employment Taxes,* to your annual Form 1040.

**Workers' compensation.** Your state may require you to provide workers' compensation insurance against job-related injuries or illnesses suffered by your employees. Check with your state department of labor or employment.

**Minimum wage and overtime.** The federal minimum hourly wage is $7.25 (2025). Your child care or elder care worker could be entitled to minimum wage, depending upon their particular hours and earnings. If your state minimum wage is higher, you will need to pay the state wage. In addition, under federal law, most domestic workers (other than live-in workers) qualify for overtime pay. Workers must be paid overtime at a rate 1.5 times the regular rate for all hours worked beyond a 40-hour workweek. You can check the U.S. Department of Labor website, www.dol.gov, for current information about federal and state minimum wage laws.

**New Hire Reporting Form.** Within a short time after you hire someone—20 days or less, depending on your state's rules—you must file a New Hire Reporting Form with a designated state agency. The information on the form becomes part of the National Directory of New Hires, used primarily to locate parents to collect child support.

**Federal ID number.** If you hire a household employee, you must obtain a federal employer identification number (EIN), required by the IRS of all employers for tax filing and reporting purposes. The form you need is IRS Form SS-4, *Application for Employer Identification Number*.

### IRS Resources

The IRS has many helpful publications and forms. Call 800-424-FORM or visit www.irs.gov to download these. Start with Publication 926, *Household Employer's Tax Guide*, which describes your major tax responsibilities. You might also want to look at:
- Form SS-8, which contains IRS definitions of independent contractor and employee, and
- Form SS-4, *Application for Employer Identification Number*.

### Reality Check

Many families don't comply with laws requiring them to pay taxes or Social Security for certain household workers, some of whom are undocumented noncitizens. This chapter isn't intended to preach about the law, but to alert you to the rules that affect your relationships with care providers and housekeeping workers. No question, if you fail to pay Social Security and to meet your other legal obligations as an employer, you might face several negative consequences:
- You might be assessed substantial financial penalties. For example, if your full-time elder care provider files for Social Security five years from now and can prove prior earnings, but no Social Security has been paid, the IRS could back-bill you at high interest rates.
- If you don't meet a state requirement to provide workers' compensation insurance and your child care worker is injured on the job and can't work for a few months, you might be in hot water if the worker files for workers' compensation. You'll probably be held liable for the worker's medical costs and a portion of any lost wages. You could also be fined for not having obtained the insurance in the first place.
- You will not be able to take a child care tax credit on your federal income taxes. The credit is based on your work-related expenses and income, but can actually offset the amount you might save by paying under the table.

## Form 77: Child Care Agreement

A provider who takes care of your children in your house, either part time or full time, may live out (often called a "caregiver" or "babysitter") or live in (a "nanny"). Their responsibilities could vary widely, from performing a whole range of housekeeping services to only taking care of children.

> **CAUTION**
> **Do not use this form if you hire a care provider or house cleaner through a placement agency.** If you use an agency that sets and collects the worker's fee from you, pays the worker, and controls the terms of the work, the agency will have its own contract for you to complete. People you hire through an agency are not your employees—they are the employees of their agencies.

> **CAUTION**
> **Special rules govern hiring of au pairs.** If you hire an au pair from another country (on a J-1 cultural exchange visa), you'll need to comply with federal laws governing the au pair's responsibilities, working hours, rate of pay, and more. An au pair agency will help you with this process. For these reasons, we don't recommend using the child care agreement provided here if you're hiring an au pair from another country.

Use this form to spell out your agreement about the child care worker's responsibilities, hours, benefits, amount and pay schedule, and other important aspects of the job. The best approach is to be as detailed as possible.

Start by filling in your name, address, phone numbers, and other contact information, both for yourself and a second parent (you'll both be signing the Child Care Agreement) and for your child care provider. List your children's names and birth dates.

Here's some advice on filling in various sections of the Child Care Agreement.

**Location and Schedule of Care (Clause 4).** Provide the address where child care will be provided (most likely, your home) and the days and hours of care, such as 8 a.m. to 6 p.m. weekdays. Live-in nannies often work some weeknights and weekends.

**Beginning Date (Clause 5)** and **Training or Probation Period (Clause 6).** Specify the date employment will begin and the length of any training or probation period, such as the first 15 or 30 days of child care. This is the time to make sure that the relationship will work for everyone involved. A training period helps your child care provider get to know your home and neighborhood and the exact way you want things done. If there will be no training or probation period, skip this clause.

**Responsibilities (Clause 7).** The responsibilities of the child care position may vary depending on many factors, including the number and ages of your children, whether the child care worker lives in or out, the hours worked, your family situation and needs, and the provider's skills and background. In some households, particularly with infants and toddlers, the babysitter only takes care of the children and doesn't do housework, except for the children's laundry. In other families, especially with older children, the employee functions more as a housekeeper, cook, and chauffeur. You should specify the child care worker's responsibilities in as much detail as possible, including cooking, bathing, and personal care for your children, social and recreational activities (such as arranging the children's play dates), transportation (driving kids to and from school or practices), shopping and errands for the family, housecleaning, ironing, and laundry.

**EXAMPLE:** Here's sample language describing responsibilities for a live-in nanny taking care of an infant (Kate) and a preschooler (Tom):

> The child care provider's primary responsibility is to provide loving care for Kate and Tom. This includes playing with and reading to them, taking them to the park as weather permits, making sure they have naps as needed, and preparing their meals and snacks. The care provider will bathe Kate and Tom every other day, more frequently if necessary. Other responsibilities include driving Tom to "Baby Gym" twice a week, doing the children's laundry, and keeping their rooms tidy.

**Wage or Salary (Clause 8).** Specify exactly how the child care provider will be paid, such as an hourly rate or weekly salary. The amount you pay depends on many factors. These include the number and ages of your children; the type of care provided and responsibilities; the number of hours, time of day, and regularity of the schedule; the experience and training of the employee; benefits such as room and board; and the going rate in your community. Check local sources to compare, such as neighborhood websites and social media groups. Before you fill in this section, be sure you understand your legal obligations when hiring an employee, such as minimum wage and overtime rules, as described above.

**Payment Schedule (Clause 9).** You can decide to pay your child care provider weekly (say, on Friday), twice per month (such as on the 15th and on the last day of the month), or once per month.

**Benefits (Clause 10).** In addition to payment, you may offer the child care provider any benefits you wish, such as paid vacations and holidays, health insurance, and sick leave. Make sure your employee understands what the various terms in this contract mean (for example, that "paid vacations" mean you pay their wage or salary while they're away, not that you pay for the entire vacation). Spell out the rules for using these benefits, such as how much advance notice you need of planned vacation time, and what happens if the child care provider gets sick after having used up all their sick leave.

**Termination Policy (Clause 11).** If things don't work out, the Child Care Agreement provides a termination policy that allows either the parents or the child care provider to terminate the agreement at any time, for any reason, and without notice.

**Confidentiality (Clause 12).** This protects your privacy and, potentially, that of your friends, coworkers, and clients.

**Additional Provisions (Clause 13).** Describe any additional terms of this agreement, such as a schedule for salary reviews, house rules, such as a no-smoking and no personal visitors policy, or a requirement that the child care provider take a first aid course (and mention who pays for it).

**Modifications (Clause 14).** This agreement provides that any changes to it must be made in writing and signed by all parties to it. This protects both the parents and the child care provider against misunderstandings over major issues that were agreed to verbally.

### Signing Instructions

To make the Child Care Agreement valid, the parent(s) and the child care provider must sign it. (If you and your children's other parent are living in the same home and raising your kids together, it's best if both of you sign this document.) Print out two copies of the form. You, your children's other parent (if signing the form), and the caregiver must sign and date the form where indicated. Give one of the signed originals to the child care provider and keep the other for your records.

---

**Shared In-Home Care**

Some families pool their resources and share an in-home child care provider. These arrangements are ideal for neighbors or coworkers with children who are close in age. Just as a written agreement between a family and a child care worker can clarify expectations and prevent conflicts, a written understanding between the two families who are sharing a child care provider can accomplish the same objectives. If you share in-home care with another family, be sure you agree on the key issues before drafting your contract with the child care worker, including location of the care, splitting expenses, termination procedures, and supervision. The other parents should make their own child care arrangements with the care provider.

---

## Form 78: Child Care Instructions

Use this form to provide important information for babysitters and child care providers (including au pairs), such as phone numbers of doctors, instructions about meals and naps, and other details of your child's care, including any allergies or health conditions your child has.

This form has space for you to fill in the names, addresses, and phone numbers of people that your babysitter or child care provider can contact if they can't reach you in an emergency. We suggest that you list at least two or three friends, relatives, or neighbors who live nearby and are well known to your children and family. The form will print out with a reminder to call 911 in case of emergency. If you wish to list another emergency number for the police, fire department, or poison control, you may do so.

Finally, the Child Care Instructions form has space to provide additional important information your family or home, such as the location of first aid supplies, the phone number of a local taxi service, or the fact that you have a rule against smoking, drinking alcohol, or entertaining personal visitors in the house.

 **RELATED TOPIC**
**Use a separate form to authorize medical care.** While these Child Care Instructions provide important medical information about your child, such as any medications or allergies, this form doesn't authorize your babysitter or child care provider to arrange medical care for your child. For that, you will need to use the Authorization for Minor's Medical Treatment (see Chapter 1).

### Signing Instructions

You don't need to sign the Child Care Instructions. Simply fill in the information and print out the form after reading it carefully to make sure all information is complete and correct. Give the babysitter or child care provider a copy and keep one posted in a prominent place, such as on your refrigerator. Be sure to review and update your Child Care Instructions from time to time.

## Form 79: Elder Care Agreement

Many older people remain at home or live with relatives rather than entering a residential facility for extended recovery or long-term care. Often this requires hiring someone (an elder care provider) to help with their personal and medical care, cooking, housekeeping, and other services.

An elder care provider (sometimes called a "home health aide") can either live out or live in, and work full or part time. The responsibilities of this position can vary, from performing a wide range of housekeeping services to attending to the personal and health care needs of the older adult (or adults, in case the elder care worker is taking care of two people, such as both of your parents). Responsibilities might range from dispensing medicine to helping with bathing to driving to doctor's appointments, activities, or social functions.

Use this form to spell out your written agreement about the elder care worker's responsibilities, hours, benefits, amount and schedule of payment, and other important aspects of the job. The best approach is to be as detailed as possible. Follow the directions for the Child Care Agreement when completing this form.

### Signing Instructions

To make the Elder Care Agreement valid, the employer(s) and the elder care provider must sign it. Start by printing out two copies of the form. You (the employer) and the caregiver must sign and date the form where indicated. Give one of the signed originals to the elder care provider and keep the other for your records.

## Form 80: Housekeeping Services Agreement

If you hire the same person every week to clean your house, a written contract can be a valuable way to define the worker's responsibilities and benefits. For a house cleaner who will be your employee, use this form to spell out hours, benefits, amount and schedule of payment, termination policy, and other aspects of the job. Your agreement should cover regular weekly cleaning tasks (Clause 5)—for example, cleaning the bathroom and mopping the kitchen floor—as well as occasional projects, such as washing blinds. Be sure to spell out other responsibilities as well (Clause 6), such as cooking, laundry, ironing, shopping, gardening, and yard work. The best approach is to be as detailed as possible. Follow the directions for the Child Care Agreement when completing this form.

### Signing Instructions

To make the Housekeeping Services Agreement valid, the employer(s) and the housekeeper must sign it. Finalizing your Housekeeping Services Agreement is easy. Start by printing out two copies. You (the employer) and the housekeeper must sign and date each form where indicated. Give one of the signed originals to the housekeeper and keep the other for your records.

CHAPTER 12

# Handling Legal Disputes

**Form 81: Demand Letter** ........................................................................................................ 112

**Form 82: Online Auction Buyer Demand Letter** ............................................................... 113

**Form 83: Request for Refund or Repair of Goods Under Warranty** ............................ 113

**Form 84: Accident Claim Worksheet** .................................................................................. 116

**Forms 85–90: Releases** ........................................................................................................... 116

    Form 85: General Release ................................................................................................. 118

    Form 86: General Mutual Release .................................................................................. 118

    Form 87: Release for Damage to Real Estate ............................................................... 118

    Form 88: Release for Property Damage in Auto Accident ....................................... 119

    Form 89: Release for Personal Injury ............................................................................. 119

    Form 90: Mutual Release of Contract Claims ............................................................. 119

**Form 91: Complaint Letter to a Government Agency** ..................................................... 119

**Form 92: Notice to Cancel Certain Contracts** ................................................................... 121

**Form 93: Identity Theft Worksheet** ..................................................................................... 122

Becoming involved in any legal or commercial dispute can be harrowing. Fortunately, most disputes can be resolved long before anyone sees the inside of a courtroom—using tools such as those found in this chapter. We'll provide everything from demand letters to an accident claim worksheet to several releases that you or the other party should sign so neither of you risks being hauled into court after you write or receive the check you believe settles the matter.

**RESOURCE**
**Additional information and sample forms for settling disputes** can be found in *Everybody's Guide to Small Claims Court*, by Cara O'Neill. For a detailed discussion of representing yourself in a lawsuit, see *Represent Yourself in Court: Prepare & Try a Winning Civil Case*, by Paul Bergman and Sarah Berman. Both titles are published by Nolo.

## Form 81: Demand Letter

Assuming your dispute has escalated to the point where you and the other party can no longer civilly discuss a compromise, your next step in trying to resolve it is to send a demand letter clearly stating what you want. That's the purpose of this form. Studies show that in as many as one-third of all disputes, a demand letter serves as a catalyst to arriving at a settlement. It is fair to ask why demand letters work so frequently to resolve disputes that couldn't simply be talked out. The answer seems to be that a written document often serves as a wake-up call, convincing the other party you really are serious about going to court if you can't settle the matter. Your demand letter also gives you a chance to organize the facts of your case, so if you wind up in mediation, arbitration, or court (such as small claims court), you will have already done much of your preparation.

When writing your demand letter, here are some suggestions:

- Be polite. Avoid personally attacking your adversary.
- Concisely review the main facts of the dispute—including who, what, where, and when. (See "How to Word a Demand," below.) Even though your adversary knows this information, a judge, mediator, or other third party may eventually see your letter.
- Ask for exactly what you want—the return of property, a specific amount of money, or whatever.
- Conclude by stating that if the problem isn't resolved within a set period of time (7 to 10 days is often good), you will take further action, such as filing a court case.

### How to Word a Demand

When writing a demand letter, describe in your own words exactly what happened. Specify dates, names of people with whom you dealt, and the damages you have suffered. Here's an example:

> On September 21, 20xx, I took my car to your garage for service. Shortly after I picked it up the next day, the engine caught fire because of your failure to connect the fuel line to the fuel injector properly. Fortunately, I was able to douse the fire without injury. As a direct result of the engine fire, I paid ABC Garage $3,281 for necessary repair work. I enclose a copy of the invoice. Also, I was without the use of my car for three days and had to rent a car to get to work. I enclose a copy of an invoice showing the rental cost of $345. In total, I was out $3,426.

The Demand Letter included here indicates that you are willing to try mediation. Mediation, a nonadversarial process involving a neutral person (a mediator), is usually a great way for people to resolve differences. If you're not willing to try mediation (that is, you plan to sue if your demands aren't met), delete the mediation language in the demand letter.

### Signing Instructions

Sign the Demand Letter and send it certified mail (return receipt requested) to the person with whom you're having a dispute. Keep a copy of the letter. You might need it later if you end up filing a lawsuit.

## Form 82: Online Auction Buyer Demand Letter

Not everyone who buys goods via an online auction has a satisfactory experience. If you have a dispute with an online auction seller (on eBay or elsewhere), use this demand letter to alert the seller of your complaint and to establish your claim.

This demand letter gives you the option of proposing to the seller that the two of you use an online dispute resolution service to resolve your claim. Make sure to research these services (suggested sites are listed on this form) to understand how they work before proposing this option to the seller.

### Signing Instructions

If you have the seller's physical address, sign the Online Auction Buyer Demand Letter and send it via certified mail, return receipt requested. If not, send it by email. Keep a copy of the letter. You might need it later if you wind up filing a lawsuit.

---

**Online Auctions: Think Before You Bid**

Before buying an item through an online auction, be sure to review the auction site's rules and find out what the company does if a problem occurs. Also, compare the price of the item elsewhere—not every item for sale at an online auction is a bargain.

Most important, learn as much as you can about the seller. Use common sense. Possible danger signs are if the seller:
- has a history of negative feedback
- is using a post office box
- wants payment in cash
- is outside the United States, or
- wants your Social Security or driver's license number.

For more advice on how to protect yourself, check out Fraud.org's Fake Merchandise Scams page at https://fraud.org/fake-merchandise.

---

## Form 83: Request for Refund or Repair of Goods Under Warranty

Use this form to request compensation when an item you purchased is defective. Most new products (and even some used ones) come with a warranty that offers protection if the product fails during the warranty period. Here are the basic rules regarding warranties:

- If a product comes with a written warranty from either the seller or the manufacturer, you have the right to rely on it.
- If a seller makes a statement describing a product's feature—for example, "This sleeping bag will keep you warm at 25 degrees below zero"—and you make your purchase because of the statement, then the statement is an express warranty that you have a right to rely on.

- For most purchases, you automatically have an implied warranty of merchantability, meaning that the item will work for its intended use—for example, a lawn mower will cut grass. If the item doesn't work, you should be able to return it for a refund or replacement.

If a warranty is breached—for example, a TV with a one-year warranty breaks after two weeks—ask the seller for redress. Simply contact or visit the store, explain the problem, and ask for a refund or replacement of the defective TV. If the seller refuses, use this form to notify the seller and manufacturer of your demand for them to make good under the warranty. Give them a reasonable chance—such as 30 days—to make necessary repairs, replace the defective product, or refund the purchase price. Most reputable sellers and manufacturers will. This form states that you may take further action, such as filing a court action, if your request is unmet.

### TIP

**If you are using this form to request warranty coverage, make sure the product warranty covers your situation.** Read the warranty to see how long it lasts; whom you contact for warranty service (seller or manufacturer); your options if the product fails (refund, replacement, or repair); what parts and problems are covered (some warranties cover replacement of parts but not labor, or cover only problems due to faulty material or workmanship); and any conditions (such as registration) or limitations that might apply.

Here's how to prepare a Request for Refund or Repair of Goods form.

**Start by filling in the name(s) and address(es) of the seller or manufacturer (depending upon the particular warranty and your complaint).** If you have a written manufacturer's warranty, check it for the appropriate address (physical or email) to send requests for warranty coverage; this might be the seller/dealer or the manufacturer. If you're not sure, ask the seller from whom you purchased the item. This might be a retail store or website. You might need to mail or deliver the product along with your request for warranty coverage to either the seller/dealer or the manufacturer.

If you don't have a written manufacturer's warranty and the dispute is with the seller, send this form to the seller. It shouldn't be too hard for you to determine the name and address of the seller, if you made an in-person purchase. For online purchases, you might have to search the seller's website to locate an address or do a more general online search.

**Fill in the item name or description.** If possible, include the model number—for example, Tasty Toaster Model 9333.

**Next, fill in the purchase price, date, and place of purchase.**

**Describe the problem (reason you are demanding redress) and why you are dissatisfied with your purchase.** Provide as much detail as possible, including what your written warranty (if any) says; what you were told (and by whom) when you made the purchase; how you have used the product; what has gone wrong; and what efforts you have made to obtain a new item or refund. For example, if you called the seller, provide the date and details of the phone conversation. If you have already sent the seller an informal note about the problem (via email or through a submission on the company's website, for example), mention that and attach a copy of the note to this form, if possible. If you are enclosing anything, such as a copy of the purchase receipt as proof of purchase or a copy of the written warranty, be sure to say so in this section of the form. (See "How to Complain About a Defective Product," below.)

**Indicate whether or not the item is enclosed.** Whether you are seeking redress by mail or in person, you might need to return the item, such as a broken toaster or punctured tires. This will not always be feasible—for example, in the case of a shattered mirror.

**Specify what type of compensation you want.** Read your warranty (if any) to find out what kind of redress might be available and to make sure that the warranty covers your situation. Some manufacturer warranties promise only to repair or replace a defective item; others will give you the additional choice of seeking a full or partial refund of your purchase price. If you don't care, or don't have a written warranty, ask for either a refund or a replacement item.

**Indicate when you want to receive the requested compensation.** We suggest 30 days, after which you will take further action such as filing a lawsuit.

## Signing Instructions

Sign the Request for Refund or Repair of Goods form and include any relevant material, such as a copy of the written warranty (often part of the owner's manual that came with the item from the manufacturer), the advertisement that you relied on when making your purchase, your receipt, previous correspondence with the seller, or the item itself. If you are addressing this form to the manufacturer, send a copy to the seller, too. You might also want to send a copy of this letter to a state or local consumer agency or the Better Business Bureau. (See "How to Complain to Government Agencies," below.)

Keep a copy of your form and any attached materials for your records. You might need this if you end up filing a small claims court case.

---

### How to Complain About a Defective Product

Here are a couple of examples of how to explain your dissatisfaction with a product you've purchased and why you're seeking redress.

**Complaint about manufacturer's warranty.**

> On May 21, 20xx, I purchased a Tasty Toaster (Model 9333) from the Toaster Store, 195 Main Street, Columbus, Ohio. This toaster came with a one-year warranty (copy enclosed). Last week the toaster coils overheated, and the toaster simply does not work. I have owned the toaster only four months, have used it only occasionally, and have not subjected it to any extraordinary usage.

**Complaint about store's warranty.**

> On April 16, 20xx, I purchased an UpHill Bicycle (model number 12345ht) from CycLeader, 3300 Sharper Avenue, Denver, Colorado. In the presence of my friend, Randy Jacobs, I explained to the store clerk, "Mark," that I planned to use the bicycle for off-road mountain cycling throughout Colorado. The clerk assured me that the tires on this particular UpHill bicycle could "handle any surface." Just last week, less than a month after I purchased the bike, both tires punctured while I was cycling on a much-used mountain bike trail near Greeley. When I asked for a partial refund so as to purchase new tires, the store manager claimed that no one named Mark currently works at CycLeader and claimed that this model UpHill bicycle would never have been sold for off-road use.

## Form 84: Accident Claim Worksheet

Many legal disputes involve claims against a person, business, or insurance company arising out of an accident where a person was injured or had their property damaged (or both). These include both car accidents and "slip-and-fall incidents." If you are the victim, use the Accident Claim Worksheet to keep track of the names, addresses, and phone numbers of parties and witnesses involved, along with communications with them, dates of relevant events and conversations, details from insurance companies, and other information you will need to process an accident claim. This worksheet is for your personal reference and isn't intended to become part of your claim.

CAUTION

**Get witness statements in writing as soon as possible.** Don't count on an eyewitness's memory for too long, especially given the fact that the witness is likely to be contacted by the other party. Ask witnesses to make and sign a note or send you an email containing their observations about the accident as soon afterward as possible.

### Signing Instructions

There are no signing instructions for the Accident Claim Worksheet. Simply fill it in for use in preparing a claim after an accident.

RELATED TOPIC

**Use the Notice of Insurance Claim** to notify the appropriate insurance company of the accident.

## Forms 85–90: Releases

A common means of settling minor disputes (such as an argument about an unpaid loan, a minor fender bender, or a golf ball crashing through a window) is for one party to pay the other a sum of money in exchange for giving up any legal claim related to the incident. Another way to settle a claim is for the person who was in the wrong to do something of benefit for the other. For example, if your neighbor's dog destroys your garden, you might agree to take no further action if your neighbor agrees to replace your most valuable plants and build a fence.

In either situation, you'll want to write out your agreement in the form of a contract, commonly called a "release." A release usually consists of no more than one party saying, "I'll pay a certain amount or do a certain thing," and the other party saying, "In exchange, I'll forever give up my legal claim against you."

### What Makes a Release Legally Enforceable?

To be legally enforceable, a release must satisfy two contract law requirements:

- **The release must be voluntary.** Each side must enter into the agreement voluntarily. If a party was coerced into signing an agreement because of the other's threats or intimidation, a court may consider it involuntary and therefore unenforceable. Courts are quite leery about tossing out a release for this reason, however. For example, in a dispute involving the repair of a bicycle, one party telling the other "I'll sue for $100,000 tomorrow if you don't agree to this release" is not the kind of threat that will make a release unenforceable. The threat or coercion must be both significant and within the realm of possibility.
- **The agreement must be arrived at fairly.** Judges are usually unwilling to enforce any agreement that is the product of deceit or the result of one side taking undue advantage of the other. For example, if a person is persuaded to sign a release two hours after an accident that left her groggy, or doesn't understand the meaning of the document or the rights being waived because of a language barrier, a court will likely not uphold it.

Releases are powerful documents. If you sign one forever giving up a legal claim in exchange for $500, and learn six months later that the extent of what you lost is much greater than you realized when you signed the release, you are out of luck unless a court declares the release unenforceable for one of the above reasons.

## Questions to Ask Before Signing a Release

In most situations where both sides understand the dispute and the consequences of various settlement options, you can confidently sign a release, knowing that the dispute will finally be put to rest. But it is always wise for you and the other party to answer the following questions before signing on the dotted line:

- Do you both understand the issues that underlie the dispute?
- Do you both understand what the release accomplishes?

If the answer to these questions is "yes," it's wise to ask another three additional questions, but this time just of yourself:

- Do I understand the alternative to a settlement—the legal result I am likely to obtain (and the time and dollars I am likely to spend to get it) if I go to court rather than accepting the release and settling the matter?
- Have I discussed my decision to sign the release with someone who has good business sense and is not emotionally involved with the issue or parties?
- If a lot of money is involved, have I consulted an attorney with practical experience in this field?

If big bucks are at stake and the answer to either of the last three questions is "no," or even a waffling "maybe," do the necessary homework before agreeing to release the other party.

This chapter contains several release forms, including a General Release (to settle a dispute when only one party is alleged to have been injured or suffered damages) and a General Mutual Release (to settle a dispute when both parties claim the other is at fault and that each has suffered injury or damage). We also include specific releases for damage to real estate, property damage in an automobile accident, personal injury, and contract claims. Review them all to see which one is most appropriate to your situation.

## Note on Legal Terminology

The person with the claim who releases the other is called the "releasor." The "releasee" is the person responsible for the injury or the claim who agrees to pay money or promises to do something of value (or not to do anything) in exchange for the release. This is called "paying consideration." To be binding, all contracts, including releases, require an exchange of consideration. The exchange of consideration (such as payment of a specific sum of money) should ideally occur before the release is signed. If this is not possible or feasible, the release should specify when the payment or consideration will be provided.

## Making the Release Binding on Others

If one of the parties dies, you want the release to be binding on that person's heirs. Our release forms include language about "successors, assigns, and heirs." In addition, in all community property states (and in some non-community property states), one spouse is generally liable for the debts of the other spouse, and is entitled to recover monies owed to the other—even if the first spouse had nothing to do with the event leading up to the liability. For this reason, our release forms are binding on spouses and require the spouse's signature signifying consent to the deal. The discussion of promissory notes, in Chapter 5, explains the basics of the community property system.

### Signing Instructions for Release Forms

You must sign the release for it to be valid. Print out two copies of the form. All parties to the release, including spouses (if any), should sign and date both copies of the document in the appropriate spaces. Print the name(s) of the spouse(s) in the blank line provided; if one or both of the parties is not married, write "N/A" on the blank line. Each party should keep one copy of the release, signed by all parties.

**FORM**

**Notarization of these release forms is optional.** You can choose to have any of these release forms notarized. While notarization will add a measure of legal credibility to the release, it's not required to make the agreement enforceable. (See the Introduction for general advice on having a form notarized.) If you do decide to sign your release in front of a licensed notary public, attach the notary certificate where indicated on the form.

### Form 85: General Release

A General Release is appropriate for settling personal disputes over a contract, debt, or minor personal injury when only one party is alleged to have been injured or suffered damage. (This form is not appropriate, however, if both parties claim the other is at fault and that each has suffered damage or injury as a result. This requires a mutual release, in which case you would use the General Mutual Release, below.)

**TIP**

**You can't release what you don't own.** If you've assigned your rights to someone else, that person becomes the releasor, not you. Paragraph 4 of the General Release form represents your promise that you own the right that is the subject of the release.

### Form 86: General Mutual Release

This form is appropriate for settling disputes—for example, over a debt or minor personal injury—where both parties say the other is at fault and each claims damage or injury as a result. Here the main point is often to trade legal releases—in which case the value or consideration is each person's relinquishment of the legal rights involved in the dispute (Clause 3 of this form). It is not unusual, however, for the person who has suffered the more serious loss (or who was less at fault) to receive additional consideration (Clause 4 of this form). This may be a cash payment or other benefit—for example, free use of a spa facility owned by one of the parties.

If the dispute concerns an oral or written contract, use the Mutual Release of Contract Claims, below.

### Form 87: Release for Damage to Real Estate

This form is appropriate for settling disputes between landowners that arise when one owner's property is damaged by another's action or inaction. Common examples include one person's tree overhanging another's yard or pool, or an uphill neighbor digging a ditch that diverts rain runoff onto a downhill neighbor's property. And, of course, walls, fences, view-blocking trees, and noise can all lead to serious disagreements between neighbors.

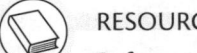

**RESOURCE**

**Before you settle a neighbor dispute, it will help if you understand the legal issues**—for example, if a tree grows on a property line, which neighbor owns it? For answers to this and similar questions, see *Neighbor Law: Fences, Trees, Boundaries & Noise*, by the Editors of Nolo.

## Form 88: Release for Property Damage in Auto Accident

Use this form to settle claims over minor property damage from an auto accident. Do not use it if personal injuries are involved. In that case, use the Release for Personal Injury, below.

## Form 89: Release for Personal Injury

Use this form when one party has suffered a relatively minor personal injury because of another's actions.

Here are a few examples of language describing an injury for use in Clause 2:
- Cat scratches sustained on both arms after Releasor was attacked by Releasee's cat, Roscoe.
- Cuts Releasor sustained from a shattered window when a baseball hit by Releasee's son broke a window in Releasor's house.

**CAUTION**
Don't sign a release involving personal injuries unless the parties are sure that the scope of the injury is fully known. For example, be sure that an injury has completely healed and your doctor has examined you, clearly established the scope of your injury, and unequivocally stated that you have recovered as much as is possible. It is almost never wise to sign very soon after an injury—you never know what problems might develop later.

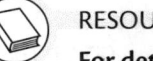

**RESOURCE**
For detailed advice on filing a personal injury claim, see *How to Win Your Personal Injury Claim*, by Joseph Matthews (Nolo).

## Form 90: Mutual Release of Contract Claims

This final release can be used to settle a disagreement that arises from the breach of a written or oral contract. Unlike the General Release or the General Mutual Release, this release is useful only for dealing with contract disputes.

> ### What If One of the Parties to a Release Doesn't Follow Through?
>
> If either of the people signing the release doesn't pay the money or do the promised deed, the other has a choice. The wronged party can take the appropriate legal steps concerning the original dispute as though no release had been signed. Or, either person could go to court and ask a judge to enforce the release (after all, it's a contract). A judge will consider whether the release was voluntary and whether the agreement was arrived at fairly.
>
> You can use small claims court to enforce the release if the amount is within the jurisdictional limits of the court. This is a good option, especially if money is the basis for the dispute.

## Form 91: Complaint Letter to a Government Agency

In every state, and at the federal level, unfair or deceptive trade acts or practices are prohibited by law. This means that it is illegal for a seller to deceive, abuse, mislead, defraud, or otherwise cheat you. If you think you've been cheated by someone selling a service or product, start by contacting the company directly.

If you're unable to resolve the problem directly, it's worth letting the appropriate federal, state, and local government offices know. Although law enforcement in the area of consumer fraud is not uniformly great, many hardworking investigators do their jobs well. The more agencies you notify, the more likely it is that someone will take notice of your complaint and act on it—especially if more than one consumer has registered a complaint about the same company.

> **How to Word a Complaint**
>
> Here's an example of language to include in a complaint letter to a government agency:
>
> > I wish to complain about a business called Celebrity Cards located in your state. About three months ago, I received a package of cards from this company, unsolicited. I received a second package two months ago. Last month I received a bill from the company for $50 plus shipping and handling. I never ordered these cards and I wrote to the company to say so. (A copy of my letter is attached.) I also stated that I considered the unsolicited items sent to my home to be a gift. Just this week, I received a second bill and a threat to send this debt to a collection agency and report it to a credit bureau.

Your initial step is to draft a complaint letter to the relevant government agencies, using this form. Be as detailed as possible, including the name and title of the person you dealt with, the dates and details of the service or product problem, and any follow-up communication. Keep your language neutral and state the facts of the situation. (See "How to Word a Complaint," below, for sample language.) To back up your complaint, attach copies (never the originals) of all purchase receipts, contracts, warranties, advertisements, and other written documents relating to your complaint.

Finally, your letter will be more persuasive if you suggest a solution, such as a refund, or at least request a reply from the person investigating your complaint.

Compile a list of agencies and their addresses where you will send your complaint letter. Start by checking www.usa.gov for information about federal, state, and local agencies. This will help you identify the appropriate federal agency to receive your complaint, depending on the nature of your problem. For example, a complaint about an online auction would go to the Federal Trade Commission (www.ftc.gov; see "How to Complain to Government Agencies," below, for a list of resources).

> **How to Complain to Government Agencies**
>
> Depending on the problem, you can send a copy of your complaint letter to one or more of the following agencies:
> - **Local district attorney's consumer fraud division.** Ask about local consumer protection services available, including mediation.
> - **Local Better Business Bureau.** Find yours at www.bbb.org.
> - **State Attorney General.** You can find contact information for your state Attorney General's office from the National Association of Attorneys General at www.naag.org.
> - **State Consumer Protection Office.** Your state consumer protection office can also provide advice, including the name of the appropriate licensing board that handles consumer complaints (for example, if your complaint concerns a licensed professional, such as a contractor or lawyer). Find your state consumer protection agency at www.usa.gov/state-consumer. (This website also has information on other useful government offices and consumer organizations.)
> - **Federal Trade Commission (FTC).** The FTC handles fraudulent, deceptive, and unfair business practices, but does not resolve individual complaints. It enters all complaints into an online database used by law enforcement agencies. For details, see the "File a Consumer Complaint" section at www.ftc.gov.

Many government agencies have their own online complaint form, but it doesn't hurt to follow up with a written complaint letter, such as the one included in this book.

Be sure to send a copy of your letter to the company you are complaining about.

### Signing Instructions

There are no specific signing instructions for this Complaint Letter to a Government Agency. Simply sign the form and send it to the appropriate government agencies with a copy to the company you're complaining about. Be sure to include copies of any relevant material such as previous correspondence with the seller or service provider. Keep a copy of your complaint letter and attached materials for your records. You might need this if you end up filing a small claims court case or taking other legal action.

## Form 92: Notice to Cancel Certain Contracts

Under the Federal Trade Commission (FTC) "cooling-off rule," consumers have the right to cancel certain types of consumer contracts within three days of signing. This right-to-cancel law applies to door-to-door sales contracts for $25 or more and contracts for $130 or more made anywhere other than the seller's normal place of business—for instance, at a sales presentation at a friend's house, hotel or restaurant, outdoor exhibit, computer show, or trade show. (Real estate, insurance, public car auctions, and craft fairs are exempted from coverage.)

The cooling-off rule applies only to goods or services primarily intended for personal, family, or household purposes. It does not apply to sales made entirely by mail, by telephone, or online. The cooling-off rule also does not apply to sales made as part of a request for a seller to do home repairs or maintenance (but purchases made beyond the maintenance or repair request are covered).

To take advantage of this right to cancel, you have until midnight of the third business day following the day you signed the contract to cancel the contract either in person or by mail. If you were not given notice of this right and a cancellation form when you signed the contract, simply use this form.

After canceling, the seller must refund your money within 10 business days. Then, the seller must either pick up the items purchased or reimburse you within 20 days for your expense of mailing the goods back to the seller. If the seller doesn't come for the goods or make arrangements for you to mail them back, you can keep them.

> **Consumer Rights to Cancel Other Types of Contracts**
>
> Federal law (the Truth in Lending Act) lets you cancel a home improvement loan, second mortgage, or other loan where you pledge your home as security (except for a first mortgage or first deed of trust). Again, you have until midnight of the third business day after you signed the contract to cancel it. Contact the FTC for more information on the Truth in Lending Act. In addition, contact your state office of consumer protection regarding state laws that allow consumers to cancel contracts for other types of goods and services (such as a health club membership) within a few days of signing. You can find your state agency at www.usa.gov/state-consumer.

**RESOURCE**

**For more information on the federal cooling-off rule, see www.ftc.gov or call 877-FTC-HELP.** Also, contact your state consumer protection office to see if your state law gives you more rights than the FTC's cooling-off rule. (See "How to Complain to Government Agencies," above, for contact information.)

### Signing Instructions

To cancel a contract under the FTC cooling-off rule, fill in the number of days the seller has to refund your money (10 under the FTC rule, or perhaps less under your state rule), and the number of days the seller has to reimburse you for any mailing expenses (20 under the FTC rule, or perhaps less under state rules). Sign and date one copy of the Notice to Cancel Certain Contracts. Mail it to the seller or the address given for cancellation (if different from the place of purchase). Keep a copy of the notice for your file. Be sure your envelope is postmarked before midnight of the third business day after the contract date. (Saturday is considered a business day, while Sundays and federal holidays are not.) It is a good idea to send this form by certified mail or some courier service with tracking and proof of delivery. You might need this later as proof that you properly canceled the contract.

## Form 93: Identity Theft Worksheet

Despite the millions of people affected by identity theft each year, many don't know what to do if it happens to them. If you believe that you are a victim of identity theft or fear that you might soon become one—for example, if you lost your wallet, had your home burglarized, or divulged your financial information to an email scammer—take these simple steps immediately. The order in which you take these steps will depend on your situation. For instance, if someone stole your wallet, you would likely want to start by contacting the relevant authorities and canceling all financial accounts that are tied to the stolen cards.

This form will help you keep track of what you've done, whom you've spoken to, and what else you'll need to do to protect your personal information.

Regardless of your situation, be sure to follow every step:

1. **Start a log.** Keep notes of your conversations and correspondence with authorities and financial institutions, including dates, names, and phone numbers. Also keep track of all time spent and expenses you incur; you can deduct theft-related expenses on your income tax return if you itemize deductions, and you might be able to seek compensation if you ever sue the thief.

2. **Check your homeowners' insurance policy.** Many now include coverage for certain administrative costs of dealing with identity theft, including attorneys' fees. Give your carrier a call to find out how it can help and what you'll need to keep track of. Unfortunately, the insurance typically won't cover any amounts that were actually stolen.

3. **Contact the credit bureaus to place a fraud alert.** Contact one of the three major credit bureaus (Equifax, Experian, or TransUnion), and ask to have a free credit report sent to you, and to have your account flagged with an initial 90-day fraud alert. Activating a fraud alert (also called a security alert) removes you from all preapproved credit and insurance offers, and requests that creditors contact you before opening any new accounts or making any changes to your existing

accounts. When activating a fraud alert, whichever one of three main credit bureaus you contact is required to notify the other two (but follow up to make sure this happens). You can request 90-day extensions or, with proof that you're an actual victim of identity theft, get an extended seven-year fraud alert. If you make additional calls to the credit bureaus on other subjects, be sure to contact all three, as they are not required to communicate with each other after your initial fraud-alert call. Here are the places to contact:

- Equifax: 888-378-4329 or www.equifax.com
- Experian: 888-397-3742 or www.experian.com, and
- TransUnion: 800-916-8800 or www.transunion.com

4. **Review your credit reports.** After you receive your credit reports from the three credit bureaus, review them thoroughly. Make sure that all your personal information, including name, address, and Social Security number, is correct and that there are no fraudulent accounts or inquiries. Immediately report any suspicious information or activity to the credit bureau that issued the credit report. And in two to three months, order another report to ensure that no new fraudulent activity has occurred. Depending on where you live, a nominal fee might apply when you order a follow-up credit report.

5. **Close any accounts that have been accessed fraudulently.** Contact all creditors, including banks, credit card companies, and other service providers, with whom there has been fraudulent activity. Close all accounts the thief opened or used fraudulently. Request that creditors notate closed accounts as "account closed at consumer's request," because a mark of "card lost or stolen" can reflect poorly on your credit report.

If a thief stole checks or opened bank accounts in your name, contact one of the major check verification companies (such as ChexSystems) to report the fraudulent activity and to stop payment on stolen checks.

**TIP**
**If your ATM or debit card was stolen, do not use your old PIN for your new card.** Choose a password that is obscure but that you will remember. Do not use obvious numbers, such as your or your spouse's birth date.

6. **Call the police.** File a report of the crime with your local police department. Provide as much evidence as you can, and ask the officer to list all fraudulently accessed accounts on the police report. Be sure to ask for a copy of the police report, because creditors will probably ask to see it. Remember to log the phone numbers and names of all the law enforcement agents with whom you speak; creditors may want this information. It's also recommended that you file a police report in the community where the crime occurred.

7. **Report the fraud to the FTC.** Go to www.identitytheft.gov, the agency's dedicated site for reporting identity theft and getting a recovery plan. Start by answering a few questions about your situation. The information you provide will be used to generate a personalized recovery plan, and you'll get step-by-step help with putting that plan into action. The FTC also uses identity theft claims to assist law enforcement agencies in finding and arresting identity thieves.

### Further Steps

Depending on the severity of your identity theft case, there are several other actions you may wish to pursue.

- **Contact the postal inspector.** If you believe that someone has changed your address through the post office or has committed mail fraud, contact the U.S. Postal Inspection Service at www.uspis.gov/. If you discover that mail in your name is being sent to an address other than your own, ask the local postmaster to forward all mail in your name to your own address.
- **Contact the Social Security Administration (SSA).** If you believe that your Social Security number (SSN) has been used to fraudulently obtain welfare or Social Security benefits and you wish to get a new SSN, visit www.ssa.gov/ssnumber.
- **Deal with debt collectors.** While you are handling your identity theft case, debt collectors may ask you to pay outstanding bills from fraudulently activated credit accounts. Inform the debt collector by phone and in writing that you are a victim of identity theft and that you are not responsible for the unpaid bill. In your letter, be sure to include copies of documents, such as a police report, that demonstrate that you are the victim of identity theft. With some exceptions, the company is legally prohibited from contacting you once it receives your letter. Request all pertinent information (for example, name, phone number, address, account number) relating to both the debt collector and the referring credit issuer, and ask whether they want you to report the incident using the FTC's "report and recovery" tool at www.identifytheft.gov. Finally, ask the debt collector to confirm in writing that you are not responsible for the outstanding debt and that the account has been closed.
- **Contact the U.S. State Department.** If your passport was stolen or if you believe someone could be fraudulently ordering a passport in your name, contact the U.S. State Department at https://travel.state.gov/content/passports/en/passports/lost-stolen.html.
- **Contact the Department of Motor Vehicles (DMV).** If your driver's license was stolen or if someone is using the number to facilitate fraud, contact your state's DMV. Most states will put a fraud alert on your license if you ask for one. You should also request a new license number and fill out the DMV's complaint form.

 **RESOURCE**

**Where to go for more information.** For a one-stop resource on reporting and recovering from identity theft, visit the federal government's dedicated identity theft site at www.identitytheft.gov.

### Signing Instructions

There are no specific signing instructions for the Identity Theft Worksheet. Simply use the form to keep track of what you've done to follow up on an identity theft.

APPENDIX

# How to Use the Downloadable Forms on the Nolo Website

**Editing RTFs** .................................................................................................................................. 126

**List of Forms Available on the Nolo Website** ................................................................... 127

This book comes with downloadable files that you can access online at: **www.nolo.com/back-of-book/SPOT.html**

Here is a list of types of files provided by this book, as well as the software programs you'll need to access them:

- **RTF.** You can open, edit, print, and save these form files with most word processing programs such as Microsoft *Word*, Windows *WordPad*, and recent versions of *WordPerfect*. On a Mac, you can use Apple *TextEdit* or Apple *Pages*. You can also work with the forms through a word processing app such as Google Docs (www.docs.google.com).
- **PDF.** You can view these files with Adobe *Reader*, free software from www.adobe.com. Government PDFs are sometimes fillable using your computer, but most PDFs are designed to be printed out and completed by hand.

## Editing RTFs

Here are some general instructions about editing RTF forms in your word processing program. Refer to the book's instructions and sample agreements for help about what should go in each blank:

- **Underlines.** Underlines indicate where to enter information. After filling in the needed text, delete the underline.
- **Bracketed and italicized text.** Bracketed and italicized text indicates instructions. Be sure to remove all instructional text before you finalize your document.
- **Optional text.** Optional text gives you the choice to include or exclude text. Delete any optional text you don't want to use. Renumber numbered items, if necessary.
- **Alternative text.** Alternative text gives you the choice between two or more text options. Delete those options you don't want to use. Renumber numbered items, if necessary.
- **Signature lines.** Signature lines should appear on a page with at least some text from the document itself.

Every word processing program uses different commands to open, format, save, and print documents, so refer to your software's help documents for help using your program. Nolo cannot provide technical support for questions about how to use your computer or your software.

> **CAUTION**
> **In accordance with U.S. copyright laws, the forms provided by this book are for your personal use only.**

## List of Forms Available on the Nolo Website

To download any of the files listed on the following pages go to: **www.nolo.com/back-of-book/SPOT.html**

| Form No. | Title | File Name |
|---|---|---|
| N/A | Dispute Resolution Clause | Disputes.rtf |
| 1 | Temporary Guardianship Authorization for Care of Minor | Form1.rtf |
| 2 | Authorization for Minor's Medical Treatment | Form2.rtf |
| 3 | Authorization for International Travel With Minor | Form3.rtf |
| 4 | House-Sitting Instructions | Form4.rtf |
| 5 | Children's Carpool Agreement | Form5.rtf |
| 6 | Pet Care Agreement | Form6.rtf |
| 7 | Authorization to Drive a Motor Vehicle | Form7.rtf |
| 8 | Power of Attorney for Finances (Limited Power) | Form8.rtf |
| 8NY | New York Power of Attorney for Finances (Limited Power) | Form8NY.rtf |
| 8PA | Pennsylvania Power of Attorney for Finances (Limited Power) | Form8PA.rtf |
| 9 | Power of Attorney for Real Estate | Form9.rtf |
| 9NY | New York Power of Attorney for Real Estate | Form9NY.rtf |
| 9PA | Pennsylvania Power of Attorney for Real Estate | Form9PA.rtf |
| 10 | Notice of Revocation of Power of Attorney | Form10.rtf |
| 11 | Request to Begin Special Education Process | Form11.rtf |
| 12 | Property Worksheet | Form12.rtf |
| 13 | Beneficiary Worksheet | Form13.rtf |
| 14 | Will for Adult With No Children | Form14.rtf |
| 15 | Will for Adult With Child(ren) | Form15.rtf |
| 16 | Will Codicil | Form16.rtf |
| 17 | Notice to Creditor of Death | Form17.rtf |
| 18 | Executor's Checklist | Form18.pdf |
| 19 | General Notice of Death | Form19.rtf |
| 20 | Obituary Information Fact Sheet | Form20.rtf |
| 21 | Notice to Deceased's Homeowners' Insurance Company | Form21.rtf |

| Form No. | Title | File Name |
|---|---|---|
| 22 | Notice to Deceased's Vehicle Insurance Company | Form22.rtf |
| 23 | Rental Application | Form23.rtf |
| 24 | Tenant References | Form24.rtf |
| 25 | Landlord-Tenant Checklist | Form25.rtf |
| 26 | Move-In Letter | Form26.rtf |
| 27 | Resident's Maintenance/Repair Request | Form27.rtf |
| 28 | Semiannual Safety and Maintenance Update | Form28.rtf |
| 29 | Landlord-Tenant Agreement to Terminate Lease | Form29.rtf |
| 30 | Consent to Assignment of Lease | Form30.rtf |
| 31 | Month-to-Month Tenant's Notice of Intent to Move Out | Form31.rtf |
| 32 | Demand for Return of Security Deposit | Form32.rtf |
| 33 | Loan Comparison Worksheet | Form33.rtf |
| 34 | Authorization to Check Credit and Employment References | Form34.rtf |
| 35 | Monthly Payment Record | Form35.rtf |
| 36 | Promissory Note—Installment Payments With Interest | Form36.rtf |
| 37 | Promissory Note—Installment Payments With Interest and Balloon Payment | Form37.rtf |
| 38 | Promissory Note—Installment Payments Without Interest | Form38.rtf |
| 39 | Promissory Note—Lump-Sum Payment With Interest | Form39.rtf |
| 40 | Promissory Note—Lump-Sum Payment Without Interest | Form40.rtf |
| 41 | Cosigner Provision | Form41.rtf |
| 42 | Security Agreement Provision for Promissory Note | Form42.rtf |
| 43 | Security Agreement for Borrowing Money | Form43.rtf |
| 44 | U.C.C. Financing Statement | Form44.rtf |
| 45 | Release of U.C.C. Financing Statement | Form45.rtf |
| 46 | Agreement to Modify Promissory Note | Form46.rtf |
| 47 | Overdue Payment Demand | Form47.rtf |
| 48 | Demand to Make Good on Bad Check | Form48.rtf |
| 49 | Ideal House Profile | Form49.rtf |

| Form No. | Title | File Name |
|---|---|---|
| 50 | House Priorities Worksheet | Form50.rtf |
| 51 | House Comparison Worksheet | Form51.rtf |
| 52 | Family Financial Statement | Form52.rtf |
| 53 | Monthly Carrying Costs Worksheet | Form53.rtf |
| 54 | Mortgage Rates and Terms Worksheet | Form54.rtf |
| 55 | Moving Checklist | Form55.rtf |
| 56 | Motor Vehicle Bill of Sale | Form56.rtf |
| 57 | Boat Bill of Sale | Form57.rtf |
| 58 | General Bill of Sale | Form58.rtf |
| 59 | Bill of Sale for Dog | Form59.rtf |
| 60 | Personal Property Rental Agreement | Form60.rtf |
| 61 | Notice of Termination of Personal Property Rental Agreement | Form61.rtf |
| 62 | Storage Contract | Form62.rtf |
| 63 | Home Maintenance Agreement | Form63.rtf |
| 64 | Home Repairs Agreement | Form64.rtf |
| 65 | Contractor Mid-Job Worksheet | Form65.rtf |
| 66 | Daily Expenses | Form66.rtf |
| 67 | Monthly Income | Form67.rtf |
| 68 | Monthly Budget | Form68.rtf |
| 69 | Statement of Assets and Liabilities | Form69.rtf |
| 70 | Assignment of Rights | Form70.rtf |
| 71 | Notice to Terminate Joint Account | Form71.rtf |
| 72 | Notice to Stop Payment of Check | Form72.rtf |
| 73 | Request for Credit Report | Form73.rtf |
| 74 | Request Reinvestigation of Credit Report Entry | Form74.rtf |
| 75 | Dispute Credit Card Charge | Form75.rtf |
| 76 | Demand Collection Agency Cease Contact | Form76.rtf |
| 77 | Child Care Agreement | Form77.rtf |

| Form No. | Title | File Name |
|---|---|---|
| 78 | Child Care Instructions | Form78.rtf |
| 79 | Elder Care Agreement | Form79.rtf |
| 80 | Housekeeping Services Agreement | Form80.rtf |
| 81 | Demand Letter | Form81.rtf |
| 82 | Online Auction Buyer Demand Letter | Form82.rtf |
| 83 | Request for Refund or Repair of Goods Under Warranty | Form83.rtf |
| 84 | Accident Claim Worksheet | Form84.rtf |
| 85 | General Release | Form85.rtf |
| 86 | General Mutual Release | Form86.rtf |
| 87 | Release for Damage to Real Estate | Form87.rtf |
| 88 | Release for Property Damage in Auto Accident | Form88.rtf |
| 89 | Release for Personal Injury | Form89.rtf |
| 90 | Mutual Release of Contract Claims | Form90.rtf |
| 91 | Complaint Letter to a Government Agency | Form91.rtf |
| 92 | Notice to Cancel Certain Contracts | Form92.rtf |
| 93 | Identity Theft Worksheet | Form93.rtf |

APPENDIX B

# Forms in This Book

| Form No. | Name | Chapter (discussed in) |
|---|---|---|
| Form 1: | Temporary Guardianship Authorization for Care of Minor | 1 |
| Form 2: | Authorization for Minor's Medical Treatment | 1 |
| Form 3: | Authorization for International Travel With Minor | 1 |
| Form 4: | House-Sitting Instructions | 1 |
| Form 5: | Children's Carpool Agreement | 1 |
| Form 6: | Pet Care Agreement | 1 |
| Form 7: | Authorization to Drive a Motor Vehicle | 1 |
| Form 8: | Power of Attorney for Finances (Limited Power) | 1 |
| Form 8NY: | New York Power of Attorney for Finances (Limited Power) | 1 |
| Form 8PA: | Pennsylvania Power of Attorney for Finances (Limited Power) | 1 |
| Form 9: | Power of Attorney for Real Estate | 1 |
| Form 9NY: | New York Power of Attorney for Real Estate | 1 |
| Form 9PA: | Pennsylvania Power of Attorney for Real Estate | 1 |
| Form 10: | Notice of Revocation of Power of Attorney | 1 |
| Form 11: | Request to Begin Special Education Process | 1 |
| Form 12: | Property Worksheet | 2 |
| Form 13: | Beneficiary Worksheet | 2 |
| Form 14: | Will for Adult With No Children | 2 |
| Form 15: | Will for Adult With Child(ren) | 2 |
| Form 16: | Will Codicil | 2 |
| Form 17: | Notice to Creditor of Death | 3 |
| Form 18: | Executor's Checklist | 3 |
| Form 19: | General Notice of Death | 3 |
| Form 20: | Obituary Information Fact Sheet | 3 |
| Form 21: | Notice to Deceased's Homeowners' Insurance Company | 3 |
| Form 22: | Notice to Deceased's Vehicle Insurance Company | 3 |
| Form 23: | Rental Application | 4 |
| Form 24: | Tenant References | 4 |
| Form 25: | Landlord-Tenant Checklist | 4 |
| Form 26: | Move-In Letter | 4 |
| Form 27: | Resident's Maintenance/Repair Request | 4 |

| Form No. | Name | Chapter (discussed in) |
|---|---|---|
| Form 28: | Semiannual Safety and Maintenance Update | 4 |
| Form 29: | Landlord-Tenant Agreement to Terminate Lease | 4 |
| Form 30: | Consent to Assignment of Lease | 4 |
| Form 31: | Month-to-Month Tenant's Notice of Intent to Move Out | 4 |
| Form 32: | Demand for Return of Security Deposit | 4 |
| Form 33: | Loan Comparison Worksheet | 5 |
| Form 34: | Authorization to Check Credit and Employment References | 5 |
| Form 35: | Monthly Payment Record | 5 |
| Form 36: | Promissory Note—Installment Payments With Interest | 5 |
| Form 37: | Promissory Note—Installment Payments With Interest and Balloon Payment | 5 |
| Form 38: | Promissory Note—Installment Payments Without Interest | 5 |
| Form 39: | Promissory Note—Lump-Sum Payment With Interest | 5 |
| Form 40: | Promissory Note—Lump-Sum Payment Without Interest | 5 |
| Form 41: | Cosigner Provision | 5 |
| Form 42: | Security Agreement Provision for Promissory Note | 5 |
| Form 43: | Security Agreement for Borrowing Money | 5 |
| Form 44: | U.C.C. Financing Statement | 5 |
| Form 45: | Release of U.C.C. Financing Statement | 5 |
| Form 46: | Agreement to Modify Promissory Note | 5 |
| Form 47: | Overdue Payment Demand | 5 |
| Form 48: | Demand to Make Good on Bad Check | 5 |
| Form 49: | Ideal House Profile | 6 |
| Form 50: | House Priorities Worksheet | 6 |
| Form 51: | House Comparison Worksheet | 6 |
| Form 52: | Family Financial Statement | 6 |
| Form 53: | Monthly Carrying Costs Worksheet | 6 |
| Form 54: | Mortgage Rates and Terms Worksheet | 6 |
| Form 55: | Moving Checklist | 6 |
| Form 56: | Motor Vehicle Bill of Sale | 7 |
| Form 57: | Boat Bill of Sale | 7 |
| Form 58: | General Bill of Sale | 7 |
| Form 59: | Bill of Sale for Dog | 7 |
| Form 60: | Personal Property Rental Agreement | 8 |

| Form No. | Name | Chapter (discussed in) |
|---|---|---|
| Form 61: | Notice of Termination of Personal Property Rental Agreement | 8 |
| Form 62: | Storage Contract | 8 |
| Form 63: | Home Maintenance Agreement | 9 |
| Form 64: | Home Repairs Agreement | 9 |
| Form 65: | Contractor Mid-Job Worksheet | 9 |
| Form 66: | Daily Expenses | 10 |
| Form 67: | Monthly Income | 10 |
| Form 68: | Monthly Budget | 10 |
| Form 69: | Statement of Assets and Liabilities | 10 |
| Form 70: | Assignment of Rights | 10 |
| Form 71: | Notice to Terminate Joint Account | 10 |
| Form 72: | Notice to Stop Payment of Check | 10 |
| Form 73: | Request for Credit Report | 10 |
| Form 74: | Request Reinvestigation of Credit Report Entry | 10 |
| Form 75: | Dispute Credit Card Charge | 10 |
| Form 76: | Demand Collection Agency Cease Contact | 10 |
| Form 77: | Child Care Agreement | 11 |
| Form 78: | Child Care Instructions | 11 |
| Form 79: | Elder Care Agreement | 11 |
| Form 80: | Housekeeping Services Agreement | 11 |
| Form 81: | Demand Letter | 12 |
| Form 82: | Online Auction Buyer Demand Letter | 12 |
| Form 83: | Request for Refund or Repair of Goods Under Warranty | 12 |
| Form 84: | Accident Claim Worksheet | 12 |
| Form 85: | General Release | 12 |
| Form 86: | General Mutual Release | 12 |
| Form 87: | Release for Damage to Real Estate | 12 |
| Form 88: | Release for Property Damage in Auto Accident | 12 |
| Form 89: | Release for Personal Injury | 12 |
| Form 90: | Mutual Release of Contract Claims | 12 |
| Form 91: | Complaint Letter to a Government Agency | 12 |
| Form 92: | Notice to Cancel Certain Contracts | 12 |
| Form 93: | Identity Theft Worksheet | 12 |

# Temporary Guardianship Authorization for Care of Minor

## Child
Name: _____
Permanent address: _____
Phone: _____ Birth date: _____

## Child's School or Day Care
[Leave this section blank if your child is not in school or any type of child care program.]
School or day care program: _____
Teacher or day care provider: _____ Grade: _____
School or day care address: _____
_____ Phone: _____

## Child's Doctor, Dentist, and Insurance
Doctor (or HMO): _____
Address: _____
_____ Phone: _____
Name of medical insurer/health plan: _____
Policy or medical records number: _____
Phone: _____

Dentist: _____
Address: _____
_____ Phone: _____
Name of dental insurer/dental plan: _____
Policy number: _____ Phone: _____

## Parents (or Legal Guardians)

### Parent/Guardian 1
Name: _____
Address: _____
_____
Home phone: _____ Work phone: _____
Cell phone: _____ Email: _____

### Parent/Guardian 2
Name: _____
Address: _____
_____
Home phone: _____ Work phone: _____
Cell phone: _____ Email: _____

**Temporary Guardian**

Name: _____

Address: _____

_____

Home phone: _____ Work phone: _____

Cell phone: _____ Email: _____

**Emergency Contact Information**

In case of emergency, if a parent, guardian, or temporary guardian cannot be reached, contact:

Name: _____

Phone: _____ Email: _____

Additional contact information: _____

_____

_____

## Authorization and Consent of Parent(s) or Legal Guardian(s)

1. I am the parent or legal guardian of, and have legal custody of, the minor child named above. I authorize my child to live with and travel with the temporary guardian. I give the temporary guardian permission to care for my child in my place and make decisions pertaining to my child's care, including educational, recreational, and religious activities.

2. I give the temporary guardian permission to authorize medical and dental care for my child, including but not limited to medical examinations, X-rays, tests, anesthesia, surgical operations, hospital care, or other treatments that, in the temporary guardian's sole opinion, are needed or useful for my child. Such medical treatment shall be provided only upon the advice of and supervision by a physician, surgeon, dentist, or other medical practitioner licensed to practice in the United States.

3. This authorization shall cover the period from _____ to _____ .

4. While the temporary guardian cares for my child, the costs of my child's upkeep, living expenses, and medical and dental expenses shall be paid as follows: _____

_____

Parent/Guardian 1's signature: _____ Date: _____

Parent/Guardian 2's signature: _____ Date: _____

## Consent of Temporary Guardian

I solemnly affirm that I will assume full responsibility for the minor who will live with me during the period designated above.

Temporary Guardian's signature: _____ Date: _____

[OPTIONAL: ATTACH NOTARY CERTIFICATE]

# Authorization for Minor's Medical Treatment

## Child

Name: _____

Birth date: _____ Age: _____ Grade in school: _____

Doctor (or HMO): _____

Address: _____

_____ Phone: _____

Name of medical insurer/health plan: _____

Policy number: _____ Phone: _____

Allergies (medications): _____

Allergies (other): _____

Medications the child is currently taking: _____

_____

Other important medical information: _____

_____

Dentist: _____

Address: _____

_____ Phone: _____

Name of dental insurer/dental plan: _____

Policy number: _____ Phone: _____

## Parents (or Legal Guardians)

### Parent/Guardian 1

Name: _____

Address: _____

_____

Home phone: _____ Work phone: _____

Cell phone: _____ Email: _____

Additional contact information: _____

### Parent/Guardian 2

Name: _____

Address: _____

_____

Home phone: _____ Work phone: _____

Cell phone: _____ Email: _____

Additional contact information: _____

**Emergency Contact**

Name: _____

Address: _____

_____

Home phone: _____ Work phone: _____

Cell phone: _____ Email: _____

Additional contact information: _____

## Authorization and Consent of Parent(s) or Legal Guardian(s)

I am the parent or legal guardian of _____ [name of the child] and have legal custody of, the minor child named above. If I cannot be reached to give consent to medical or dental care for my child, I authorize _____ [name of the person to whom you want to give authority to get medical care for your child] to give consent to such care in my place.

    This authorization includes permission to consent to medical and dental care for my child, including but not limited to medical examinations, X-rays, tests, anesthesia, surgical operations, hospital care, or other treatments that in the opinion of _____ [name of the person to whom you want to give authority to get medical care for your child] are needed or useful for my child. Such medical treatment shall be provided only upon the advice of and shall be supervised by a physician, surgeon, dentist, or other medical practitioner licensed to practice in the United States.

Parent/Guardian 1's signature: _____ Date: _____

Parent/Guardian 2's signature: _____ Date: _____

[OPTIONAL: ATTACH NOTARY CERTIFICATE]

# Authorization for International Travel With Minor

To Whom It May Concern:

This letter concerns my child, _____ [name of child], a U.S. citizen and a minor born on _____ , _____ , [child's date of birth], who has been issued a U.S. passport with the number _____ .

I affirm that I have legal custody of my child, and that there are no pending divorce or child custody proceedings that involve my child. I give my full authorization and consent for my child to travel outside of the United States with _____ [name of adult with whom child will travel], who is the _____ [state adult's relationship with child] of my child. The purpose of the travel is _____ _____ [specify vacation, touring, to visit relatives, to accompany adult on business trip, or other reason].

I have approved the following travel plans:

| Dates of travel | Destinations/Accommodations |
|---|---|
| _____ | _____ |
| _____ | _____ |
| _____ | _____ |
| _____ | _____ |
| _____ | _____ |

Furthermore, I hereby authorize _____ [name of adult with whom child will travel] to modify the travel plans specified above as he/she deems necessary.

I declare under penalty of perjury under the laws of the state of _____ [the U.S. state in which you and the child live] that the foregoing is true and correct.

Parent/Guardian 1's signature: _____ Date: _____

Printed name: _____

Address: _____

Home phone: _____ Work phone: _____

Cell phone: _____ Email: _____

Parent/Guardian 2's signature: _____ Date: _____

Printed name: _____

Address: _____

Home phone: _____ Work phone: _____

Cell phone: _____ Email: _____

[OPTIONAL: ATTACH NOTARY CERTIFICATE]

# House-Sitting Instructions

**Homeowner(s)**

Name(s): _____

Home address: _____

Cell phone: _____ Home phone: _____

Temporary address(es) and phone numbers while house sitter is staying at home [*or attach schedule*]:

_____

**Plants and Garden.** [*What to water, when.*] _____

_____

**Newspapers and Mail.** [*What to do about mail and newspapers; what to save, what to throw out.*]

_____

**Garbage and Recycling.** [*Details of garbage pickup and recycling—what, where, when.*] _____

_____

**Appliances.** [*Where to find manuals/booklets on major and minor appliances, plus odds and ends of information as to location and operation of vacuum cleaner, television, stove, etc.*] _____

_____

**Lights.** [*Any special details on regular lights, smart lights, timers, automatic night lights, and external motion-sensitive lights.*] _____

**Windows, Doors, Security Systems, and Keys.** [*Details on how locks and security system work, and who has extra keys.*] _____

_____

**Smoke Detectors and Fire Extinguishers.** [*Details on location and functioning of smoke detectors and fire extinguishers.*] _____

_____

**Wireless Network.** [*Network name and password; location of router; instructions for resetting*]

_____

**Utilities.** [*Details on location and use of thermostat, gas and water shut-off valves, fuse box, and spare fuses.*]

_____

**Tools and Supplies.** [*Location of house supplies, such as tools, lightbulbs, batteries, iron, cleaning supplies, and first aid kit.*] _____

_____

**Vehicles.** [*Details on cars, location of extra keys, maintenance instructions, local parking restrictions, and so on.*] _____
_____
_____

**Neighbors and Friends.** [*Names and phone numbers of neighbors and friends who can help with any questions.*] _____
_____

**Repair People and Service Contacts.** [*Names and phone numbers of repair person, plumber, insurance agent, etc.*] _____
_____

**Miscellaneous.** [*Anything else you want the housesitter to know.*] _____
_____

Signature: _____ Date: _____

# Children's Carpool Agreement

1. The purpose of this carpool is to transport children to _____ [name of activity], located at _____ [address].

2. The carpool will begin on _____ [date] and end on _____ [date].

3. Inbound trip: The carpool will pick up _____ [the first child to be picked up] at _____ [time] and pick up the rest of the children in this order: _____ _____ [list the pickup order].

4. Return trip: The carpool will meet the children at _____ [time] and deliver the children to the addresses listed below in this order: _____ _____ [list the drop-off order].

5. Special agreements (waiting time, alternate drop-off sites, etc.): _____ _____ .

6. The members of the carpool and the riders are:

   ### Child 1

   Child's name: _____ Cell phone: _____
   Inbound pickup address: _____
   Outbound drop-off address: _____
   Parents'/Guardians' name(s): _____
   Parents'/Guardians' home address: _____
   Parents'/Guardians' work address: _____

   **Parents'/Guardians' contact information:**
   Home phone: _____ Work phone: _____
   Cell phone: _____ Email: _____
   Names, phone numbers, and relationship to you/child of two people, other than those listed above, to call in an emergency: _____
   _____

   Name and phone number of child's physician: _____
   Driver's name: _____
   Driver's license number: _____
   Driver's address, if different from above: _____
   Driver's phone, if different from above: _____
   Model, make, and license number of vehicle(s) driver expects to use: _____
   _____

   Name of insurance company: _____

## Child 2

Child's name: _____ Cell phone: _____
Inbound pickup address: _____
Outbound drop-off address: _____
Parents'/Guardians' name(s): _____
Parents'/Guardians' home address: _____
Parents'/Guardians' work address: _____

### Parents'/Guardians' contact information:

Home phone: _____ Work phone: _____
Cell phone: _____ Email: _____
Names, phone numbers, and relationship to you/child of two people, other than those listed above, to call in an emergency: _____
_____

Name and phone number of child's physician: _____
Driver's name: _____
Driver's license number: _____
Driver's address, if different from above: _____
Driver's phone, if different from above: _____
Model, make, and license number of vehicle(s) driver expects to use: _____
_____

Name of insurance company: _____

## Child 3

Child's name: _____ Cell phone: _____
Inbound pickup address: _____
Outbound drop-off address: _____
Parents'/Guardians' name(s): _____
Parents'/Guardians' home address: _____
Parents'/Guardians' work address: _____

### Parents'/Guardians' contact information:

Home phone: _____ Work phone: _____
Cell phone: _____ Email: _____
Names, phone numbers, and relationship to you/child of two people, other than those listed above, to call in an emergency: _____
_____

Name and phone number of child's physician: _____
Driver's name: _____

Driver's license number: _____

Driver's address, if different from above: _____

Driver's phone, if different from above: _____

Model, make, and license number of vehicle(s) driver expects to use: _____

_____

Name of insurance company: _____

## Child 4

Child's name: _____ Cell phone: _____

Inbound pickup address: _____

Outbound drop-off address: _____

Parents'/Guardians' name(s): _____

Parents'/Guardians' home address: _____

Parents'/Guardians' work address: _____

### Parents'/Guardians' contact information:

Home phone: _____ Work phone: _____

Cell phone: _____ Email: _____

Names, phone numbers, and relationship to you/child of two people, other than those listed above, to call in an emergency: _____

_____

Name and phone number of child's physician: _____

Driver's name: _____

Driver's license number: _____

Driver's address, if different from above: _____

Driver's phone, if different from above: _____

Model, make, and license number of vehicle(s) driver expects to use: _____

_____

Name of insurance company: _____

7. By signing this Agreement, I agree to abide by its terms to the best of my ability. I understand that any member of the carpool can stop participating without notice but agree to give as much notice as is possible under the circumstances. I understand that if a member is not fulfilling his or her responsibilities, that member may be asked to leave. I understand that this document is not a legally binding agreement and is entered into in a spirit of cooperation and a shared desire to make the carpool work well for the benefit of the children and their parents or guardians.

Parent or Guardian signature: _____ Date: _____

Parent or Guardian signature: _____ Date: _____

Parent or Guardian signature: _____ Date: _____

Parent or Guardian signature: _____ Date: _____

# Pet Care Agreement

## Owner

Name: _____

Home address: _____
_____

Home phone: _____  Work phone: _____

Cell phone: _____  Email: _____

Temporary address while pet is in Caregiver's care: _____
_____  Phone: _____

[if more than one temporary address, attach itinerary]

## Caregiver

Name: _____

Home address: _____
_____

Home phone: _____  Work phone: _____

Cell phone: _____  Email: _____

Temporary address while pet is in Caregiver's care: _____
_____  Phone: _____

## Pet(s)

Caregiver will take care of: [list name, species, breed, age, and, if necessary, any distinguishing characteristics]
_____
_____
_____
_____

## Dates of Care

Caregiver will care for the animal(s) at _____
[location, either Caregiver's home or your home] from _____ [beginning date] until _____ [ending date].

## Reimbursement and Compensation

Owner will reimburse Caregiver for reasonable out-of-pocket expenses, including veterinary bills incurred while caring for the animal(s). Owner will also compensate Caregiver as follows:

☐ no compensation

☐ payment of $_____

☐ other: _____

## Care Instructions

Caregiver will exercise reasonable care to protect the animal(s) from sickness, injury, and theft, and will follow these instructions:

### Food

Type of food: _____

Amount: _____

Frequency: _____

Special instructions: _____

_____

### Medication

1. Name: _____ Dosage: _____

    Special instructions: _____

2. Name: _____ Dosage: _____

    Special instructions: _____

### Exercise

Frequency and type: _____

Special instructions: _____

### Grooming

Frequency and type: _____

Special instructions: _____

### Veterinary Care

Name: _____

Address: _____

_____ Phone: _____

Veterinary insurance company and policy no.: _____

Special instructions: _____

### Other Care Instructions

_____

_____

_____

_____

## Emergency Contact

If Caregiver becomes unable to care for the pet(s), Caregiver will contact _____
_____ [name] at _____ [phone number]
to try to make substitute arrangements for care of the pet(s) and will promptly notify Owner. If arrangements cannot be made, Caregiver will turn the pet(s) over to _____
_____ [name] at _____ [phone number]
and promptly notify Owner.

## Disputes

If any dispute arises under this agreement, the parties agree to select a mutually agreeable third party to help them mediate it, and to share equally any costs of mediation.

## Additional Terms

_____
_____
_____
_____

## Entire Agreement

This agreement contains the entire agreement between Owner and Caregiver. Any modifications must be in writing.

## Signatures

Owner's name: _____

Signature: _____ Date: _____

Caregiver's name: _____

Signature: _____ Date: _____

# Authorization to Drive a Motor Vehicle

## Vehicle Owner ("Owner")

Name: _____

Address: _____

_____

Home phone: _____ Work phone: _____

Cell phone: _____ Email: _____

## Vehicle

Make, model, and year of vehicle: _____

Vehicle license plate number: _____ State of registration: _____

Vehicle identification number (VIN): _____

Insurance company: _____

Insurance policy number: _____

Odometer reading when authorization begins: _____

## Person Authorized to Drive ("Borrower")

Name: _____

Address: _____

_____

Home phone: _____ Work phone: _____

Cell phone: _____ Email: _____

Driver's license number: _____

Motor vehicle insurance company (if any): _____

Insurance policy number (if any): _____

## Authorization and Consent of Owner

I am the lawful owner of the vehicle indicated above. I give my authorization and consent for Borrower to use this vehicle as follows:

Dates of use: _____

Area in which vehicle may be used: _____

Any restrictions or conditions on use: _____

I declare under penalty of perjury under the laws of the state of _____ that the foregoing is true and correct.

Owner's signature: _____ Date: _____

# Power of Attorney for Finances (Limited Power)

I, _____ [your name] (principal),
of _____ [your city and state],
appoint _____ [name of your
attorney-in-fact] to act in my place for the purposes of: _____
_____
_____.

This power of attorney takes effect on _____,
and shall continue until terminated in writing, or until _____,
whichever comes first. In the event of my incapacity or death, this power of attorney shall terminate immediately.

I grant my attorney-in-fact full authority to act in any manner both proper and necessary to the exercise of the foregoing powers, and I ratify every act that my attorney-in-fact may lawfully perform in exercising those powers.

I agree that any third party who receives a copy of this document may act under it. Revocation of the power of attorney is not effective as to a third party until the third party has actual knowledge of the revocation. I agree to indemnify the third party for any claims that arise against the third party because of reliance on this power of attorney.

Signed: This _____ day of _____, _____
State of: _____, County of: _____
Signature: _____, Principal

## Witnesses

[*Witnesses are required in some states, optional in others*]

On the date written above, the principal declared to me that this instrument is his or her financial power of attorney, and that he or she willingly executed it as a free and voluntary act. The principal signed this instrument in my presence.

**Witness 1**
Signature: _____
Name: _____
Address: _____
_____

**Witness 2**
Signature: _____
Name: _____
Address: _____
_____

## Acknowledgment of Attorney-in-Fact

By accepting or acting under the appointment, I assume the fiduciary and other legal responsibilities and liabilities of an agent. I understand that I owe a duty of loyalty and good faith to the principal and must use the powers granted to me only for the benefit of the principal. I acknowledge that my authority to act on behalf of the principal ceases at the death of the principal.

Name of attorney-in-fact: _____

Signature of attorney-in-fact: _____

[ATTACH NOTARY CERTIFICATE OF ACKNOWLEDGMENT]

# New York Power of Attorney for Finances (Limited Power)

**CAUTION TO THE PRINCIPAL:** Your Power of Attorney is an important document. As the "principal," you give the person whom you choose (your "agent") authority to spend your money and sell or dispose of your property during your lifetime without telling you. You do not lose your authority to act even though you have given your agent similar authority.

When your agent exercises this authority, he or she must act according to any instructions you have provided or, where there are no specific instructions, in your best interest. "Important Information for the Agent" at the end of this document describes your agent's responsibilities.

Your agent can act on your behalf only after signing the Power of Attorney before a notary public.

You can request information from your agent at any time. If you are revoking a prior Power of Attorney, you should provide written notice of the revocation to your prior agent(s) and to any third parties who may have acted upon it, including the financial institutions where your accounts are located.

You can revoke or terminate your Power of Attorney at any time for any reason as long as you are of sound mind. If you are no longer of sound mind, a court can remove an agent for acting improperly.

Your agent cannot make health care decisions for you. You may execute a "Health Care Proxy" to do this.

The law governing Powers of Attorney is contained in the New York General Obligations Law, Article 5, Title 15. This law is available at a law library, or online through the New York State Senate or Assembly websites, www.nysenate.gov or www.nyassembly.gov.

If there is anything about this document that you do not understand, you should ask a lawyer of your own choosing to explain it to you.

I, _____ [your name],
of _____ [your city and state],
appoint _____ [name of your agent]
to act in my place for the purposes of: _____ .

This power of attorney takes effect on _____ and shall continue until terminated in writing or until _____ , whichever comes first.

I grant my agent full authority to act in any manner both proper and necessary to the exercise of the foregoing powers, and I ratify every act that my agent may lawfully perform in exercising those powers.

I agree that any third party who receives a copy of this document may act under it. Revocation of the power of attorney is not effective as to a third party until the third party has actual knowledge of the revocation. I agree to indemnify the third party for any claims that arise against the third party because of reliance on this power of attorney.

Signed: This _____ day of _____ , _____
State of: _____ , County of: _____
Signature: _____ , Principal

## Signature of Witnesses

By signing as a witness, I acknowledge that the principal signed the Power of Attorney in my presence and in the presence of the other witness, or that the principal acknowledged to me that the principal's signature was affixed by him or her or at his or her direction. I also acknowledge that the principal has stated that this Power of Attorney reflects his or her wishes and that he or she has signed it voluntarily. I am not named herein as an agent or as a permissible recipient of gifts.

**Witness 1**

Signature: _____

Name: _____

Address: _____

**Witness 2**

Signature: _____

Name: _____

Address: _____

STATE OF NEW YORK            )
                             ) ss:
COUNTY OF _____ )

On the _____ day of _____, 20____, before me, the undersigned, personally appeared _____, personally known to me or proved to me on the basis of satisfactory evidence to be the individual whose name is subscribed to the within instrument and acknowledged to me that he/she executed the same in his/her capacity, and that by his/her signature on the instrument, the individual, or the person upon behalf of which the individual acted, executed the instrument.

Notary Public: _____

## IMPORTANT INFORMATION FOR THE AGENT:

When you accept the authority granted under this Power of Attorney, a special legal relationship is created between you and the principal. This relationship imposes on you legal responsibilities that continue until you resign or the Power of Attorney is terminated or revoked. You must:

(1) act according to any instructions from the principal, or, where there are no instructions, in the principal's best interest;

(2) avoid conflicts that would impair your ability to act in the principal's best interest;

(3) keep the principal's property separate and distinct from any assets you own or control, unless otherwise permitted by law;

(4) keep a record of all transactions conducted for the principal or keep all receipts of payments, and transactions conducted for the principal; and

(5) disclose your identity as an agent whenever you act for the principal by writing or printing the principal's name and signing your own name as "agent" in either of the following manners: (Principal's Name) by (Your Signature) as Agent, or (your signature) as Agent for (Principal's Name).

You may not use the principal's assets to benefit yourself or anyone else or make gifts to yourself or anyone else unless the principal has specifically granted you that authority in this document. If you have that authority, you must act according to any instructions of the principal or, where there are no such instructions, in the principal's best interest.

You may resign by giving written notice to the principal and to any co-agent, successor agent, monitor if one has been named in this document, or the principal's guardian if one has been appointed. If there is anything about this document or your responsibilities that you do not understand, you should seek legal advice.

Liability of agent: The meaning of the authority given to you is defined in New York's General Obligations Law, Article 5, Title 15. If it is found that you have violated the law or acted outside the authority granted to you in the Power of Attorney, you may be liable under the law for your violation.

## AGENT'S SIGNATURE AND ACKNOWLEDGMENT OF APPOINTMENT:

It is not required that the principal and the agent(s) sign at the same time, nor that multiple agents sign at the same time.

I, _____, have read the foregoing Power of Attorney. I am the person identified therein as agent for the principal named therein.

I acknowledge my legal responsibilities.

In Witness Whereof I have hereunto signed my name on _____, 20____.

Agent(s) sign(s) here:   ==>_____

STATE OF NEW YORK         )
                          ) ss:
COUNTY OF _____ )

On the _____ day of _____, 20____, before me, the undersigned, personally appeared _____, personally known to me or proved to me on the basis of satisfactory evidence to be the individual whose name is subscribed to the within instrument and acknowledged to me that he/she executed the same in his/her capacity, and that by his/her signature on the instrument, the individual, or the person upon behalf of which the individual acted, executed the instrument.

Notary Public: _____

# Pennsylvania Power of Attorney for Finances (Limited Power)

## NOTICE

THE PURPOSE OF THIS POWER OF ATTORNEY IS TO GIVE THE PERSON YOU DESIGNATE (YOUR "AGENT") BROAD POWERS TO HANDLE YOUR PROPERTY, WHICH MAY INCLUDE POWERS TO SELL OR OTHERWISE DISPOSE OF ANY REAL OR PERSONAL PROPERTY WITHOUT ADVANCE NOTICE TO YOU OR APPROVAL BY YOU.

THIS POWER OF ATTORNEY DOES NOT IMPOSE A DUTY ON YOUR AGENT TO EXERCISE GRANTED POWERS, BUT WHEN POWERS ARE EXERCISED, YOUR AGENT MUST USE DUE CARE TO ACT FOR YOUR BENEFIT AND IN ACCORDANCE WITH THIS POWER OF ATTORNEY.

YOUR AGENT MAY EXERCISE THE POWERS GIVEN HERE THROUGHOUT YOUR LIFETIME, EVEN AFTER YOU BECOME INCAPACITATED, UNLESS YOU EXPRESSLY LIMIT THE DURATION OF THESE POWERS OR YOU REVOKE THESE POWERS OR A COURT ACTING ON YOUR BEHALF TERMINATES YOUR AGENT'S AUTHORITY.

YOUR AGENT MUST ACT IN ACCORDANCE WITH YOUR REASONABLE EXPECTATIONS TO THE EXTENT ACTUALLY KNOWN BY YOUR AGENT AND, OTHERWISE, IN YOUR BEST INTEREST, ACT IN GOOD FAITH AND ACT ONLY WITHIN THE SCOPE OF AUTHORITY GRANTED BY YOU IN THE POWER OF ATTORNEY.

THE LAW PERMITS YOU, IF YOU CHOOSE, TO GRANT BROAD AUTHORITY TO AN AGENT UNDER POWER OF ATTORNEY, INCLUDING THE ABILITY TO GIVE AWAY ALL OF YOUR PROPERTY WHILE YOU ARE ALIVE OR TO SUBSTANTIALLY CHANGE HOW YOUR PROPERTY IS DISTRIBUTED AT YOUR DEATH. BEFORE SIGNING THIS DOCUMENT, YOU SHOULD SEEK THE ADVICE OF AN ATTORNEY AT LAW TO MAKE SURE YOU UNDERSTAND IT.

A COURT CAN TAKE AWAY THE POWERS OF YOUR AGENT IF IT FINDS YOUR AGENT IS NOT ACTING PROPERLY.

THE POWERS AND DUTIES OF AN AGENT UNDER A POWER OF ATTORNEY ARE EXPLAINED MORE FULLY IN 20 PA.C.S. CH. 56.

IF THERE IS ANYTHING ABOUT THIS FORM THAT YOU DO NOT UNDERSTAND, YOU SHOULD ASK A LAWYER OF YOUR OWN CHOOSING TO EXPLAIN IT TO YOU.

I have read or had explained to me this notice and I understand its contents.

Signature: _____, Principal

Date: _____

I, _____ [your name],

(principal) of _____ [your city and state], appoint

[name of your agent] _____ to act in my place for the purposes of:

_____ .

This power of attorney takes effect on _____ and shall continue until terminated in writing or until _____, whichever comes first. In the event of my incapacity or death, this power of attorney shall terminate immediately.

I grant my agent full authority to act in any manner both proper and necessary to the exercise of the foregoing powers, and I ratify every act that my agent may lawfully perform in exercising those powers.

I agree that any third party who receives a copy of this document may act under it. Revocation of the power of attorney is not effective as to a third party until the third party has actual knowledge of the revocation. I agree to indemnify the third party for any claims that arise against the third party because of reliance on this power of attorney.

Signed: This _____ day of _____, _____

State of Pennsylvania, County of _____

Signature: _____, Principal

## Witnesses

On the date written above, the principal declared to me that this instrument is his or her financial power of attorney, and that he or she willingly executed it as a free and voluntary act. The principal signed this instrument in my presence.

**Witness 1**

Signature: _____

Name: _____

Address: _____

**Witness 2**

Signature: _____

Name: _____

Address: _____

## Certificate of Acknowledgment of Notary Public

State of Pennsylvania _____

County of _____  } ss

This record was acknowledged before me on (date) _____, by (name(s) of individual(s)), _____ _____, and _____.

[NOTARIAL SEAL]  Signature of Notarial Officer: _____
Title of Office: _____
My commission expires: _____

## Acknowledgment of Agent

I, _____, have read the attached power of attorney and am the person identified as the agent for the principal. I hereby acknowledge that when I act as agent I shall act in accordance with the principal's reasonable expectations to the extent actually known by me and, otherwise, in the principal's best interest, act in good faith and act only within the scope of authority granted to me by the principal in the power of attorney.

Name of Agent: _____
Signature of Agent: _____
Date: _____

# Power of Attorney for Real Estate

RECORDING REQUESTED BY
AND WHEN RECORDED MAIL TO

_____

_____

_____

## Power of Attorney for Real Estate

I, _____ [name of principal],
of _____ [city], _____ [county],
_____ [state], appoint _____
_____ [name of attorney-in-fact], of _____ [city],
_____ [county], _____ [state]
to act in my place with respect to the real property described as follows:
_____
_____
_____

My attorney-in-fact may act for me in any manner to deal with all or any part of any interest in the real property described in this document, under such terms, conditions, and covenants as my attorney-in-fact deems proper. My attorney-in-fact's powers include but are not limited to the power to:

1. Accept as a gift or as security for a loan, reject, demand, buy, lease, receive, or otherwise acquire ownership or possession of any estate or interest in real property.

2. Sell, exchange, convey with or without covenants, quitclaim, release, surrender, mortgage, encumber, partition or consent to the partitioning of, grant options concerning, lease, sublet, or otherwise dispose of any interest in the real property described in this document.

3. Maintain, repair, improve, insure, rent, lease, and pay or contest taxes or assessments on any estate or interest in the real property described in this document.

4. Prosecute, defend, intervene in, submit to arbitration, settle, and propose or accept a compromise with respect to any claim in favor of or against me based on or involving the real property described in this document.

However, my attorney-in-fact shall not have the power to:
_____
_____
_____

I further grant to my attorney-in-fact full authority to act in any manner both proper and necessary to the exercise of the foregoing powers, including _____
_____
_____,
and I ratify every act that my attorney-in-fact may lawfully perform in exercising those powers.

This power of attorney takes effect on _____, and shall continue until terminated in writing, or until _____, whichever comes first. In the event of my incapacity or death, this power of attorney shall terminate immediately.

I agree that any third party who receives a copy of this document may act under it. Revocation of the power of attorney is not effective as to a third party until the third party has actual knowledge of the revocation. I agree to indemnify the third party for any claims that arise against the third party because of reliance on this power of attorney.

Signed this _____ day of _____, _____

State of _____, County of _____

Signature: _____

## Witnesses

On the date written above, the principal declared to me that this instrument is his or her power of attorney for real estate, and that he or she willingly executed it as a free and voluntary act. The principal signed this instrument in my presence.

Signature: _____  Signature: _____
Name: _____  Name: _____
Address: _____  Address: _____
County: _____  County: _____

## Preparation Statement

This document was prepared by:

Print name: _____

Signature: _____

Address: _____

## Signature of Attorney-in-Fact

By accepting or acting under the appointment, the attorney-in-fact assumes the fiduciary and other legal responsibilities of an agent.

Signature of attorney-in-fact: _____

[ATTACH NOTARY CERTIFICATE OF ACKNOWLEDGMENT]

Form 9NY

RECORDING REQUESTED BY
AND WHEN RECORDED MAIL TO
_____
_____
_____

# New York Power of Attorney for Real Estate

**CAUTION TO THE PRINCIPAL:** Your Power of Attorney is an important document. As the "principal," you give the person whom you choose (your "agent") authority to spend your money and sell or dispose of your property during your lifetime without telling you. You do not lose your authority to act even though you have given your agent similar authority.

When your agent exercises this authority, he or she must act according to any instructions you have provided or, where there are no specific instructions, in your best interest. "Important Information for the Agent" at the end of this document describes your agent's responsibilities.

Your agent can act on your behalf only after signing the Power of Attorney before a notary public.

You can request information from your agent at any time. If you are revoking a prior Power of Attorney, you should provide written notice of the revocation to your prior agent(s) and to any third parties who may have acted upon it, including the financial institutions where your accounts are located.

You can revoke or terminate your Power of Attorney at any time for any reason as long as you are of sound mind. If you are no longer of sound mind, a court can remove an agent for acting improperly.

Your agent cannot make health care decisions for you. You may execute a "Health Care Proxy" to do this.

The law governing Powers of Attorney is contained in the New York General Obligations Law, Article 5, Title 15. This law is available at a law library, or online through the New York State Senate or Assembly websites, www.nysenate.gov or www.nyassembly.gov.

If there is anything about this document that you do not understand, you should ask a lawyer of your own choosing to explain it to you.

I, _____ [name of principal], of
_____ [city] , _____ [county],
_____ [state], appoint _____
_____ [name of agent], of _____ [city],
_____ [county], _____ [state],
to act in my place with respect to the real property described as follows: _____
_____ .

My agent may act for me in any manner to deal with all or any part of any interest in the real property described in this document, under such terms, conditions, and covenants as my agent deems proper. My agent's powers include but are not limited to the power to:

1. Accept as a gift or as security for a loan, reject, demand, buy, lease, receive, or otherwise acquire ownership or possession of any estate or interest in real property.

2. Sell, exchange, convey with or without covenants, quitclaim, release, surrender, mortgage, encumber, partition or consent to the partitioning of, grant options concerning, lease, sublet, or otherwise dispose of any interest in the real property described in this document.

3. Maintain, repair, improve, insure, rent, lease, and pay or contest taxes or assessments on any estate or interest in the real property described in this document.
4. Prosecute, defend, intervene in, submit to arbitration, settle, and propose or accept a compromise with respect to any claim in favor of or against me based on or involving the real property described in this document.

However, my attorney-in-fact shall not have the power to: _____
_____
_____ .

I further grant to my agent full authority to act in any manner both proper and necessary to the exercise of the foregoing powers, including _____
_____ and I ratify every act that my agent may lawfully perform in exercising those powers.

This power of attorney takes effect on _____, and shall continue until terminated in writing, or until _____, whichever comes first. In the event of my incapacity or death, this power of attorney shall terminate immediately.

I agree that any third party who receives a copy of this document may act under it.

Revocation of the power of attorney is not effective as to a third party until the third party has actual knowledge of the revocation. I agree to indemnify the third party for any claims that arise against the third party because of reliance on this power of attorney.

Signed: This _____ day of _____, _____
State of: _____, County of: _____
Signature: _____, Principal

## Signature of Witnesses

By signing as a witness, I acknowledge that the principal signed the Power of Attorney in my presence and in the presence of the other witness, or that the principal acknowledged to me that the principal's signature was affixed by him or her or at his or her direction. I also acknowledge that the principal has stated that this Power of Attorney reflects his or her wishes and that he or she has signed it voluntarily. I am not named herein as an agent or as a permissible recipient of gifts.

**Witness 1**

Signature: _____
Name: _____
Address: _____

**Witness 2**

Signature: _____
Name: _____
Address: _____

STATE OF NEW YORK     )
                      ) ss:
COUNTY OF _____ )

On the _____ day of _____ , 20____ , before me, the undersigned, personally appeared _____ , personally known to me or proved to me on the basis of satisfactory evidence to be the individual whose name is subscribed to the within instrument and acknowledged to me that he/she executed the same in his/her capacity, and that by his/her signature on the instrument, the individual, or the person upon behalf of which the individual acted, executed the instrument.

Notary Public: _____

IMPORTANT INFORMATION FOR THE AGENT:

When you accept the authority granted under this Power of Attorney, a special legal relationship is created between you and the principal. This relationship imposes on you legal responsibilities that continue until you resign or the Power of Attorney is terminated or revoked. You must:

(1) act according to any instructions from the principal, or, where there are no instructions, in the principal's best interest;

(2) avoid conflicts that would impair your ability to act in the principal's best interest;

(3) keep the principal's property separate and distinct from any assets you own or control, unless otherwise permitted by law;

(4) keep a record of all transactions conducted for the principal or keep all receipts of payments, and transactions conducted for the principal; and

(5) disclose your identity as an agent whenever you act for the principal by writing or printing the principal's name and signing your own name as "agent" in either of the following manners: (Principal's Name) by (Your Signature) as Agent, or (your signature) as Agent for (Principal's Name).

You may not use the principal's assets to benefit yourself or anyone else or make gifts to yourself or anyone else unless the principal has specifically granted you that authority in this document. If you have that authority, you must act according to any instructions of the principal or, where there are no such instructions, in the principal's best interest.

You may resign by giving written notice to the principal and to any co-agent, successor agent, monitor if one has been named in this document, or the principal's guardian if one has been appointed. If there is anything about this document or your responsibilities that you do not understand, you should seek legal advice.

Liability of agent: The meaning of the authority given to you is defined in New York's General Obligations Law, Article 5, Title 15. If it is found that you have violated the law or acted outside the authority granted to you in the Power of Attorney, you may be liable under the law for your violation.

AGENT'S SIGNATURE AND ACKNOWLEDGMENT OF APPOINTMENT:

It is not required that the principal and the agent(s) sign at the same time, nor that multiple agents sign at the same time.

I, _____, have read the foregoing Power of Attorney. I am the person identified therein as agent for the principal named therein.

I acknowledge my legal responsibilities.

In Witness Whereof I have hereunto signed my name on _____ 20____.

Agent(s) sign(s) here:   ==> _____

STATE OF NEW YORK                                    )
                                                     ) ss:
COUNTY OF _____                  )

On the _____ day of _____, 20____, before me, the undersigned, personally appeared _____, personally known to me or proved to me on the basis of satisfactory evidence to be the individual whose name is subscribed to the within instrument and acknowledged to me that he/she executed the same in his/her capacity, and that by his/her signature on the instrument, the individual, or the person upon behalf of which the individual acted, executed the instrument.

Notary Public: _____

## Preparation Statement

This document was prepared by:

Print Name: _____

Signature: _____

Address: _____

# Pennsylvania Power of Attorney for Real Estate

RECORDING REQUESTED BY _____

AND WHEN RECORDED MAIL TO _____

_____

## NOTICE

THE PURPOSE OF THIS POWER OF ATTORNEY IS TO GIVE THE PERSON YOU DESIGNATE (YOUR "AGENT") BROAD POWERS TO HANDLE YOUR PROPERTY, WHICH MAY INCLUDE POWERS TO SELL OR OTHERWISE DISPOSE OF ANY REAL OR PERSONAL PROPERTY WITHOUT ADVANCE NOTICE TO YOU OR APPROVAL BY YOU.

THIS POWER OF ATTORNEY DOES NOT IMPOSE A DUTY ON YOUR AGENT TO EXERCISE GRANTED POWERS, BUT WHEN POWERS ARE EXERCISED, YOUR AGENT MUST USE DUE CARE TO ACT FOR YOUR BENEFIT AND IN ACCORDANCE WITH THIS POWER OF ATTORNEY.

YOUR AGENT MAY EXERCISE THE POWERS GIVEN HERE THROUGHOUT YOUR LIFETIME, EVEN AFTER YOU BECOME INCAPACITATED, UNLESS YOU EXPRESSLY LIMIT THE DURATION OF THESE POWERS OR YOU REVOKE THESE POWERS OR A COURT ACTING ON YOUR BEHALF TERMINATES YOUR AGENT'S AUTHORITY.

YOUR AGENT MUST ACT IN ACCORDANCE WITH YOUR REASONABLE EXPECTATIONS TO THE EXTENT ACTUALLY KNOWN BY YOUR AGENT AND, OTHERWISE, IN YOUR BEST INTEREST, ACT IN GOOD FAITH AND ACT ONLY WITHIN THE SCOPE OF AUTHORITY GRANTED BY YOU IN THE POWER OF ATTORNEY.

THE LAW PERMITS YOU, IF YOU CHOOSE, TO GRANT BROAD AUTHORITY TO AN AGENT UNDER POWER OF ATTORNEY, INCLUDING THE ABILITY TO GIVE AWAY ALL OF YOUR PROPERTY WHILE YOU ARE ALIVE OR TO SUBSTANTIALLY CHANGE HOW YOUR PROPERTY IS DISTRIBUTED AT YOUR DEATH. BEFORE SIGNING THIS DOCUMENT, YOU SHOULD SEEK THE ADVICE OF AN ATTORNEY AT LAW TO MAKE SURE YOU UNDERSTAND IT.

A COURT CAN TAKE AWAY THE POWERS OF YOUR AGENT IF IT FINDS YOUR AGENT IS NOT ACTING PROPERLY.

THE POWERS AND DUTIES OF AN AGENT UNDER A POWER OF ATTORNEY ARE EXPLAINED MORE FULLY IN 20 PA.C.S. CH. 56.

IF THERE IS ANYTHING ABOUT THIS FORM THAT YOU DO NOT UNDERSTAND, YOU SHOULD ASK A LAWYER OF YOUR OWN CHOOSING TO EXPLAIN IT TO YOU.

I have read or had explained to me this notice and I understand its contents.

Signature: _____ , Principal

Date: _____

## Power of Attorney for Real Estate

I, _____ [name of principal], of _____ [city],
_____ [county], _____ [state],
appoint _____ [name of attorney-in-fact], of _____
[city], _____ [county], _____ [state] to act in
my place with respect to the real property described as follows:

_____
_____
_____

My attorney-in-fact may act for me in any manner to deal with all or any part of any interest in the real property described in this document, under such terms, conditions, and covenants as my attorney-in-fact deems proper. My attorney-in-fact's powers include but are not limited to the power to:

1. Accept as a gift or as security for a loan, reject, demand, buy, lease, receive, or otherwise acquire ownership or possession of any estate or interest in real property.

2. Sell, exchange, convey with or without covenants, quitclaim, release, surrender, mortgage, encumber, partition or consent to the partitioning of, grant options concerning, lease, sublet, or otherwise dispose of any interest in the real property described in this document.

3. Maintain, repair, improve, insure, rent, lease, and pay or contest taxes or assessments on any estate or interest in the real property described in this document.

4. Prosecute, defend, intervene in, submit to arbitration, settle, and propose or accept a compromise with respect to any claim in favor of or against me based on or involving the real property described in this document.

However, my attorney-in-fact shall not have the power to:

_____
_____
_____

I further grant to my attorney-in-fact full authority to act in any manner both proper and necessary to the exercise of the foregoing powers, including _____
and I ratify every act that my attorney-in-fact may lawfully perform in exercising those powers.

This power of attorney takes effect on _____, and shall continue until terminated in writing, or until _____, whichever comes first. In the event of my incapacity or death, this power of attorney shall terminate immediately.

I agree that any third party who receives a copy of this document may act under it. Revocation of the power of attorney is not effective as to a third party until the third party has actual knowledge of the revocation. I agree to indemnify the third party for any claims that arise against the third party because of reliance on this power of attorney.

Signed: This _____ day of _____,
State of _____, County of _____
Signature: _____

## Witnesses

On the date written above, the principal declared to me that this instrument is his or her financial power of attorney, and that he or she willingly executed it as a free and voluntary act. The principal signed this instrument in my presence.

**Witness 1**
Signature: _____
Name: _____
Address: _____

**Witness 2**
Signature: _____
Name: _____
Address: _____

## Certificate of Acknowledgment of Notary Public

STATE OF PENNSYLVANIA        )
                             ) ss:
COUNTY OF _____    )

This record was acknowledged before me on (date) _____, by (name(s) of individual(s)), _____,
_____, and _____.

[NOTARIAL SEAL]    Signature of Notarial Officer: _____
                   Title of Office: _____
                   My commission expires: _____

## Acknowledgment of Agent

I, _____ , have read the attached power of attorney and am the person identified as the agent for the principal. I hereby acknowledge that when I act as agent I shall act in accordance with the principal's reasonable expectations to the extent actually known by me and, otherwise, in the principal's best interest, act in good faith and act only within the scope of authority granted to me by the principal in the power of attorney.

Name of Agent: _____

Signature of Agent: _____

Date: _____

## Preparation Statement

This document was prepared by:

Print Name: _____

Signature: _____

Address: _____

# Notice of Revocation of Power of Attorney

I, _____ [your name],

of _____ [your city and state],

revoke the power of attorney dated _____, empowering

_____ [name of your attorney-in-fact]

to act as my attorney-in-fact. I revoke and withdraw all power and authority granted under that power of attorney.

[*if applicable:*] That power of attorney was recorded on _____, _____.
The reference number is _____.

Signed: This _____ day of _____, _____

State of: _____ County of: _____

Signature: _____, Principal

[ATTACH NOTARY CERTIFICATE OF ACKNOWLEDGMENT]

# Request to Begin Special Education Process

Date: _____

To: _____
_____
_____
_____
[name and address of special education administrator]

Re: _____ [name of child]

Child's school: _____

Child's teacher: _____ Child's grade: _____

I am writing because my child is experiencing difficulties in school, including [describe difficulties] _____
_____
_____
_____
_____
_____
_____
_____
_____ .

I am formally requesting that the school immediately begin its special education process, including initial assessment for eligibility. I understand that you will send me an assessment plan explaining the tests that may be given to my child. Because I realize the assessment can take some time, I would appreciate receiving the assessment plan within 10 days. I would also appreciate any other information you have regarding assessments, how eligibility is determined, and the general IEP process.

I am also requesting that you make available to me a complete copy of my child's school file, including all tests, reports, assessments, grades, notes by teachers or other staff members, and any other information contained in the file. I understand that I am entitled to these records under the Family Educational Rights and Privacy Act (FERPA) (20 U.S.C. § 1232g). I would greatly appreciate having these files within the next five days. I will call you to discuss how and when I will get the copies.

Thank you very much for your assistance. I look forward to working with you and your staff.

Sincerely,

Signature of parent: _____

Printed name: _____

Address: _____
_____

Email: _____ Cell phone: _____

Home phone: _____

**Form 11: Request to Begin Special Education Process**

Form 12

# Property Worksheet

**Property**             **Name of Any Existing Beneficiary**

**Real Estate** [*list each piece of real estate by address*]

_____     _____

_____     _____

**Cash and Other Liquid Assets**

Cash

_____     _____

_____     _____

Checking accounts

_____     _____

_____     _____

Savings and money market accounts

_____     _____

_____     _____

Certificates of deposit

_____     _____

_____     _____

Alternative currencies (Bitcoin, local currencies, barter units)

_____     _____

_____     _____

Precious metals

_____     _____

_____     _____

**Securities (Not in Retirement Accounts)**

Mutual funds

_____     _____

_____     _____

Listed and unlisted stocks

_____     _____

_____     _____

Government, corporate, and municipal bonds

_____     _____

_____     _____

| Property | Name of Any Existing Beneficiary |
|---|---|

**Securities (continued)**

Annuities

**Retirement Plan Assets (IRAs, Keoghs, Roth IRAs, 401(k) and 403(b) Plans)**

**Vehicles**

Automobiles, trucks, and recreational vehicles

Planes, boats, and other vehicles

**Other Personal Property**

Household goods

Valuable clothing, jewelry, and furs

Collectibles, including artworks, and antiques

Tools and equipment

**Property**              **Name of Any Existing Beneficiary**

**Other Personal Property (continued)**

Livestock or other valuable animals

_____

_____

Money owed you (personal loans, etc.)

_____

_____

_____

Death benefits

_____

_____

_____

Life insurance (other than term insurance)

_____

_____

Miscellaneous (any personal property not listed above)

_____

_____

**Digital Assets**

[*Use this section to make notes about your digital accounts and property. If you want to provide access to your survivors, leave usernames and passwords in a separate, secured document.*]

Email accounts

_____

_____

Social media accounts (Facebook, Instagram, LinkedIn, Twitter)

_____

_____

Subscriptions (journals, Amazon Prime, Netflix)

_____

_____

Marketplace accounts (eBay, Etsy, Craigslist, Amazon)

_____

_____

Apps (for phone or tablet)

_____

_____

Photos, books, music, videos (online, on your phone, computer, or external drive)

_____

_____

File sharing and storage accounts (Dropbox, Google Docs)

_____

_____

| Property | Name of Any Existing Beneficiary |
|---|---|

### Digital Assets (continued)

Financial accounts (online banking, budget programs, trading, credit monitoring)

_____

_____

Medical accounts (HMO/doctor's portals, online pharmacies)

_____

_____

Insurance accounts (online accounts for car, home, life)

_____

_____

Blogs and websites (domain names, third-party hosts)

_____

_____

Utilities (online accounts for gas and electric, phone, internet)

_____

_____

Data stored on your computer (contact lists, tax prep or financial software)

_____

_____

_____

### Business Personal Property

Business ownerships (partnerships, sole proprietorships, limited partnerships, limited liability companies, corporations)

| _____ | _____ |
| _____ | _____ |
| _____ | _____ |
| _____ | _____ |

Intellectual property (domain names, patents, copyrights, and trademarks—including the right to receive royalties)

| _____ | _____ |
| _____ | _____ |
| _____ | _____ |
| _____ | _____ |

Miscellaneous receivables (mortgages, deeds of trust, or promissory notes held by you; any rents due from income property you own; and payments due for professional or personal services or property sold by you for which you have not been fully paid by the purchaser)

| _____ | _____ |
| _____ | _____ |
| _____ | _____ |
| _____ | _____ |

# Beneficiary Worksheet

## Beneficiaries of Specific Gifts in Your Will

Item: _____
    Beneficiary(ies): _____
    Address(es): _____
    Alternate beneficiary(ies): _____
    Address(es): _____

Item: _____
    Beneficiary(ies): _____
    Address(es): _____
    Alternate beneficiary(ies): _____
    Address(es): _____

Item: _____
    Beneficiary(ies): _____
    Address(es): _____
    Alternate beneficiary(ies): _____
    Address(es): _____

Item: _____
    Beneficiary(ies): _____
    Address(es): _____
    Alternate beneficiary(ies): _____
    Address(es): _____

Item: _____
    Beneficiary(ies): _____
    Address(es): _____
    Alternate beneficiary(ies): _____
    Address(es): _____

Item: _____
    Beneficiary(ies): _____
    Address(es): _____
    Alternate beneficiary(ies): _____
    Address(es): _____

Item: _____
    Beneficiary(ies): _____
    Address(es): _____
    Alternate beneficiary(ies): _____
    Address(es): _____

**Item:** _____

    Beneficiary(ies): _____

    Address(es): _____

    Alternate beneficiary(ies): _____

    Address(es): _____

**Item:** _____

    Beneficiary(ies): _____

    Address(es): _____

    Alternate beneficiary(ies): _____

    Address(es): _____

## Debts Forgiven

Amount forgiven: _____ Date of loan: _____

Debtor: _____

Amount forgiven: _____ Date of loan: _____

Debtor: _____

Amount forgiven: _____ Date of loan: _____

Debtor: _____

Amount forgiven: _____ Date of loan: _____

Debtor: _____

## Residuary Beneficiary or Beneficiaries

Residuary beneficiary(ies) and percentage each one receives:

_____ _____%
_____ _____%
_____ _____%
_____ _____%
_____ _____%
_____ _____%
_____ _____%

## Alternate Residuary Beneficiary or Beneficiaries

Alternate residuary beneficiary(ies) and percentage each one receives:

_____ _____%
_____ _____%
_____ _____%
_____ _____%
_____ _____%
_____ _____%
_____ _____%

# Form 14

> **!** ***Do not just fill in and sign this form.*** To be legally valid, your will must be printed out (using the e-form that you can access with this book) or typed, eliminating all items that don't apply to you. You cannot just fill in the blanks of this form and try to use the completed form as your will.

## Will for Adult With No Children

Will of _____

I, _____,
a resident of _____ [county], State of _____,
declare that this is my will.

1. **Revocation.** I revoke all wills that I have previously made.

2. **Marital Status.** I am ☐ married ☐ single ☐ in a registered domestic partnership or civil union.

3. **Specific Gifts.** I make the following specific gifts:

    I leave _____

    to _____

    or, if that/those beneficiary/beneficiaries does/do not survive me, to _____
    _____.

    I leave _____

    to _____

    or, if that/those beneficiary/beneficiaries does/do not survive me, to _____
    _____.

    I leave _____

    to _____

    or, if that/those beneficiary/beneficiaries does/do not survive me, to _____
    _____.

    I leave _____

    to _____

    or, if that/those beneficiary/beneficiaries does/do not survive me, to _____
    _____.

    I leave _____

    to _____

    or, if that/those beneficiary/beneficiaries does/do not survive me, to _____
    _____.

    [repeat as needed]

4. **Residuary Estate.** I leave my residuary estate, that is, the rest of my property not otherwise specifically and validly disposed of by this will, including lapsed or failed gifts, to _____

    or, if that/those beneficiary/beneficiaries does/do not survive me, to _____
    _____.

5. **Beneficiary Provisions.** The following terms and conditions apply to the beneficiary clauses of this will.

    A. **45-Day Survivorship Period.** As used in this will, the phrase "survive me" means to be alive or in existence as an organization on the 45th day after my death. Any beneficiary, except any alternate residuary beneficiary, must survive me to take property under this will.

    B. **Shared Gifts.** If I leave property to be shared by two or more beneficiaries, it shall be shared equally by them unless this will provides otherwise.

    If any beneficiary of a shared specific gift left in a single paragraph of the Specific Gifts clause, above, does not survive me, the gift shall be given to the surviving beneficiaries in equal shares.

    If any beneficiary of a shared residuary gift does not survive me, the residue shall be given to the surviving residuary beneficiaries in equal shares.

    C. **Encumbrances.** All property that I leave by this will shall pass subject to any encumbrances or liens on the property.

6. **Executor.** I name _____ as executor, to serve without bond. If that person does not qualify, or ceases to serve, I name _____ _____ as executor, also to serve without bond.

    I direct that my executor take all actions legally permissible to probate this will, including filing a petition in the appropriate court for the independent administration of my estate.

    I grant to my executor the following powers, to be exercised as the executor deems to be in the best interests of my estate:

    A. To retain property, without liability for loss or depreciation resulting from such retention.

    B. To sell, lease, or exchange property and to receive or administer the proceeds as a part of my estate.

    C. To vote stock; convert bonds, notes, stocks, or other securities belonging to my estate into other securities; and to exercise all other rights and privileges of a person owning similar property.

    D. To deal with and settle claims in favor of or against my estate.

    E. To continue, maintain, operate, or participate in any business that is a part of my estate, and to incorporate, dissolve, or otherwise change the form of organization of the business.

    F. To pay all debts and taxes that may be assessed against my estate, as provided under state law.

    G. To do all other acts, which in the executor's judgment may be necessary or appropriate for the proper and advantageous management, investment, and distribution of my estate.

    These powers, authority, and discretion are in addition to the powers, authority, and discretion vested in an executor by operation of law, and may be exercised as often as deemed necessary, without approval by any court in any jurisdiction.

**Form 14**

## Signature

I subscribe my name to this will this _____ day of _____, _____, at _____ [county], State of _____.

I declare that it is my will, that I sign it willingly, that I execute it as my free and voluntary act for the purposes expressed, and that I am of the age of majority or otherwise legally empowered to make a will and under no constraint or undue influence.

Signature: _____

## Witnesses

On this _____ day of _____, _____, the testator, _____ declared to us, the undersigned, that this instrument was the testator's will and requested us to act as witnesses to it. The testator signed this will in our presence, all of us being present at the same time. We now, at the testator's request, in the testator's presence, and in the presence of each other, subscribe our names as witnesses and each declare that we are of sound mind and of proper age to witness a will. We further declare that we understand this to be the testator's will, and that to the best of our knowledge the testator is of the age of majority, or is otherwise legally empowered to make a will, and appears to be of sound mind and under no constraint or undue influence.

We declare under penalty of perjury that the foregoing is true and correct, this _____ day of _____, _____, at _____ [county], State of _____.

**Witness 1**

Signature: _____

Typed or printed name: _____

Residing at: _____

City, state, zip: _____

**Witness 2**

Signature: _____

Typed or printed name: _____

Residing at: _____

City, state, zip: _____

**Form 15**

> ⚠ ***Do not just fill in and sign this form.*** To be legally valid, your will must be printed out (using the e-form that you can access with this book) or typed, eliminating all items that don't apply to you. You cannot just fill in the blanks of this form and try to use the completed form as your will.

## Will for Adult With Child(ren)

Will of _____

I, _____ ,
a resident of _____ [county], State of _____ ,
declare that this is my will.

1. **Revocation.** I revoke all wills that I have previously made.

2. **Marital Status.** I am ☐ married ☐ single ☐ in a registered domestic partnership or civil union.

3. **Children.** I have the following natural and legally adopted children:

   | Name | Date of Birth |
   |---|---|
   | _____ | _____ |
   | _____ | _____ |
   | _____ | _____ |
   | _____ | _____ |
   | _____ | _____ |
   | _____ | _____ |
   | _____ | _____ |
   | _____ | _____ |

   [repeat as needed]

4. **Specific Gifts.** I make the following specific gifts:

   I leave _____
   _____
   to _____
   or, if that/those beneficiary/beneficiaries does/do not survive me, to _____
   _____ .

   I leave _____
   _____
   to _____
   or, if that/those beneficiary/beneficiaries does/do not survive me, to _____
   _____ .

   I leave _____
   _____
   to _____
   or, if that/those beneficiary/beneficiaries does/do not survive me, to _____
   _____ .

I leave _____

to _____

or, if that/those beneficiary/beneficiaries does/do not survive me, to _____ .

I leave _____

to _____

or, if that/those beneficiary/beneficiaries does/do not survive me, to _____ .

[repeat as needed]

5. **Residuary Estate.** I leave my residuary estate, that is, the rest of my property not otherwise specifically and validly disposed of by this will, including lapsed or failed gifts, to _____

or, if that/those beneficiary/beneficiaries does/do not survive me, to _____ .

6. **Beneficiary Provisions.** The following terms and conditions apply to the beneficiary clauses of this will.

   A. **45-Day Survivorship Period.** As used in this will, the phrase "survive me" means to be alive or in existence as an organization on the 45th day after my death. Any beneficiary, except any alternate residuary beneficiary, must survive me to take property under this will.

   B. **Shared Gifts.** If I leave property to be shared by two or more beneficiaries, it shall be shared equally by them unless this will provides otherwise.
   
   If any beneficiary of a shared specific gift left in a single paragraph of the Specific Gifts clause, above, does not survive me, the gift shall be given to the surviving beneficiaries in equal shares.
   
   If any beneficiary of a shared residuary gift does not survive me, the residue shall be given to the surviving residuary beneficiaries in equal shares.

   C. **Encumbrances.** All property that I leave by this will shall pass subject to any encumbrances or liens on the property.

7. **Executor.** I name _____
   as executor, to serve without bond. If that person does not qualify, or ceases to serve, I name
   _____ as executor, also to serve without bond.
   
   I direct that my executor take all actions legally permissible to probate this will, including filing a petition in the appropriate court for the independent administration of my estate.
   
   I grant to my executor the following powers, to be exercised as the executor deems to be in the best interests of my estate:
   
   A. To retain property, without liability for loss or depreciation resulting from such retention.
   
   B. To sell, lease, or exchange property and to receive or administer the proceeds as a part of my estate.
   
   C. To vote stock; convert bonds, notes, stocks, or other securities belonging to my estate into other securities; and to exercise all other rights and privileges of a person owning similar property.
   
   D. To deal with and settle claims in favor of or against my estate.

- E. To continue, maintain, operate, or participate in any business that is a part of my estate, and to incorporate, dissolve, or otherwise change the form of organization of the business.
- F. To pay all debts and taxes that may be assessed against my estate, as provided under state law.
- G. To do all other acts, which in the executor's judgment may be necessary or appropriate for the proper and advantageous management, investment, and distribution of my estate.

These powers, authority, and discretion are in addition to the powers, authority, and discretion vested in an executor by operation of law, and may be exercised as often as deemed necessary, without approval by any court in any jurisdiction.

8. **Personal Guardian.** If at my death any of my children are minors, and a personal guardian is needed, I nominate _____ to be appointed personal guardian of my minor children. If that person cannot serve as personal guardian, I nominate _____ to be appointed personal guardian.

    I direct that no bond be required of any personal guardian.

9. **Property Guardian.** If at my death any of my children are minors, and a property guardian is needed, I appoint _____ as the property guardian of my minor children. If that person cannot serve as property guardian, I appoint _____ as property guardian.

    I direct that no bond be required of any property guardian.

10. **Gifts Under the Uniform Transfers to Minors Act.** All property left by this will to _____ [name of minor] shall be given to _____ [name of custodian] as custodian for _____ [name of minor] under the Uniform Transfers to Minors Act of _____ [your state].

    If _____ [name of custodian] cannot serve as custodian, _____ [name of successor custodian] shall serve as custodian. If _____ [your state] allows testators to choose the age at which the custodianship ends, I choose the oldest age allowed by my state's Uniform Transfers to Minors Act.

    [repeat as needed for each young person]

## Signature

I subscribe my name to this will this _____ day of _____, _____, at _____ [county], State of _____.

I declare that it is my will, that I sign it willingly, that I execute it as my free and voluntary act for the purposes expressed, and that I am of the age of majority or otherwise legally empowered to make a will and under no constraint or undue influence.

Signature: _____

**Form 15**

## Witnesses

On this _____ day of _____ , _____ , the testator, _____

declared to us, the undersigned, that this instrument was the testator's will and requested us to act as witnesses to it. The testator signed this will in our presence, all of us being present at the same time. We now, at the testator's request, in the testator's presence, and in the presence of each other, subscribe our names as witnesses and each declare that we are of sound mind and of proper age to witness a will. We further declare that we understand this to be the testator's will, and that to the best of our knowledge the testator is of the age of majority, or is otherwise legally empowered to make a will, and appears to be of sound mind and under no constraint or undue influence.

We declare under penalty of perjury that the foregoing is true and correct, this _____ day of _____ , _____ , at _____ [county], State of _____ .

**Witness 1**

Signature: _____

Typed or printed name: _____

Residing at: _____

City, state, zip: _____

**Witness 2**

Signature: _____

Typed or printed name: _____

Residing at: _____

City, state, zip: _____

**Do not just fill in and sign this form.** To be legally valid, your will must be printed out (using the e-form that you can access with this book) or typed, eliminating all items that don't apply to you. You cannot just fill in the blanks of this form and try to use the completed form as your will.

# Will Codicil

**First Codicil to the Will of** _____

I, _____,
a resident of _____ [county], State of _____,
declare this to be the first codicil to my will dated _____, _____.

FIRST: I revoke the provision of Clause _____ of my will that provided:
[include the exact will language you wish to revoke]

_____
_____
_____
_____
_____
_____
_____

SECOND: I add the following provision to Clause _____ of my will:
[add whatever is desired]

_____
_____
_____
_____
_____
_____
_____

THIRD: In all other respects I confirm and republish my will dated _____, _____.

Dated: _____, _____.

## Signature

I subscribe my name to this codicil this _____ day of _____, _____, at
_____ [county], State of _____.
I declare that it is my will, that I sign it willingly, that I execute it as my free and voluntary act for the purposes expressed, and that I am of the age of majority or otherwise legally empowered to make a codicil and under no constraint or undue influence.

Signature: _____

## Witnesses

On this _____ day of _____, _____, _____ [codicil maker's name] declared to us, the undersigned, that this instrument was a codicil to _____ _____ s' [codicil maker's name] will and requested us to act as witnesses to it. The testator signed this codicil in our presence, all of us being present at the same time. We now, at the testator's request, in the testator's presence, and in the presence of each other, subscribe our names as witnesses and declare we understand this to be the testator's codicil and that to the best of our knowledge the testator is of the age of majority, or is otherwise legally empowered to make a codicil, and appears to be of sound mind and is under no constraint or undue influence.

We declare under penalty of perjury that the foregoing is true and correct, this _____ day of _____, _____, at _____ [county], State of _____.

**Witness 1**

Signature: _____

Typed or printed name: _____

Residing at: _____

City, state, zip: _____

**Witness 2**

Signature: _____

Typed or printed name: _____

Residing at: _____

City, state, zip: _____

# Notice to Creditor of Death

Date: _____

_____
_____
_____
_____

[*insert name and address of creditor*]

Name of deceased: _____
Deceased's address: _____
Account number: _____ Date of death: _____

To whom it may concern:

I am the representative of the decedent. Please cancel this account at once.

Please also acknowledge that you received this notice by signing a copy of this letter and returning it to me in the enclosed stamped, self-addressed envelope.

If there is any outstanding balance on this account, please notify me promptly at the address below.

Thank you for your assistance.

Signature: _____
Printed or typed name: _____
Address: _____
_____

Home phone: _____ Work phone: _____

**Receipt acknowledged by:**

Signature: _____
Printed or typed name: _____
Title: _____
Date: _____

# Executor's Checklist

☐ **1. Inventory and Safeguard Property**

☐ Find the deceased person's assets and keep them safe until you distribute them.

☐ Using money left by the deceased person, pay necessary continuing expenses—for example, mortgage payments, utility bills, and homeowners' insurance premiums.

☐ If the deceased person left enough money, pay debts. If there isn't enough money to pay them all, consult a lawyer before you pay anything. State law gives certain creditors priority.

☐ File the will in the local probate court. You should do this whether or not you think probate court proceedings will be required.

☐ **2. Handle Day-to-Day Details**

☐ Terminate leases (if the deceased person was a renter), credit cards, utilities that are no longer needed, and other services (like cell phone, television subscriptions, and internet).

☐ Head off fraud by reporting the death to the major credit reporting agencies and canceling the deceased person's passport and driver's license.

☐ Notify the Social Security Administration of the death if the funeral director hasn't done so. You might also need to notify other agencies, such as the Department of Veterans Affairs or the state Medicaid agency.

☐ Get mail forwarded to you, if necessary.

☐ **3. Decide Whether or Not Probate Is Necessary**

☐ Probate isn't necessary for many common assets. No probate is necessary to:
- pass real estate and other assets owned in joint tenancy to the surviving joint tenant
- transfer real estate left by a transfer-on-death deed
- transfer property (bank accounts, securities, or vehicles) registered in "payable-on-death" or "transfer-on-death" form to beneficiaries
- transfer funds in IRAs and other retirement plans to named beneficiaries
- transfer property left to the surviving spouse (in some states)
- claim life insurance proceeds with named beneficiaries, or
- transfer assets held in trust (such as revocable living trusts or bypass trusts) to named beneficiaries.

Most states also offer streamlined probate procedures for small estates. Whether probate is necessary commonly depends upon the value of everything in the estate, minus all the assets that can be transferred outside of probate.

☐ **4. Pay Taxes**

☐ You must file an income tax return for the year in which the person died. If the estate goes through probate and has a certain amount of income, you'll have to file an income tax return for it, too.

☐ Pay estate taxes if necessary. It's unlikely, but state and federal estate tax returns may be required. For deaths in 2022, estates worth less than $12.06 million do not owe federal estate tax. (This amount increases each year with inflation.) However, some states collect their own estate tax on smaller estates. And a few states also impose inheritance tax, which is paid by the people who inherit—though close family members are often exempt or pay low rates. Check with your state's taxing authority for details about your state's tax laws. And learn more about estate and inheritance taxes in the Legal Articles section of Nolo.com.

## ☐ 5. Handle Probate Proceedings, If Necessary

If probate is necessary, you'll need to:

- ☐ Ask the probate court to confirm you as executor (personal representative). You might want to hire a lawyer to prepare the paperwork or to help you with the process. (See below.)

- ☐ Send notice of the probate proceeding to the beneficiaries named in the will and, if necessary, to certain close relatives—in most cases, a surviving spouse and children—who would have been entitled to property had there been no valid will.

- ☐ During the probate process, which in many places takes about nine months to a year, you must manage the deceased person's property. Depending on the contents of the will and the financial condition of the estate, you might need to sell real estate or securities owned by the deceased person.

- ☐ Set up an estate bank account to hold money that belonged to or is owed to the deceased person—for example, paychecks or stock dividends.

- ☐ Notify creditors of the probate proceeding in the manner required by state law. They then have a certain amount of time—about six months, in most states—to file a claim for payment of any bills or other obligations you haven't voluntarily paid. As executor, you decide whether or not a claim is valid.

- ☐ Supervise the distribution of property, such as cash, personal belongings, and real estate, to the people or organizations entitled to inherit.

- ☐ When debts and taxes have been paid and all the property distributed to the beneficiaries, ask the probate court to formally close the estate.

## ☐ 6. Decide Whether to Hire a Lawyer

Many people think that probate requires hiring a lawyer. Although this is often a sensible choice, especially for estates with lots of different types of property, significant tax liabilities, or the potential for disputes among inheritors, it is not mandatory. Many courts now provide lots of useful information and instructions online. You might decide that you can handle the paperwork yourself, particularly if you are a main (or sole) beneficiary and you don't expect any complications collecting and transferring the assets.

Handling a probate court proceeding requires shuffling a lot of papers through the court clerk's office; in the vast majority of cases, there are no disputes that require a decision by a judge. You might even be able to do everything by mail. Doing a good job requires persistence and attention to tedious detail—not necessarily a law degree.

Here are some ways to get help if you decide to handle the probate yourself:

- Find out what your probate court offers. Many give out packets of forms or publish good information and forms on their websites. Court clerks commonly answer basic questions about court procedure, but they staunchly avoid saying anything that could be construed as legal advice. Some courts, however, have lawyers on staff who look over probate documents; they may point out errors in your papers and tell you how to fix them.

- In some areas of the country, experienced legal document preparers (paralegals) have set up shop to help people deal with probate paperwork. These document preparers do not offer legal advice; they just prepare documents as you instruct them. They can also file papers with the court for you.
- To find one, search online for "legal document preparation" or similar terms. Make sure that the person you hire has lots of probate experience and can provide you with references to check out.
- Consult books written for nonlawyers. *The Executor's Guide: Settling a Loved One's Estate or Trust*, by Mary Randolph (Nolo), provides a guide to executors' duties. For Californian estates, *How to Probate an Estate in California*, by Lisa Fialco (Nolo), leads you through the process step by step. And for estates that also involve a living trust, *The Trustee's Legal Companion*, by Liza Hanks and Carol Elias Zolla (Nolo), explains how to be a successor trustee.
- Get free legal information from Nolo.com. Its Wills, Trusts & Probate section offers straightforward and easy-to-understand information about the job of an executor, small estate procedures, transferring property without probate, state and federal estate taxes, how to work with a lawyer and much more.

☐ **7. Working With a Lawyer**

You might want some expert help, at least once in a while. There are two basic ways to work with a lawyer:

- Hire a lawyer to act as a coach, answering your legal questions as they come up. You might also want the lawyer to do some research for you or look over documents before you file them.
- Hire a lawyer to do everything. The lawyer will be paid out of the estate. In most states, lawyers charge either a lump sum or an hourly rate—$200 to $400 per hour is common, but be sure you negotiate this in advance. In a few states (California, for example), a lawyer may take a certain percentage of the gross value of the deceased person's estate unless you agree, in writing, to a different fee arrangement. You should be able to find a competent lawyer who will agree to a lower fee.

Some ways to find a good lawyer:

- Talk to friends who have small businesses to see if they have a good relationship with a lawyer. That lawyer can probably recommend someone with estate planning and probate experience.
- Ask whether a local senior center has a list of recommended probate lawyers.
- Use an online lawyer directory to search for lawyers in your area.

# General Notice of Death

Date: _____

_____
_____
_____
_____
[insert name and address of organization]

This is to notify you that _____ [name]
of _____
_____ [address]
died on _____ [date]. Please let me know if you would like further information.

Signature: _____
Printed or typed name: _____
Relationship to deceased: _____
Address: _____
_____

# Obituary Information Fact Sheet

Name of deceased: _____

Date of death: _____ Age at death: _____

Location of death: _____

Cause of death: _____

Birthplace: _____

Address: _____

_____ Length of time in community: _____

Religious affiliation or membership: _____

High school, college, or graduate degrees: _____

_____

Professional degrees or affiliations: _____

_____

Military service: _____

Profession: _____

Interesting personal facts: _____

_____

_____

_____

_____

Survived by: [*Names of survivors—spouses, siblings, in-laws, children, grandchildren, etc.—and their relationship to deceased*] _____

_____

Predeceased by: [*Names of spouses, siblings, and children who predeceased and when deaths occurred*]

_____

_____

_____

Time and location of funeral arrangements and services: _____

_____

_____

_____

For further information, contact: _____

_____

_____

# Notice to Deceased's Homeowners' Insurance Company

Date: _____

_____

_____

_____

_____

[*insert insurance company name and address*]

Name of deceased: _____

Address: _____

_____ Date of death: _____

Homeowners' insurance policy number: _____

This letter is to notify you that your insured, _____

_____ [*deceased's name*], has died. I am the executor of the estate and would like to be added as a named insured to this homeowners' insurance policy. Enclosed with this letter you will find a certified death certificate, along with documentation that I am the executor.

Please contact me so that we may discuss this matter. I can be reached using the information below. Please sign and return the copy of this letter in the enclosed stamped and self-addressed envelope.

Thank you for your assistance.

Signature: _____

Printed or typed name: _____

Relationship to deceased: _____

Address: _____

_____ Home phone: _____

Work phone: _____ Email: _____

**Receipt acknowledged by:**

Signature: _____

Printed or typed name: _____

Title: _____

Date of receipt of notice: _____

# Notice to Deceased's Vehicle Insurance Company

Date: _____

_____

_____

_____

[*insert insurance company name and address*]

Name of deceased: _____

Address: _____

Date of death: _____

Vehicle insurance policy number: _____

Make, model, and year of vehicle: _____

This letter is to notify you that your insured, _____
_____ [*deceased's name*], has died.
I am the executor of the estate and would like to be added as a named insured to this insurance policy. Enclosed with this letter you will find a certified death certificate for _____
_____ [*deceased's name*], documentation of my status as executor, and a state-certified copy of my driving record.

Please contact me so that we may discuss this matter. I can be reached using the information below. Please sign and return the second copy of this letter in the enclosed stamped and self-addressed envelope.

Thank you for your assistance.

Signature: _____

Printed or typed name: _____

Relationship to deceased: _____

Address: _____

_____ Home phone: _____

Work phone: _____ Email: _____

**Receipt acknowledged by:**

Signature: _____

Printed or typed name: _____

Title: _____

Date of receipt of notice: _____

# Rental Application

*A separate application is required from each applicant aged 18 or older.*

Date and time received by Landlord _____

---

**THIS SECTION TO BE COMPLETED BY LANDLORD**

Address of property to be rented: _____

Rental term: ☐ month-to-month  ☐ lease from _____ to _____

**Amounts Due Prior to Occupancy**

First month's rent: ............................................................................... $ _____

Security deposit: ................................................................................ $ _____

Credit check fee: ................................................................................ $ _____

Other (specify): _____ $ _____

TOTAL  $ _____

---

## Applicant

Full Name—include all names you use or have used in the past: _____

Home Phone: _____ Work Phone: _____

Cell Phone: _____ Email: _____

Social Security number: _____ Driver's License Number/State: _____

Other Identifying Information: _____

Vehicle Make: _____ Model: _____ Color: _____ Year: _____

License Plate Number/State: _____

## Additional Occupants

List everyone, including minor children, who will live with you:

| **Full Name** | **Relationship to Applicant** |
|---|---|
| _____ | _____ |
| _____ | _____ |
| _____ | _____ |
| _____ | _____ |
| _____ | _____ |

## Rental History

FIRST-TIME RENTERS: INSTEAD ATTACH A DESCRIPTION OF YOUR HOUSING FOR THE PAST FIVE YEARS.

Current Address: _____

Dates Lived at Address: _____ Rent $ _____ Security Deposit $ _____

Landlord/Manager: _____ Landlord/Manager's Phone: _____

Reason for Leaving: _____

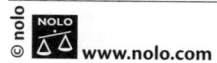

Form 23: Rental Application

Previous Address: _____
Dates Lived at Address: _____ Rent $ _____ Security Deposit $ _____
Landlord/Manager: _____ Landlord/Manager's Phone: _____
Reason for Leaving: _____

Previous Address: _____
Dates Lived at Address: _____ Rent $ _____ Security Deposit $ _____
Landlord/Manager: _____ Landlord/Manager's Phone: _____
Reason for Leaving: _____

### Employment History

EMPLOYEES: ATTACH TAX RETURNS FROM THE MOST RECENT TWO YEARS, PLUS PAY STUBS FROM THE PAST SIX MONTHS.
SELF-EMPLOYED APPLICANTS: INSTEAD ATTACH TAX RETURNS FOR THE PAST TWO YEARS.

Name and Address of Current Employer: _____
_____ Phone: ( ) _____
Name of Supervisor: _____ Supervisor's Phone: ( ) _____
Dates Employed at This Job: _____ Position or Title: _____

Name and Address of Previous Employer: _____
_____ Phone: ( ) _____
Name of Supervisor: _____ Supervisor's Phone: ( ) _____
Dates Employed at This Job: _____ Position or Title: _____

### Income

1. Your gross monthly employment income (before deductions):     $ _____
2. Average monthly amounts of other income (specify sources):     $ _____
   _____ $ _____
   _____ $ _____

                                          TOTAL:   $ _____

### Bank/Financial Accounts

|  | Account Number | Bank/Institution | Branch |
|---|---|---|---|
| Savings Account: | | | |
| Checking Account: | | | |
| Money Market or Similar Account: | | | |

## Credit Card Accounts

Major Credit Card: ☐ VISA ☐ MC ☐ Discover Card ☐ Am Ex ☐ Other: _____

Issuer: _____ Account No. _____

Balance $ _____ Average Monthly Payment $ _____

Major Credit Card: ☐ VISA ☐ MC ☐ Discover Card ☐ Am Ex ☐ Other: _____

Issuer: _____ Account No. _____

Balance $ _____ Average Monthly Payment $ _____

## Loans

| Type of Loan (mortgage, car, student loan, etc.) | Name of Creditor | Account Number | Amount Owed | Monthly Payment |
|---|---|---|---|---|
| | | | | |
| | | | | |
| | | | | |

## Other Major Obligations (such as child support, alimony, tax liens, etc.)

| Type | Payee | Amount Owed | Monthly Payment |
|---|---|---|---|
| | | | |
| | | | |
| | | | |

## Pets

| Type | Breed | Sex | Age | Neutered/spayed? | Weight | Years owned |
|---|---|---|---|---|---|---|
| | | | | | | |
| | | | | | | |
| | | | | | | |

## Miscellaneous

Describe water-filled furniture you want to have in the rental property: _____.

Do you smoke? ☐ yes ☐ no

Have you ever: Filed for bankruptcy? ☐ yes ☐ no How many times _____

Been sued? ☐ yes ☐ no How many times _____

Sued someone else? ☐ yes ☐ no How many times _____

Been evicted? ☐ yes ☐ no How many times _____

Explain (include dates) any "yes" listed above: _____

_____

_____

## References and Emergency Contact

Personal Reference: _____ Relationship: _____

Address: _____

Email: _____ Phone: ( ) _____

Personal Reference: _____ Relationship: _____

Address: _____

Email: _____ Phone: ( ) _____

Contact in Emergency: _____ Relationship: _____

Address: _____

Email: _____ Phone: ( ) _____

## Source

Where did you learn of this vacancy? _____

_____

I certify that all the information given above is true and correct and understand that my lease or rental agreement may be terminated if I have made any material false or incomplete statements in this application. I authorize verification of the information provided in this application from my credit sources, credit bureaus, current and previous landlords and employers, and personal references. This permission will survive the expiration of my tenancy.

_____     _____

Applicant                                                                       Date

Notes (Landlord/Manager): _____

_____

_____

_____

_____

_____

_____

_____

_____

# Tenant References

Name of Applicant: _____

Address of Rental Unit: _____

## Previous Landlord or Manager

Contact (name, property owner or manager, address of rental unit): _____

_____

_____

Date: _____

## Questions

When did tenant rent from you (move-in and move-out dates)? _____

What was the monthly rent? _____ Did tenant pay rent on time? ☐ yes ☐ no

If rent was not paid on time, did you have to give tenant a legal notice demanding the rent? ☐ yes ☐ no

If rent was not paid on time, provide details: _____

_____

Did you give tenant notice of any lease violation for other than nonpayment of rent? ☐ yes ☐ no

If you gave a lease violation notice, what was the outcome? _____

Was tenant considerate of neighbors—that is, no loud parties and fair, careful use of common areas?

_____

Did tenant have any pets? ☐ yes ☐ no

If so, were there any problems? _____

Did tenant make any unreasonable demands or complaints? ☐ yes ☐ no

If so, explain: _____

_____

Why did tenant leave? _____

Did tenant give the proper amount of notice before leaving? ☐ yes ☐ no

Did tenant leave the place in good condition? ☐ yes ☐ no

Did you need to use the security deposit to cover damage? ☐ yes ☐ no

Any particular problems you'd like to mention? _____

Would you rent to this person again? ☐ yes ☐ no

Other comments: _____

_____

## Previous Landlord or Manager

When did tenant rent from you (move-in and move-out dates)? _____

What was the monthly rent? _____ Did tenant pay rent on time? ☐ yes ☐ no

If rent was not paid on time, did you have to give tenant a legal notice demanding the rent? ☐ yes ☐ no

If rent was not paid on time, provide details: _____

_____

Did you give tenant notice of any lease violation for other than nonpayment of rent? ☐ yes ☐ no

If you gave a lease violation notice, what was the outcome? _____

Was tenant considerate of neighbors—that is, no loud parties and fair, careful use of common areas?

_____

Did tenant have any pets? ☐ yes ☐ no

If so, were there any problems? _____

Did tenant make any unreasonable demands or complaints? ☐ yes ☐ no

If so, explain: _____

_____

Why did tenant leave? _____

Did tenant give the proper amount of notice before leaving? ☐ yes ☐ no

Did tenant leave the place in good condition? ☐ yes ☐ no

Did you need to use the security deposit to cover damage? ☐ yes ☐ no

Any particular problems you'd like to mention? _____

Would you rent to this person again? ☐ yes ☐ no

Other comments: _____

## Employment Verification

Contact (name, company, position): _____

Date: _____

Salary: _____

Dates of Employment: _____

Comments: _____

_____

## Personal Reference

Contact (name and relationship to applicant): _____

Date: _____

How long have you known the applicant? _____

Would you recommend this person as a prospective tenant? ☐ yes ☐ no

Comments: _____

_____

**Credit and Financial Information**

**Notes, Including Reasons for Rejecting Applicant**

Form 25

# Landlord-Tenant Checklist

Property Address: _____

## General Condition of Rental Unit and Premises

|  | Move-In Condition<br>Date of Walk-Through: | Move-Out Condition<br>Date of Walk-Through: |
|---|---|---|
| **Living Room** | | |
| Flooring | | |
| Walls & ceiling | | |
| Light fixtures | | |
| Window treatments | | |
| Windows & screens | | |
| Doors & handles/locks | | |
| Fireplace | | |
| Smoke detector & CO detector | | |
| Other | | |
| **Kitchen** | | |
| Flooring | | |
| Walls & ceiling | | |
| Light fixtures | | |
| Window treatments | | |
| Windows & screens | | |
| Doors & handles/locks | | |
| Cabinets | | |
| Counters | | |
| Stove/oven/range | | |
| Refrigerator | | |
| Dishwasher | | |
| Garbage disposal | | |
| Microwave | | |
| Stove hood | | |
| Sink & plumbing | | |
| Other appliances | | |
| Smoke detector & CO detector | | |
| Other | | |

|  | Move-In Condition<br>Date of Walk-Through: | Move-Out Condition<br>Date of Walk-Through: |
|---|---|---|
| **Dining Room** | | |
| Flooring | | |
| Walls & ceiling | | |
| Light fixtures | | |
| Window treatments | | |
| Windows & screens | | |
| Doors & handles/locks | | |
| Smoke detector & CO detector | | |
| Other | | |
| **Bathroom** | | |
| Flooring | | |
| Walls & ceiling | | |
| Light fixtures | | |
| Window treatments | | |
| Windows & screens | | |
| Doors & handles/locks | | |
| Bathtub/shower (incl. attached door) | | |
| Sink, counters & plumbing | | |
| Cabinets & storage | | |
| Mirror(s) | | |
| Toilet | | |
| Ceiling fan/ventilation | | |
| Other | | |
| **Bedroom #1** | | |
| Flooring | | |
| Walls & ceiling | | |
| Lighting fixtures | | |
| Window treatments | | |
| Windows & screens | | |
| Doors & handles/locks | | |
| Closet | | |
| Smoke detector & CO detector | | |
| Other | | |

|  | Move-In Condition<br>Date of Walk-Through: | Move-Out Condition<br>Date of Walk-Through: |
|---|---|---|
| **Bedroom #2** | | |
| Flooring | | |
| Walls & ceiling | | |
| Lighting fixtures | | |
| Window treatments | | |
| Windows & screens | | |
| Doors & handles/locks | | |
| Closet | | |
| Smoke detector & CO detector | | |
| Other | | |
| **Other Areas** | | |
| Heating & A/C (mechanical room) | | |
| Lawn/garden | | |
| Stairs and landings | | |
| Patio, terrace, deck, etc. | | |
| Basement | | |
| Garage | | |
| Attic | | |
| Entryway | | |
| Laundry room | | |
| Other | | |

☐ Tenants acknowledge that all smoke detectors were tested in their presence and found to be in working order, and that the testing procedure was explained to them. Tenants agree to promptly notify Landlord in writing should any smoke detector appear to be malfunctioning or inoperable. Tenants will not refuse Landlord access for the purpose of inspecting, maintaining, repairing, or installing legally required smoke detectors.

☐ Tenants acknowledge that all carbon monoxide detectors were tested in their presence and found to be in working order, and that the testing procedure was explained to them. Tenants agree to promptly notify Landlord in writing should any carbon monoxide detector appear to be malfunctioning or inoperable. Tenants will not refuse Landlord access for the purpose of inspecting, maintaining, repairing, or installing legally required carbon monoxide detectors.

## Checklist for Furnished Property

| | Move-In Condition<br>Date of Walk-Through: | Move-Out Condition<br>Date of Walk-Through: |
|---|---|---|
| **Living Room** | | |
| Coffee table | | |
| End tables | | |
| Lamps | | |
| Chairs | | |
| Sofa | | |
| Decorative items (unattached mirrors, rugs, pictures, vases, etc.) | | |
| Electronics | | |
| Other | | |
| **Kitchen** | | |
| Countertop appliances | | |
| Dishes, silverware & cookware | | |
| Linens | | |
| Chairs & stools | | |
| Table | | |
| Decorative items (unattached mirrors, rugs, pictures, vases, etc.) | | |
| Other | | |
| **Dining Room** | | |
| Chairs | | |
| Stools | | |
| Table | | |
| Lamps | | |
| Decorative items (unattached mirrors, rugs, pictures, vases, etc.) | | |
| Electronics | | |
| Other | | |
| **Bathroom** | | |
| Shelves & storage (unattached) | | |
| Shower curtain & rod | | |
| Hamper | | |
| Linens | | |
| Decorative items (unattached mirrors, rugs, pictures, vases, etc.) | | |
| Other | | |

|  | Move-In Condition<br>Date of Walk-Through: | Move-Out Condition<br>Date of Walk-Through: |
|---|---|---|
| **Bedroom #1** | | |
| Bed(s) | | |
| Chairs | | |
| Bureau | | |
| Chests | | |
| Dressing table | | |
| Bedside tables | | |
| Lamps | | |
| Linens | | |
| Decorative items (unattached mirrors, rugs, pictures, vases, etc.) | | |
| Electronics | | |
| Other | | |
| **Bedroom #2** | | |
| Bedroom #2 has no furnishings | | |
| **Other Areas** | | |
| Desks | | |
| Shelves | | |
| Books, games, media | | |
| Decorative items (unattached mirrors, rugs, pictures, vases, etc.) | | |
| Electronics | | |
| Tools (yard and workshop) | | |
| Trash & recycling bins | | |
| Outdoor furniture | | |
| Recreational equipment | | |
| Other | | |

Use this space to provide any additional explanation:

_____

_____

_____

_____

_____

Landlord-Tenant Checklist completed on moving in on _____
and approved by:

_____ and _____
Landlord/Manager                             Tenant

                                              _____
                                              Tenant

                                              _____
                                              Tenant

Landlord-Tenant Checklist completed on moving out on _____
and approved by:

_____ and _____
Landlord/Manager                             Tenant

                                              _____
                                              Tenant

                                              _____
                                              Tenant

னட
# Move-In Letter

Date: _____

Tenant: _____

Street Address: _____

City and State: _____

Dear: _____ ,
                      Tenant

Welcome to _____
_____ [address of rental unit]. We hope you will enjoy living here. This letter is to explain what you can expect from the management and what we'll be looking for from you.

Rent: _____
_____
_____.

New Roommates: _____
_____
_____
_____.

Notice to End Tenancy: _____
_____
_____
_____.

Deposits: _____
_____
_____.

Manager: _____
_____
_____
_____.

Landlord-Tenant Checklist: _____
_____
_____
_____
_____
_____.

Maintenance/Repair Problems: _____
_____
_____
_____
_____
_____
_____

Semiannual Safety and Maintenance Update: _____
_____
_____
_____
_____
_____

Annual Safety Inspection: _____
_____
_____
_____
_____

Insurance: _____
_____
_____
_____
_____
_____

Moving Out: _____
_____
_____
_____
_____

Changes to Your Contact Information: _____
_____
_____

Please let us know if you have any questions.

Sincerely,

_____     _____
Landlord/Manager                                                                  Date

I have read and received a copy of this statement.

_____     _____
Tenant                                                                             Date

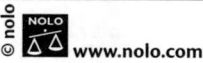

Form 27

# Resident's Maintenance/Repair Request

Date: _____

Address: _____

Resident's name: _____

Home phone: _____   Work phone: _____

Email: _____

Problem (be as specific as possible): _____

Best time to make repairs: _____

Other comments: _____

I authorize entry into my unit to perform the maintenance or repair requested above, in my absence, unless stated otherwise above.

Resident signature: _____

Date: _____

................................................................................................

## FOR MANAGEMENT USE

Work done: _____

Time spent: _____ hours

Date completed: _____   By: _____

Unable to complete on: _____, Because: _____

Notes and comments: _____

Landlord/Manager signature: _____

Date: _____

# Semiannual Safety and Maintenance Update

We're asking all tenants to complete the following checklist and note any safety or maintenance problems in your unit or on the premises. Please:

- Describe the specific problems and the rooms or areas involved. Here are some examples of the types of things we want to know about: garage roof leaks, excessive mildew in rear bedroom closet, fuses blow out frequently, doors or locks that stick, water that comes out too hot in the shower, peeling paint, and any pest infestations. This list isn't exhaustive; please let us know about any maintenance issue that is or could become a problem if not attended to, and be as specific as possible when describing it.
- Point out any potential safety and security problems in the neighborhood and anything you consider a serious nuisance.
- Indicate the approximate date when you first noticed the problem and list any other recommendations or suggestions for improvement.

Please return this form with this month's rent check. Thank you.—THE MANAGEMENT

Name: _____

Address: _____

_____

Please indicate (and explain below) problems with:

- ☐ Floors and floor coverings _____
- ☐ Walls and ceilings _____
- ☐ Windows, screens, and doors _____
- ☐ Window coverings (drapes, miniblinds, etc.) _____
- ☐ Electrical system and light fixtures _____
- ☐ Plumbing (sinks, bathtub, shower, or toilet) _____
- ☐ Heating or air-conditioning system _____
- ☐ Major appliances (stove, oven, dishwasher, refrigerator) _____
- ☐ Basement or attic _____
- ☐ Locks or security system _____
- ☐ Smoke detector _____
- ☐ Fireplace _____
- ☐ Cupboards, cabinets, and closets _____
- ☐ Furnishings (table, bed, mirrors, chairs) _____
- ☐ Laundry facilities _____
- ☐ Elevator _____
- ☐ Stairs and handrails _____
- ☐ Hallway, lobby, and common areas _____
- ☐ Garage _____

_____

- ☐ Patio, terrace, or deck _____
- ☐ Lawn, fences, and grounds _____
- ☐ Carbon monoxide detector _____
- ☐ Pool and recreational facilities _____
- ☐ Roof, exterior walls, and other structural elements _____
- ☐ Driveway and sidewalks _____
- ☐ Neighborhood _____
- ☐ Nuisances _____
- ☐ Other _____

Specifics of problems: _____
_____
_____
_____

Other comments: _____
_____
_____
_____
_____

_____          _____
Tenant                                            Date

## FOR MANAGEMENT USE

Action/Response: _____
_____
_____
_____
_____
_____
_____

_____          _____
Landlord/Manager                                  Date

# Landlord-Tenant Agreement to Terminate Lease

Landlord: _____ and

Tenant: _____

agree that the lease they entered into on _____,

for premises at _____

_____,

will terminate on _____.

Landlord's signature: _____ Date: _____
Print name: _____

Tenant 1's signature: _____ Date: _____
Print name: _____

Tenant 2's signature: _____ Date: _____
Print name: _____

Tenant 3's signature: _____ Date: _____
Print name: _____

**Form 30**

# Consent to Assignment of Lease

Landlord: _____

Tenant: _____

Assignee: _____

Landlord, Tenant, and Assignee agree as follows:

1. **Location of Premises**

   Tenant has leased the premises located at _____ from Landlord.

2. **Lease Beginning and Ending Dates**

   The lease began on _____, _____.

   It will expire on _____, _____.

3. **Assignment**

   Tenant is assigning the balance of Tenant's lease to Assignee, beginning on _____, _____. It will end on the expiration date noted in clause 2 above.

4. **Tenant's Future Liability**

   Tenant's financial responsibilities under the terms of the lease are ended by this assignment. Specifically, Tenant's responsibilities for future rent and future damage are ended.

5. **Tenant's Right to Occupy**

   As of the effective date of the assignment, Tenant permanently gives up the right to occupy the premises.

6. **Binding Nature of Agreement**

   Assignee is bound by every term and condition in the lease that is the subject of this assignment.

Landlord's signature: _____ Date: _____

Print name: _____

Tenant's signature: _____ Date: _____

Print name: _____

Assignee's signature: _____ Date: _____

Print name: _____

# Month-to-Month Tenant's Notice of Intent to Move Out

Landlord: _____

Landlord's Street Address: _____

City and State: _____

Dear: _____ [*name of landlord*]:

This is to notify you that the undersigned tenants, _____
_____ [*tenants' names*], will be moving from
_____ [*rental address*], on
_____ [*last day of residence*], or _____
[*number of days*] days from today. This notice provides at least _____ [*number of days*] days' written notice as required by law.

Sincerely,

Tenant's signature: _____ Date: _____
_____ [*tenant's printed name*]

Tenant's signature: _____ Date: _____
_____ [*tenant's printed name*]

Tenant's signature: _____ Date: _____
_____ [*tenant's printed name*]

# Demand for Return of Security Deposit

Dear _____ [name of landlord]:

On _____ [date], we vacated the rental unit at _____
_____ [address]
and gave you our new address and phone number. As of today, we haven't received our $ _____
[amount of security deposit owed] security deposit, nor any accounting from you for that money. We were entitled to receive our deposit by _____ [date when deposit return was due]. You are now _____ [number of days or weeks] late.

We left our rental unit clean and undamaged, paid all of our rent, and gave you proper notice of our intention to move.

Perhaps your check is in the mail. If not, please send it promptly. Should we fail to hear from you by _____ [date], we'll take this matter to small claims court. If we are compelled to do this, we will also sue you for any costs and additional punitive damages allowed by state law.

Please mail our deposit immediately to our new address. If you have any questions, please contact us at the number below.

Very truly yours,

Tenant's signature: _____ Date: _____
_____ [tenant's printed name]
Phone: _____ Email: _____

Tenant's signature: _____ Date: _____
_____ [tenant's printed name]
Phone: _____ Email: _____

# Loan Comparison Worksheet

Purpose of loan: _____

Desired amount of loan: $ _____

|  | Loan 1 | Loan 2 | Loan 3 |
|---|---|---|---|

## General Information

| | Loan 1 | Loan 2 | Loan 3 |
|---|---|---|---|
| Lender: | | | |
| Contact: | | | |
| Address: | | | |
| | | | |
| | | | |

## Loan Terms

| | Loan 1 | Loan 2 | Loan 3 |
|---|---|---|---|
| APR: | _____% | _____% | _____% |
| Interest rate: | _____% | _____% | _____% |
| Adjustable? | | | |
| Cap: | _____% | _____% | _____% |
| No. of months: | | | |
| Monthly payment (principal and interest): | $ | $ | $ |
| Total payments (# of mos. × monthly payment): | $ | $ | $ |

## Other Costs

| | Loan 1 | Loan 2 | Loan 3 |
|---|---|---|---|
| Loan application fee: | $ | $ | $ |
| Credit check fee: | $ | $ | $ |
| Credit insurance: | $ | $ | $ |
| Other: | $ | $ | $ |

## Other Features

| | Loan 1 | Loan 2 | Loan 3 |
|---|---|---|---|
| Collateral required? | | | |
| If yes, specify: | | | |
| Balloon payment? | | | |
| Prepayment penalty? | | | |
| If yes, amount: | | | |
| Cosigner required? | | | |
| Payment due date: | | | |
| Grace period? | | | |
| Late fee? | | | |
| Possible loan discounts: | | | |
| Account with lender: | | | |
| Automatic deduction: | | | |
| On-time payments: | | | |

Form 34

# Authorization to Check Credit and Employment References

I, the undersigned borrower, _____ [name of borrower],
authorize _____ [name]
_____ [address]
_____ [phone] to verify my employment, financial, and credit information provided on this form.

## Borrower

Full name—include generations (Jr., Sr., III): _____

Other names used: _____

Street address: _____

Mailing address: _____

City, state, and zip code: _____

Date moved into current address: _____

Phone: _____

Previous address: _____

City, state, and zip code: _____

Dates there: _____

Date of birth: _____ Social Security number: _____

Driver's license number: _____

## Employment History

Name and address of current employer: _____
_____

Position/title: _____

Name of supervisor: _____

Supervisor's phone: _____

Annual gross income: _____

Previous employment (if at current job less than 18 months): _____

## Credit and Financial Information

### Bank/Financial Accounts

*Provide account number, bank/institution, branch address.*

Bank savings account: _____

_____

Bank checking account: _____

_____

Bank certificate of deposit: _____

_____

Mutual fund account: _____

_____

Brokerage account: _____

_____

Other: _____

_____

Other: _____

_____

Other: _____

_____

### Credit Accounts and Loans

*Provide type of account (auto loan, Visa, etc.), account number, name and address of creditor, amount owed, and monthly payment.*

Credit card: _____

Credit card: _____

Loan (specify type): _____

Loan (specify type): _____

Loan (specify type): _____

Other (specify type): _____

I certify that the information given above is true and correct. I authorize the above employers, financial institutions, and creditors to verify my employment, financial, and credit information provided above, and to provide correct information if the above is incorrect. A copy of this signed form is valid for this purpose.

Signature of Borrower: _____ Date: _____

# Monthly Payment Record

Name of lender: _____

Name of borrower: _____

Original amount borrowed: _____ Date loan made: _____

| Month | (A) Beginning balance (or prior month ending balance) | (B) Annual interest rate divided by 12 | (C) Interest due (A) × (B) | (D) Amount of payment made | (E) Principal reduction (D) − (C) | (F) New balance (A) − (E) |
|---|---|---|---|---|---|---|
| 1 | | | | | | |
| 2 | | | | | | |
| 3 | | | | | | |
| 4 | | | | | | |
| 5 | | | | | | |
| 6 | | | | | | |
| 7 | | | | | | |
| 8 | | | | | | |
| 9 | | | | | | |
| 10 | | | | | | |
| 11 | | | | | | |
| 12 | | | | | | |
| 13 | | | | | | |
| 14 | | | | | | |
| 15 | | | | | | |
| 16 | | | | | | |
| 17 | | | | | | |
| 18 | | | | | | |
| 19 | | | | | | |
| 20 | | | | | | |
| 21 | | | | | | |
| 22 | | | | | | |
| 23 | | | | | | |
| 24 | | | | | | |
| 25 | | | | | | |
| 26 | | | | | | |
| 27 | | | | | | |
| 28 | | | | | | |
| 29 | | | | | | |
| 30 | | | | | | |

# Promissory Note—Installment Payments With Interest

## 1. Borrower(s)

_____ [name of borrower 1]
_____ [name of borrower 2]

## 2. Lender

_____ [name of lender]

## 3. Loan

In return for a loan Borrower has received from Lender, Borrower promises to pay to Lender the amount of $_____ (principal), plus interest on unpaid principal at the rate of _____% per year from the date this note is signed until it is paid in full. If there is more than one borrower, they agree to be jointly and severally liable.

## 4. Monthly Payments

Borrower will pay back the loan in monthly installments, which include principal and interest, of not less than $_____ per month until the principal and interest are paid in full. Payments will be due on the first day of each month, beginning on _____ [date on which first installment payment is due]. Borrower will send all payments to _____
_____ [address where payments are to be sent].

## 5. Prepayments

Borrower may make extra payments of principal, in addition to the monthly installment payments, at any time. Borrower will identify any such payments, in writing, as prepayments of principal. Lender will use any prepayments to reduce the amount of principal owed by Borrower. Prepayments will not change the amount or due date of any future installment payments.

## 6. Late Payments

If any installment payment due under this note is not received by Lender within _____ days of its due date, Borrower will pay a late fee of five percent (5%) of the amount of the monthly payment. The late fee will be due immediately.

If any installment payment is not received by Lender within _____ days of its due date, Lender may demand, in writing, that Borrower repay the entire amount of unpaid principal immediately. After receiving Lender's demand, Borrower will immediately pay the entire unpaid principal.

## 7. Attorneys' Fees

If Lender sues Borrower to collect on this note, and wins, Borrower agrees to pay Lender's attorneys' fees in an amount the court finds to be fair and reasonable.

## 8. Entire Agreement

This note represents the entire agreement between Borrower and Lender. Any modifications must be in writing and signed by both Borrower and Lender.

## 9. Terminology

The term Borrower refers to one or more borrowers. The term Lender refers to more than one lender and to any person who legally holds this note, including a buyer in due course.

## 10. Governing Law

This note shall be governed under the laws in the State of _____ .

## Borrower's Signature(s)

Name: _____ Date: _____

Signature: _____

Location: [city or county where signed]_____

Name: _____ Date: _____

Signature: _____

Location: [city or county where signed]_____

[ATTACH NOTARY CERTIFICATE WHERE APPLICABLE]

# Promissory Note—Installment Payments With Interest and Balloon Payment

### 1. Borrower(s)

_____ [name of borrower 1]
_____ [name of borrower 2]

### 2. Lender

_____ [name of lender]

### 3. Loan

In return for a loan Borrower has received from Lender, Borrower promises to pay to Lender the amount of $_____ (principal), plus interest on unpaid principal at the rate of _____% per year from the date this note is signed until it is paid in full. If there is more than one borrower, they agree to be jointly and severally liable.

### 4. Installment Payments and Balloon Payment

Borrower will make monthly installment payments, which include principal and interest, of not less than $_____ , beginning on _____ [date by which first installment payment must be made] and continuing on the first day of each month until _____ [date of the last regular monthly payment before "balloon" payment becomes due]. Borrower agrees to pay the remaining principal and interest on or before _____ [date on which the "balloon" payment is due]. Borrower will send all payments to _____ _____ [address where payments are to be sent].

### 5. Prepayments

Borrower may make extra payments of principal, in addition to the monthly installment payments, at any time. Borrower will identify any such payments, in writing, as prepayments of principal. Lender will use any prepayments to reduce the amount of principal owed by Borrower. Prepayments will not change the amount or due date of any future installment payments.

### 6. Late Payments

If any installment payment due under this note is not received by Lender within _____ days of its due date, Borrower will pay a late fee of five percent (5%) of the amount of the monthly payment. The late fee will be due immediately.

If any installment payment is not received by Lender within _____ days of its due date, Lender may demand, in writing, that Borrower repay the entire amount of unpaid principal immediately. After receiving Lender's demand, Borrower will immediately pay the entire unpaid principal.

### 7. Attorneys' Fees

If Lender sues Borrower to collect on this note, and wins, Borrower agrees to pay Lender's attorneys' fees in an amount the court finds to be fair and reasonable.

## 8. Entire Agreement

This note represents the entire agreement between Borrower and Lender. Any modifications must be in writing and signed by both Borrower and Lender.

## 9. Terminology

The term Borrower refers to one or more borrowers. The term Lender refers to more than one lender and to any person who legally holds this note, including a buyer in due course.

## 10. Governing Law

This note shall be governed under the laws in the State of _____ .

## Borrower's Signature(s)

Name: _____ Date: _____

Signature: _____

Location: [city or county where signed]_____

Name: _____ Date: _____

Signature: _____

Location: [city or county where signed]_____

**[ATTACH NOTARY CERTIFICATE WHERE APPLICABLE]**

# Promissory Note—Installment Payments Without Interest

## 1. Borrower(s)

_____ [name of borrower 1]
_____ [name of borrower 2]

## 2. Lender

_____ [name of lender]

## 3. Loan

In return for a loan Borrower has received from Lender, Borrower promises to pay to Lender the amount of $_____ (principal). If there is more than one borrower, they agree to be jointly and severally liable.

## 4. Monthly Payments

Borrower will make equal installments of $_____ per month until the principal is paid in full. Payments will be due on the first day of each month, beginning on _____ [date on which first payment is due]. Borrower will send all payments to _____ _____ [address where payments are to be sent].

## 5. Late Payments

If any installment payment due under this note is not received by Lender within _____ days of its due date, Borrower will pay a late fee of five percent (5%) of the amount of the monthly payment. The late fee will be due immediately.

If any installment payment is not received by Lender within _____ days of its due date, Lender may demand that Borrower repay the entire amount of unpaid principal immediately. If Lender notifies Borrower, in writing, that the entire amount is now due and payable, Borrower will immediately pay the entire unpaid principal.

## 6. Attorneys' Fees

If Lender sues Borrower to collect on this note, and wins, Borrower agrees to pay Lender's attorneys' fees in an amount the court finds to be fair and reasonable.

## 7. Entire Agreement

This note represents the entire agreement between Borrower and Lender. Any modifications must be in writing and signed by both Borrower and Lender.

## 8. Terminology

The term Borrower refers to one or more borrowers. The term Lender refers to more than one lender and to any person who legally holds this note, including a buyer in due course.

## 9. Governing Law

This note shall be governed under the laws in the State of _____ .

## Borrower's Signature(s)

Name: _____  Date: _____

Signature: _____

Location: [city or county where signed]_____

Name: _____  Date: _____

Signature: _____

Location: [city or county where signed]_____


[ATTACH NOTARY CERTIFICATE WHERE APPLICABLE]

# Promissory Note—Lump-Sum Payment With Interest

## 1. Borrower(s)

_____ [name of borrower 1]
_____ [name of borrower 2]

## 2. Lender

_____ [name of lender]

## 3. Loan

In return for a loan Borrower has received from Lender, Borrower promises to pay to Lender the amount of $ _____ (principal), plus interest on unpaid principal at the rate of _____% per year from the date this note is signed until it is paid in full. If there is more than one borrower, they agree to be jointly and severally liable.

## 4. Due Date and Repayment Terms

Borrower will repay the entire amount by _____. Borrower will send payment to _____ [address where payment is to be sent].

## 5. Prepayments

Borrower may make payments of principal at any time before the loan is due. Borrower will identify any such payments, in writing, as prepayments of principal. Lender will use any prepayments to reduce the amount of principal owed by Borrower.

## 6. Attorneys' Fees

If Lender sues Borrower to collect on this note, and wins, Borrower agrees to pay Lender's attorneys' fees in an amount the court finds to be fair and reasonable.

## 7. Entire Agreement

This note represents the entire agreement between Borrower and Lender. Any modifications must be in writing and signed by both Borrower and Lender.

## 8. Terminology

The term Borrower refers to one or more borrowers. The term Lender refers to more than one lender and to any person who legally holds this note, including a buyer in due course.

## 9. Governing Law

This note shall be governed under the laws in the State of _____ .

## Borrower's Signature(s)

Name: _____ Date: _____

Signature: _____ Location: [city or county where signed] _____

Name: _____ Date: _____

Signature: _____ Location: [city or county where signed] _____

[ATTACH NOTARY CERTIFICATE WHERE APPLICABLE]

Form 40

# Promissory Note—Lump-Sum Payment Without Interest

### 1. Borrower(s)

_____ [name of borrower 1]
_____ [name of borrower 2]

### 2. Lender

_____ [name of lender]

### 3. Loan

In return for a loan Borrower has received from Lender, Borrower promises to pay to Lender the amount of $_____ by _____ [date on which payment is due] at _____ [address where payment is to be sent]. If there is more than one borrower, they agree to be jointly and severally liable.

### 4. Attorneys' Fees

If Lender sues Borrower to collect on this note, and wins, Borrower agrees to pay Lender's attorneys' fees in an amount the court finds to be fair and reasonable.

### 5. Entire Agreement

This note represents the entire agreement between Borrower and Lender. Any modifications must be in writing and signed by both Borrower and Lender.

### 6. Terminology

The term Borrower refers to one or more borrowers. The term Lender refers to more than one lender and to any person who legally holds this note, including a buyer in due course.

### 7. Governing Law

This note shall be governed under the laws in the State of _____ .

### Borrower's Signature(s)

Name: _____  Date: _____
Signature: _____
Location: [city or county where signed] _____

Name: _____  Date: _____
Signature: _____
Location: [city or county where signed] _____

[ATTACH NOTARY CERTIFICATE WHERE APPLICABLE]

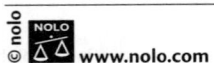

## Cosigner Provision

Name of Cosigner 1: _____

Name of Cosigner 2: _____

Name of Borrower 1: _____

Name of Borrower 2: _____

Name of Lender: _____

1. Borrower has agreed to pay Lender the amount indicated in the attached Promissory Note under the terms specified in that Note.

2. Cosigner agrees to guarantee this debt and understands this obligation means the following:
   - If Borrower doesn't pay the debt on time, that fact may become a part of Cosigner's credit record.
   - If Borrower doesn't pay the debt at all, Cosigner will be legally obligated to do so.
   - Cosigner might have to pay late fees or collection costs, which will increase the amount due.
   - Lender can collect this debt from Cosigner without first trying to collect from Borrower.
   - Lender can use the same collection methods against Cosigner that can be used against Borrower, including filing a lawsuit against Cosigner, and if the lawsuit is successful, garnishing Cosigner's wages, seizing other personal property of Cosigner, and placing a lien against Cosigner's real property.

*The term Cosigner refers to one or more cosigners. If there is more than one cosigner, they agree to be jointly and severally liable.*

Cosigner 1's signature: _____ Date: _____

Print name: _____

Location [*city or county where signed*]: _____

Address: _____


Cosigner 2's signature: _____ Date: _____

Print name: _____

Location [*city or county where signed*]: _____

Address: _____

**Form 42**

# Security Agreement Provision for Promissory Note

[*Here are some examples of the kind of language to include in the security agreement provision.*]

[*If a vehicle is security, use this language:*]

Borrower agrees that until the principal and interest owed under this note are paid in full, the note is secured by the following security agreement:

Security agreement signed by: _____ [*name of owner*] on: _____ [*date signed*], which gives title to: _____ [*date, make, model, and VIN of vehicle*].

[*If other valuable personal property is security, use this language:*]

Borrower agrees that until the principal and interest owed under this note are paid in full, the note is secured by the following security agreement:

Security agreement signed by: _____ [*name of owner*] on: _____ [*date signed*], which gives a security interest in: _____
_____ [*description of the personal property used as collateral*].

# Security Agreement for Borrowing Money

Name of Borrower: _____

Name of Lender: _____

1. **Grant of Security Interest.** Borrower grants to Lender a continuing security interest in the following personal property: _____
_____ (the Secured Property). Borrower grants this security interest to secure performance of the promissory note dated _____ that Borrower executed in favor of Lender (the Note), which obligates Borrower to pay Lender $ _____ with interest at the rate of _____% per year, on the terms stated in the Note.

2. **Financing Statement.** Until the amount due under the Note is paid in full, the Note will be further secured by a Uniform Commercial Code (U.C.C.) Financing Statement. Borrower agrees to sign any other documents that Lender reasonably requests to protect Lender's security interest in the Secured Property.

3. **Use and Care of Secured Property.** Until the amount due under the Note is paid in full, Borrower agrees to:

    A. Maintain the Secured Property in good repair.

    B. Refrain from selling, transferring, or releasing the Secured Property without Lender's prior written consent.

    C. Pay all taxes on the Secured Property as they become due.

    D. Allow Lender to inspect the Secured Property at any reasonable time.

4. **Borrower's Default.** If Borrower is more than _____ days late in making any payment due under the Note, or if Buyer fails to correct any violations of Paragraph 3 within _____ days of receiving written notice from Lender, Borrower will be in default.

5. **Lender's Rights.** If Borrower is in default, Lender may exercise the remedies contained in the U.C.C. for the State of _____ and any other remedies legally available to Lender. Before exercising such remedies, Lender will provide at least 10 days' advance notice, as provided in Paragraph 6. Lender may, for example:

    A. Remove the Secured Property from the place where it is then located.

    B. Require Borrower to make the Secured Property available to Lender at a place designated by Lender that is reasonably convenient to Borrower and Lender.

    C. Sell, lease, or otherwise dispose of the Secured Property.

6. **Notice.** Any notice may be delivered to a party at the address that follows a party's signature below, or to a new address that a party designates in writing. A notice may be delivered in person, by certified mail, or by overnight courier.

7. **Entire Agreement.** This is the entire agreement between the parties. It replaces and supersedes any and all oral agreements between the parties, as well as any prior writings.

8. **Successors and Assigns.** This agreement binds and benefits the parties' heirs, successors, and assigns.

9. **Governing Law.** This agreement will be governed by and construed in accordance with the laws of the State of _____ .

10. **Modification.** This agreement may be modified only in writing.

11. **Waiver.** If one party waives any term or provision of this agreement at any time, that waiver will be effective only for the specific instance and specific purpose for which the waiver was given. If either party fails to exercise or delays exercising any rights or remedies under this agreement, that party retains the right to enforce that term or provision at a later time.

12. **Severability.** If any court determines that any provision of this agreement is invalid or unenforceable, any such invalidity or unenforceability will affect only that provision and will not make any other provision of this agreement invalid or unenforceable, and such provision shall be modified, amended, or limited only to the extent necessary to render it valid and enforceable.

Lender's signature: _____ Date: _____

Print name: _____

Location [*city or county where signed*]: _____

Address: _____

_____

Borrower's signature: _____ Date: _____

Print name: _____

Location [*city or county where signed*]: _____

Address: _____

_____

# U.C.C. Financing Statement

This Financing Statement is presented for filing under the Uniform Commercial Code as adopted in
_____ [name of your state].

---

Name of Borrower: _____

Address of Borrower: _____

_____

Name of Lender/secured party: _____

Address of Lender/secured party: _____

_____

*The term Borrower refers to one or more borrowers. If there is more than one borrower, they agree to be jointly and severally liable. The term Lender refers to any person who legally holds the promissory note, including a buyer in due course.*

The property listed as collateral in the security agreement is as follows [*identify or describe*]:

_____

_____

This Financing Statement secures the following debt:

Promissory note dated: _____

Amount of debt: _____

Payback due date: _____

All other terms and conditions are stated in the promissory note, a copy of which is attached.

Borrower's signature: _____

Print name: _____

Location [*city or county where signed*]: _____

Date: _____

---

(*For Use by the Filing Officer*)

Date of filing: _____  Time of filing: _____

File number and address of filing office: _____

_____

Form 44: U.C.C. Financing Statement

# Release of U.C.C. Financing Statement

This Release of Financing Statement is presented for filing under the Uniform Commercial Code as adopted in _____ [*name of your state*].

---

Name of Borrower: _____

Address of Borrower: _____

_____

Name of Lender/secured party: _____

Address of Lender/secured party: _____

_____

*The term Borrower refers to one or more borrowers. The term Lender refers to any person who legally holds the promissory note, including a buyer in due course.*

The property listed as collateral in the security agreement is as follows [*identify or describe*]:

_____

_____

File number of Financing Statement: _____

Date filed: _____

Address of filing office: _____

Borrower's signature: _____

Print name: _____

Date: _____

---

*(For Use by the Filing Officer)*

Date of filing: _____ Time of filing: _____

File number and address of filing office: _____

_____

# Agreement to Modify Promissory Note

Name of Borrower 1: _____

Name of Borrower 2: _____

Name of Lender: _____

1. This Agreement modifies the original promissory note dated _____, _____, under which Borrower promised to pay to Lender the amount of $_____ at the rate of _____% per year from the date the note was signed until _____, _____.

2. Lender and Borrower agree to the following modifications [*choose all that apply*]:
   - ☐ Borrower has until _____, _____ to pay the note in full.
   - ☐ Borrower will make interest-only payments beginning on _____, _____ until _____, _____, at which time the remaining principal balance will be reamortized over the remaining months of the note.
   - ☐ Beginning on _____, _____, the interest rate will change to _____%. The new monthly payments will be in the amount of $_____.
   - ☐ Other: _____
   _____.

*The term Borrower refers to one or more borrowers. If there is more than one borrower, they agree to be jointly and severally liable. The term Lender refers to any person who legally holds the promissory note, including a buyer in due course.*

Borrower 1's signature: _____ Date: _____

Print name _____

Location [*city or county where signed*]: _____

Address: _____

_____

Borrower 2's signature: _____ Date: _____

Print name: _____

Location [*city or county where signed*]: _____

Address: _____

_____

Lender's signature: _____ Date _____

Print name: _____

Location [*city or county where signed*]: _____

Address: _____

_____

Form 47

# Overdue Payment Demand

Date: _____

To: _____
_____
_____
_____

[insert name and address of person who borrowed money]

Re: Promissory note dated _____

Dear _____:

This correspondence is to notify you that I have not received the following payment(s) due under the promissory note referenced above ("the Note").

Amount: $ _____  Due date: _____
Amount: $ _____  Due date: _____
Total:   $ _____

Please remit the outstanding balance within fifteen (15) days. If you fail to do so, I will have no choice but to assume that you do not intend to repay the amount that is due under the Note. I will proceed to enforce my rights under the Note, including possibly filing a lawsuit, to collect the entire balance.

Sincerely,

Signature of Lender: _____

Print name of Lender: _____

Address: _____
_____

Phone: _____  Work phone: _____

# Demand to Make Good on Bad Check

Date: _____

To: _____

_____

_____

_____

[*insert name and address of check writer*]

Re: Check # _____ dated _____ , _____

Issuing financial institution: _____

Dear _____ :

Your check was returned to my bank and refused payment for the following reason [*choose one*]:

☐ insufficient funds in the account on which the check was drawn to cover the amount of the check.

☐ the account on which the check was drawn has been closed

☐ you stopped payment on the check

Please pay the returned check amount of $ _____ within 30 days. If you fail to do so, I will have no choice but to assume that you do not intend to make this check good. I will proceed to enforce my rights, which may include filing a lawsuit. I will request that the court award me the maximum monetary damages allowed under state law, as well as:

☐ the amount of the check

☐ the bad-check processing fee charged by my bank

☐ the expenses incurred in attempting to collect on the check as allowed under state law

Sincerely,

Signature of check recipient: _____

Print name of check recipient: _____

Address: _____

_____

Phone: _____ Work phone: _____

# Ideal House Profile

Upper price limit: _____

Maximum down payment: _____

Special financing needs: _____

|  | Must Have | Hope to Have |
|---|---|---|

**Neighborhood or location:**

_____ ☐ ☐

_____ ☐ ☐

**School needs:**

_____ ☐ ☐

**Desired neighborhood features:**

_____ ☐ ☐

_____ ☐ ☐

_____ ☐ ☐

_____ ☐ ☐

**Length of commute:**

_____ ☐ ☐

**Access to public transportation:**

_____ ☐ ☐

**Size of house:**

_____ ☐ ☐

**Number and type of rooms:**

_____ ☐ ☐

_____ ☐ ☐

**Condition, age, and type of house:**

_____ ☐ ☐

_____ ☐ ☐

**Type of yard and grounds:**

_____ ☐ ☐

_____ ☐ ☐

**Other desired features:**

_____ ☐ ☐

_____ ☐ ☐

_____ ☐ ☐

**Absolute no ways:**

_____ ☐ ☐

_____ ☐ ☐

_____ ☐ ☐

_____ ☐ ☐

Form 50

# House Priorities Worksheet

Date visited: _____

Address: _____
_____

Price: $ _____

Agent or seller: _____ Contact info: _____

**Must haves:**

☐ _____
☐ _____
☐ _____
☐ _____
☐ _____
☐ _____
☐ _____
☐ _____

**Hope to haves:**

☐ _____
☐ _____
☐ _____
☐ _____
☐ _____
☐ _____
☐ _____
☐ _____

**Absolute no ways:**

☐ _____
☐ _____
☐ _____

**Comments about the house:**

_____
_____
_____
_____
_____
_____

## House Comparison Worksheet

House 1 _____
House 2 _____
House 3 _____
House 4 _____

|  | 1 | 2 | 3 | 4 |
|---|---|---|---|---|

**Must haves:**

| | 1 | 2 | 3 | 4 |
|---|---|---|---|---|
| _____ | ☐ | ☐ | ☐ | ☐ |
| _____ | ☐ | ☐ | ☐ | ☐ |
| _____ | ☐ | ☐ | ☐ | ☐ |
| _____ | ☐ | ☐ | ☐ | ☐ |
| _____ | ☐ | ☐ | ☐ | ☐ |
| _____ | ☐ | ☐ | ☐ | ☐ |
| _____ | ☐ | ☐ | ☐ | ☐ |
| _____ | ☐ | ☐ | ☐ | ☐ |
| _____ | ☐ | ☐ | ☐ | ☐ |
| _____ | ☐ | ☐ | ☐ | ☐ |
| _____ | ☐ | ☐ | ☐ | ☐ |
| _____ | ☐ | ☐ | ☐ | ☐ |

**Hope to haves:**

| | 1 | 2 | 3 | 4 |
|---|---|---|---|---|
| _____ | ☐ | ☐ | ☐ | ☐ |
| _____ | ☐ | ☐ | ☐ | ☐ |
| _____ | ☐ | ☐ | ☐ | ☐ |
| _____ | ☐ | ☐ | ☐ | ☐ |
| _____ | ☐ | ☐ | ☐ | ☐ |
| _____ | ☐ | ☐ | ☐ | ☐ |
| _____ | ☐ | ☐ | ☐ | ☐ |
| _____ | ☐ | ☐ | ☐ | ☐ |
| _____ | ☐ | ☐ | ☐ | ☐ |

**Absolute no ways:**

| | 1 | 2 | 3 | 4 |
|---|---|---|---|---|
| _____ | ☐ | ☐ | ☐ | ☐ |
| _____ | ☐ | ☐ | ☐ | ☐ |
| _____ | ☐ | ☐ | ☐ | ☐ |
| _____ | ☐ | ☐ | ☐ | ☐ |
| _____ | ☐ | ☐ | ☐ | ☐ |

Form 52

# Family Financial Statement

|          | Borrower | Coborrower |
|----------|----------|------------|
| Name:    |          |            |
| Address: |          |            |

Primary phone number:
Employer:
Employer's address:
Work phone number:

## Worksheet 1: Income and Expenses

| | Borrower ($) | Coborrower ($) | Total |
|---|---|---|---|
| **I. INCOME** | | | |
| A. Monthly gross income | | | |
|   1. Employment | | | |
|   2. Public benefits | | | |
|   3. Dividends | | | |
|   4. Royalties | | | |
|   5. Interest and other investment income | | | |
|   6. Other (specify): _____ | | | |
| B. Total monthly gross income | | | |
| **II. MONTHLY EXPENSES** | | | |
| A. Nonhousing | | | |
|   1. Child care | | | |
|   2. Clothing | | | |
|   3. Food | | | |
|   4. Insurance | | | |
|     a. Auto | | | |
|     b. Life | | | |
|     c. Medical & dental | | | |
|   5. Other medical | | | |
|   6. Personal | | | |
|   7. Education | | | |
|   8. Taxes (nonhousing) | | | |
|   9. Phone, cable, streaming, Wi-Fi services | | | |
|   10. Transportation | | | |
|   11. Other (specify): _____ | | | |
| B. Current Housing | | | |
|   1. Mortgage | | | |
|   2. Taxes | | | |
|   3. Insurance | | | |
|   4. Utilities | | | |
|   5. Rent | | | |
|   6. Other (specify): _____ | | | |
| C. Total monthly expenses | | | |

## Worksheet 2: Assets and Liabilities

|  | Borrower ($) | Coborrower ($) | Total |
|---|---|---|---|
| **I. ASSETS (cash or market value)** | | | |
| A. Cash & cash equivalents | | | |
|   1. Cash | _____ | _____ | _____ |
|   2. Deposits (list): | _____ | _____ | _____ |
|     _____ | _____ | _____ | _____ |
| B. Marketable securities | | | |
|   1. Stocks/bonds (bid price) | _____ | _____ | _____ |
|   2. Other securities | _____ | _____ | _____ |
|   3. Mutual funds | _____ | _____ | _____ |
|   4. Life insurance | _____ | _____ | _____ |
|   5. Other (specify): | _____ | _____ | _____ |
|     _____ | _____ | _____ | _____ |
| C. Total cash & marketable securities | _____ | _____ | _____ |
| D. Nonliquid assets | | | |
|   1. Real estate | _____ | _____ | _____ |
|   2. Retirement funds | _____ | _____ | _____ |
|   3. Business | _____ | _____ | _____ |
|   4. Motor vehicles | _____ | _____ | _____ |
|   5. Other (specify): | _____ | _____ | _____ |
|     _____ | _____ | _____ | _____ |
| E. Total nonliquid assets | _____ | _____ | _____ |
| F. Total all assets | _____ | _____ | _____ |
| **II. LIABILITIES** | | | |
| A. Debts | | | |
|   1. Real estate loans | _____ | _____ | _____ |
|   2. Student loans | _____ | _____ | _____ |
|   3. Motor vehicle loans | _____ | _____ | _____ |
|   4. Child or spousal support | _____ | _____ | _____ |
|   5. Personal loans | _____ | _____ | _____ |
|   6. Credit cards (specify): | _____ | _____ | _____ |
|     _____ | _____ | _____ | _____ |
|     _____ | _____ | _____ | _____ |
|   7. Other (specify): | _____ | _____ | _____ |
|     _____ | _____ | _____ | _____ |
| B. Total liabilities | _____ | _____ | _____ |
| **III. NET WORTH** (total assets minus total liabilities) | _____ | _____ | _____ |

Form 53

# Monthly Carrying Costs Worksheet

1. Estimated purchase price  $_____
2. Down payment  $_____
3. Loan amount  $_____
4. Interest rate  _____%
5. Monthly mortgage payment  $_____
6. Homeowners' insurance [*monthly*]  $_____
7. Property taxes [*monthly*]  $_____
8. Total monthly housing costs [*add lines 5–7*]  $_____
9. Other monthly debts

    _____ $_____

    _____ $_____

    _____ $_____

    _____ $_____

    Total monthly debts  $_____

10. Private mortgage insurance [*if any*]  $_____
11. Homeowners' association fee
    [*if in a planned unit development*]  $_____
12. Total monthly housing costs and other debts
    [*add lines 8–11*]  $_____
13. Lender qualifying ratio [*between 28% and 36%*]  _____%
14. Monthly gross income to qualify
    [*divide line 12 by line 13*]  $_____
15. Yearly gross income to qualify
    [*multiply line 14 by the number 12*]  $_____

Form 54

# Mortgage Rates and Terms Worksheet

Lender: _____  _____  _____

Loan agent: _____  _____  _____

Phone number and email: _____  _____  _____

Date: _____  _____  _____

## 1. General Information

| | | | |
|---|---|---|---|
| Fixed or adjustable? | ☐ F ☐ A | ☐ F ☐ A | ☐ F ☐ A |
| Fixed interest rate | _____ % | _____ % | _____ % |
| Government financing? | ☐ Y ☐ N | ☐ Y ☐ N | ☐ Y ☐ N |
| Minimum down payment | _____ % | _____ % | _____ % |
| PMI required? | ☐ Y ☐ N | ☐ Y ☐ N | ☐ Y ☐ N |
| Impound account? | ☐ Y ☐ N | ☐ Y ☐ N | ☐ Y ☐ N |
| Term of mortgage | _____ years | _____ years | _____ years |
| Assumable? | ☐ Y ☐ N | ☐ Y ☐ N | ☐ Y ☐ N |
| Rate lock-in available? | ☐ Y ☐ N | ☐ Y ☐ N | ☐ Y ☐ N |
| Cost to lock in | $ _____ | $ _____ | $ _____ |
| 21 days | $ _____ | $ _____ | $ _____ |
| 30 days | $ _____ | $ _____ | $ _____ |
| 45 days | $ _____ | $ _____ | $ _____ |

## 2. Debt-to-Income Ratio Information

| | | | |
|---|---|---|---|
| Allowable monthly carrying costs as % of income | _____ | _____ | _____ |
| Allowable monthly carrying costs plus long-term debts as % of monthly income | _____ | _____ | _____ |
| Maximum loan you qualify for based on debt-to-income ratio | $ _____ | $ _____ | $ _____ |

### 3. Loan Costs

| | | | |
|---|---|---|---|
| Number of points | _____ | _____ | _____ |
| Cost of points | $ _____ | $ _____ | $ _____ |
| PMI | $ _____ | $ _____ | $ _____ |
| Additional loan fee | $ _____ | $ _____ | $ _____ |
| Credit report | $ _____ | $ _____ | $ _____ |
| Application fee | $ _____ | $ _____ | $ _____ |
| Appraisal fee | $ _____ | $ _____ | $ _____ |
| Miscellaneous fees | $ _____ | $ _____ | $ _____ |
| Estimated total loan costs | $ _____ | $ _____ | $ _____ |

### 4. Time Limits

| | | | |
|---|---|---|---|
| Credit/employment check | _____ days | _____ days | _____ days |
| Lender appraisal | _____ days | _____ days | _____ days |
| Loan approval | _____ days | _____ days | _____ days |
| Loan funding | _____ days | _____ days | _____ days |
| Loan due date each month | _____ | _____ | _____ |
| Grace period | _____ days | _____ days | _____ days |
| Late fee | _____ % | _____ % | _____ % |

### 5. Other Features
[such as a discount for having an account with a certain bank, or a lender discount of interest rate on initial payments]

_____    _____    _____    _____
_____    _____    _____    _____
_____    _____    _____    _____

### 6. Fixed-Rate Two-Step Loans

| | | | |
|---|---|---|---|
| Initial annual interest rate | _____ % | _____ % | _____ % |
| Over how many years? | _____ years | _____ years | _____ years |

### 7. Fixed-Rate Balloon Payment Loans

| | | | |
|---|---|---|---|
| Interest rate | _____ % | _____ % | _____ % |
| Monthly payment | $ _____ | $ _____ | $ _____ |
| Term of loan | _____ years | _____ years | _____ years |
| Amount of balloon payment | _____ | _____ | _____ |

**8. Adjustable-Rate Mortgages (ARMs)**

Index:

| | | | |
|---|---|---|---|
| 11th District COFI Index | ☐ _____ % | ☐ _____ % | ☐ _____ % |
| 6-Month T-Bill Index | ☐ _____ % | ☐ _____ % | ☐ _____ % |
| 1-Year T-Bill Index | ☐ _____ % | ☐ _____ % | ☐ _____ % |

Other:

| | | | |
|---|---|---|---|
| _____ | ☐ _____ % | ☐ _____ % | ☐ _____ % |
| Margin | ☐ _____ % | ☐ _____ % | ☐ _____ % |
| Initial interest rate | ☐ _____ % | ☐ _____ % | ☐ _____ % |
| How long? | ____ mos. ____ yrs. | ____ mos. ____ yrs. | ____ mos. ____ yrs. |
| Interest cap rate | ☐ _____ % | ☐ _____ % | ☐ _____ % |
| Adjustment period | _____ months | _____ months | _____ months |
| Life-of-loan (overall) cap | ☐ _____ % | ☐ _____ % | ☐ _____ % |
| Initial payment | _____ months | _____ months | _____ months |
| Payment cap | ☐ _____ % | ☐ _____ % | ☐ _____ % |
| Payment cap period | _____ months | _____ months | _____ months |

Highest payment or interest rate in:

| | | | |
|---|---|---|---|
| 6 months | ____ % $_____ | ____ % $_____ | ____ % $_____ |
| 12 months | ____ % $_____ | ____ % $_____ | ____ % $_____ |
| 18 months | ____ % $_____ | ____ % $_____ | ____ % $_____ |
| 24 months | ____ % $_____ | ____ % $_____ | ____ % $_____ |
| 30 months | ____ % $_____ | ____ % $_____ | ____ % $_____ |
| 36 months | ____ % $_____ | ____ % $_____ | ____ % $_____ |

**9. Hybrid Loans**

| | | | |
|---|---|---|---|
| Initial interest rate | _____ % | _____ % | _____ % |
| Term as a fixed-rate loan | _____ years | _____ years | _____ years |
| Interest rate at first adjustment period | _____ % | _____ % | _____ % |

# Moving Checklist

*[Not all items on this list will apply to you. If you're moving within the same town, you probably won't have to transfer your kids to a new school, get references for a new job, or have your car serviced for travel. So just focus on the applicable items.]*

## I. Two Weeks Before Moving

- ☐ Check with your children's new school about what records and transcripts it will need; arrange for their transfer.
- ☐ Close or transfer bank and safe deposit box accounts.
- ☐ Cancel deliveries or change the address for newspapers and magazines, meals or fruits and vegetables, diaper service, laundry, and so on.
- ☐ Contact utility companies—gas, electric, cable, internet, phone, water, garbage—and advise them of when to transfer services (if possible) or arrange new services; request deposit refunds.
- ☐ Get recommendations for, or find in advance (especially if a medical condition needs regular attention), new doctors, dentist, and veterinarian. Arrange for transfer of medical records.
- ☐ Arrange for reference letters, if you'll need to find a job.
- ☐ Cancel membership (or transfer membership, if relevant) in religious, civic, and athletic organizations.
- ☐ Have car serviced for travel.
- ☐ Arrange to move pets. Consider having them microchipped if you haven't already (and be sure to change the address associated with their chip after you move).
- ☐ Finalize arrangements with moving and/or car-shipping company. (Ideally, you got bids and made preliminary arrangements weeks earlier.)
- ☐ Tell close friends and relatives your schedule.

## II. Things to Remember While Packing

- ☐ Before you pack, inventory and sort through things. This way you can move less and won't end up throwing things away at your new home or needing storage space. Take photos of items of any significant value you plan to have moved, for purposes of claiming reimbursement if they're damaged, lost, or stolen in transit.
- ☐ Label boxes on top and side—your name, new city, room of house they're meant for, and contents.
- ☐ Assemble moving kit—hammer, screwdriver, pliers, tape, nails, tape measure, scissors, flashlight, cleansers, cleaning cloths, rubber gloves, garbage bags, lightbulbs, and extension cords. If you're driving to your new home, pack a broom and pail in your car. Larger items that are handy when moving in, such as a step stool or vacuum cleaner, should go in the moving van, unless your new house is nearby and you're moving lots of things by car.
- ☐ Keep the basics handy—comfortable clothes, prescription medications, toiletries, towels, alarm clock, disposable plates, cups, and utensils, can opener, one pot, one pan, sponge, paper towels, dish soap, toilet paper, plastic containers, and toys for kids.

- ☐ Consider carrying jewelry, extremely fragile items, currency, and important documents with you.
- ☐ Make other arrangements if the moving company won't move antiques, art collections, crystal, wine and other liquids, other valuables, or plants.

### III. Whom to Advise of Your Change of Address

- ☐ Friends and relatives
- ☐ Subscription services or publications
- ☐ Government agencies you regularly deal with or are awaiting a decision from—Veterans Administration, IRS, USCIS, Social Security Administration, Department of State, etc.
- ☐ Charge and credit accounts
- ☐ Installment debt—such as student loan or car loan
- ☐ Frequent flyer programs
- ☐ Brokers and mutual funds
- ☐ Insurance agent/companies (if you've moved to a better neighborhood, your car insurance rates might go down!)
- ☐ Medical providers—if you'll continue as a patient there after moving
- ☐ Catalogs you want to keep receiving
- ☐ Charities you wish to continue donating to
- ☐ School alumni office
- ☐ Post office (but don't count on it for consistent forwarding. If you're trying to get off of catalog and other direct mailing lists, have only first-class mail forwarded. Give your new address to those catalog companies on whose lists you want to remain, and don't forget to tell them not to trade or sell your name. Standard USPS forwarding lasts 12 months.)

### IV. Things to Do After Moving In

- ☐ Open local bank accounts and safe deposit box account.
- ☐ Begin deliveries—oil, newspaper, meals or fruits and vegetables, diapers, laundry.
- ☐ Change the locks.
- ☐ Register to vote.
- ☐ Change (or get a new) driver's license.
- ☐ Change auto registration.
- ☐ Install new batteries in existing smoke or carbon monoxide detectors (and install any additionally needed detectors); buy fire extinguisher.
- ☐ Hold party for the people who helped you find your house and your moving helpers, and take yourself out for a congratulatory dinner!

# Motor Vehicle Bill of Sale

## 1. Seller

Seller name: _____

Seller address: _____

_____

## 2. Buyer

Buyer name: _____

Buyer address: _____

_____

## 3. Terminology

The term "Buyer" refers to one or more buyers, and the term "Seller" refers to one or more sellers.

## 4. Vehicle Being Sold

Make: _____ Model: _____

Body type: _____ [e.g. sedan, SUV]   Year: _____

Vehicle identification number (VIN): _____

Vehicle includes the following additional items: _____

_____

*[List any items that are included in the sale price of the vehicle, such as a bicycle rack or a car cover.]*

## 5. Odometer

The odometer reading for Vehicle is: _____ .

## 6. Purchase Price

The full purchase price for Vehicle is: _____ .

In exchange for Vehicle, Buyer has paid Seller: *[choose one]*

☐ the full purchase price.

☐ $_____ as a down payment. Buyer will pay the balance of the purchase price by _____ *[date on which balance is due]*.

☐ $_____ as a down payment and has executed a promissory note for the balance of the purchase price.

## 7. Legal Owner

Seller warrants that Seller is the legal owner of Vehicle and that Vehicle is free of all liens or encumbrances.

## 8. Inspections

Vehicle ☐ has been  ☐ has not been inspected by an independent mechanic at Buyer's request.

## 9. Condition of Vehicle

Vehicle is sold "as is," and Seller does not make any express or implied warranties about its condition, except that to the best of Seller's knowledge, Vehicle: [check a box for each declaration]

- ☐ is ☐ is not a salvage vehicle.
- ☐ has ☐ has not been declared a total loss by an insurance company.
- ☐ has ☐ has not been repaired under the terms of a lemon law.

## 10. Additional Terms of Sale

Additional terms of sale for Vehicle are: _____

_____

_____ [enter any additional terms, or enter "none"].

## 11. Signatures

Seller signature: _____ Date: _____

Seller signature: _____ Date: _____

Buyer signature: _____ Date: _____

Buyer signature: _____ Date: _____

[ATTACH NOTARY CERTIFICATE WHEN REQUIRED/PREFERRED]

# Boat Bill of Sale

Seller 1: _____

Address: _____

Seller 2: _____

Address: _____

Buyer 1: _____

Address: _____

Buyer 2: _____

Address: _____

[*If there is more than one buyer or seller, the use of the singular incorporates the plural.*]

1. Seller sells the boat (Boat) described here to Buyer:

   Year: _____ Make: _____

   Model: _____ Length: _____

   Serial or hull ID number: _____ General type: _____

   Registration, CF, or document number: _____

2. Boat has the following types of engine(s) (Engines) [*provide details on engines including year, make, type, model, hours, and serial numbers*]: _____
   _____
   _____
   _____ .

3. Boat contains the following equipment (Equipment) included in this sale [*list and describe all that apply, including sails and rigging, safety equipment, electronics and navigation equipment, and deck equipment*]: _____
   _____
   _____
   _____ .

4. Seller believes Boat, Engines, and Equipment to be in good condition except for the following defects:
   _____
   _____ .

5. Boat and Engines ☐ have been ☐ have not been independently inspected or surveyed at Buyer's request. If an independent inspection or marine survey has been made, the inspection report or marine survey ☐ is attached to and made part of this bill of sale ☐ is not attached.

6. The full purchase price for Boat, Engines, and Equipment is $_____ . In exchange for Boat, Engines, and Equipment, Buyer has paid Seller [*choose one*]:

   ☐ a single payment of the full purchase price.

   ☐ $_____ as a down payment, balance of the purchase price due by
   _____ [*date*].

   ☐ $_____ as a down payment and has executed a promissory note for the balance of the purchase price.

Form 57: Boat Bill of Sale

**Form 57**

7. Seller warrants that Seller is the legal owner of Boat, Engines, and Equipment and that Boat, Engines, and Equipment are free of all liens and encumbrances except _____
   _____.
   Seller agrees to remove any lien or encumbrance specified in this clause with the proceeds of this sale and other funds as necessary within _____ days of the date of this bill of sale.

8. Additional terms of sale for Boat, Engines, and Equipment are as follows: _____
   _____
   _____.

Seller 1's signature: _____ Date: _____

Seller 2's signature: _____ Date: _____

Buyer 1's signature: _____ Date: _____

Buyer 2's signature: _____ Date: _____

*[ATTACH NOTARY CERTIFICATE WHEN REQUIRED/PREFERRED]*

# General Bill of Sale

## 1. Seller and Buyer

Seller name: _____

Seller address: _____

_____

Buyer name: _____

Buyer address: _____

_____

## 2. Description of Goods

Seller sells the goods (Goods) described here to Buyer: _____

_____ [*describe goods in reasonable detail*].

## 3. Purchase Price

The full purchase price for Goods is $_____. In exchange for Goods, Buyer has paid Seller: [*choose one*]

☐ the full purchase price.

☐ _____ as a down payment. Buyer will pay the balance of the purchase price by _____ [*date on which balance is due*].

☐ _____ as a down payment and has executed a promissory note for the balance of the purchase price.

☐ other payment arrangement: _____

_____

_____ [*describe payment arrangement, i.e., exchange of goods or services*].

## 4. Ownership

Seller warrants that Seller is the legal owner of Goods and that Goods are free of all liens and encumbrances.

## 5. Condition of Goods

Seller believes Goods to be in good condition except for the following: _____

_____ [*describe any significant defects in the goods*].

## 6. Delivery of Goods

Goods will be delivered to Buyer in the following manner: [*choose one*]

☐ Buyer will take immediate possession of Goods.

☐ Buyer will pick up Goods from _____

_____ [*address*] by _____ [*pickup date*].

☐ In exchange for an additional delivery charge of $ _____ , receipt of which is hereby acknowledged, Seller will deliver goods to _____
_____ [address of delivery location]
by _____ [delivery date].

## 7. Additional Terms

Additional terms of this sale are as follows: _____
_____
_____ [enter any additional terms, or enter "none"].

## 8. Signatures

Seller signature: _____ Date: _____

Buyer: signature _____ Date: _____

[ATTACH NOTARY CERTIFICATE WHEN REQUIRED/PREFERRED]

# Bill of Sale for Dog

Seller 1: _____

Address: _____

Seller 2: _____

Address: _____

Buyer 1: _____

Address: _____

Buyer 2: _____

Address: _____

*If there is more than one buyer or seller, the use of the singular incorporates the plural.*

1. Seller sells to Buyer the dog (Dog) described as follows:

    Name: _____

    Breed: _____ Sex: _____

    Birth date [*estimate if specific date not known*]: _____

2. The full purchase price for Dog is $ _____.

3. Buyer has paid Seller [*choose one*]:

    ☐ a single payment of the full purchase price

    ☐ a down payment of $ _____ with the balance of $ _____

    due _____ [*date*], or

    ☐ other: _____

    _____ [*explain*].

4. Seller warrants that:

    a. Seller is the legal owner of Dog.

    b. Dog has had the following vaccinations [*list all the vaccinations Dog has received, including the date the vaccination was given and the name of the vet who gave it*]: _____

    _____

    _____

    _____ .

    c. Dog was [*choose one*]:

       ☐ bred by the Seller

       ☐ bought from a breeder _____

       _____

       [*name of breeder*] on _____ [*date*].

       ☐ acquired from a previous private party owner, _____

       _____

       _____ [*name*].

d. Dog has had the following special training: _____.

e. Dog ☐ is  ☐ is not purebred.

f. Dog is:
    ☐ male, neutered
    ☐ male, not neutered
    ☐ female, spayed
    ☐ female, not spayed
        ☐ pregnant
        ☐ not pregnant

g. Dog is [check one]:

    ☐ registered with the American Kennel Club or another entity [provide details as appropriate] _____.

    ☐ not registered with the American Kennel Club or another entity and is not eligible to be registered.

    ☐ not registered with the American Kennel Club or another entity but is eligible to be registered [explain] _____
_____.

Seller will provide Buyer with the necessary papers to process registration.

5. Seller believes that Dog is healthy and in good condition, except for the following known problems: _____
_____
_____.

6. If a licensed veterinarian certifies, in writing, that Dog has a serious disease or congenital defect that was present when Buyer took possession of Dog, Buyer may, within 14 days of taking possession of Dog [choose one]:
    ☐ return Dog to Seller. In this case, Seller will refund the purchase price plus any sales tax and reimburse Buyer for the cost of reasonable veterinary services directly related to the examination that showed Dog was ill, and emergency treatment to relieve suffering plus any sales tax.
    ☐ keep Dog. In this case, Seller will reimburse Buyer for the cost of reasonable veterinary services directly related to the examination that showed Dog was ill, and emergency treatment to relieve suffering, up to the amount of the purchase price plus any sales tax.

7. Dog will be delivered to Buyer in the following manner [choose one]:
    ☐ Buyer will take immediate possession of Dog.
    ☐ Buyer assumes responsibility for picking up Dog from _____
    by _____ [date].
    ☐ In exchange for an additional delivery charge of $_____, Seller will deliver Dog by _____ [date] to the following location: _____
_____.

8. Additional terms: _____
_____
_____
_____
_____
_____
_____ .

Seller 1's signature: _____ Date: _____

Seller 2's signature: _____ Date: _____

Buyer 1's signature: _____ Date: _____

Buyer 2's signature: _____ Date: _____

*[ATTACH NOTARY CERTIFICATE WHEN REQUIRED/PREFERRED]*

# Personal Property Rental Agreement

Owner's name: _____ Phone: _____
Address: _____ Phone: _____
Renter's name: _____ Phone: _____
Address: _____

*If there is more than one owner or renter, the use of the singular incorporates the plural.*

## 1. Property Being Rented; Use

Owner agrees to rent to Renter, and Renter agrees to rent from Owner, the following property ("the Property"): _____.

Renter will use the Property for the following purpose only: _____
_____.

Owner may cancel this agreement and require that Renter return the Property immediately if it is used for any other purpose.

## 2. Duration of Rental Period

This rental will begin at _____ o'clock a.m./p.m. on _____, _____
and will end at _____ o'clock a.m./p.m. on _____, _____.

## 3. Rental Amount

The rental amount will be $_____ per _____ [*specify hour, day, week, or month*].

## 4. Payment

Renter has paid $_____ to Owner to cover the rental period specified in Clause 2.

☐ **Security deposit** [*optional*]. In addition to the rent, Renter has deposited $_____ with Owner. This deposit will be applied toward any additional rent, late return fees, and any amounts owed for damage to or loss of the Property, which Owner and Renter agree has the current value stated in Clause 8. Owner will return to Renter any unused portion of the deposit within 24 hours of the return of the Property. Owner will deposit in the U.S. mail a refund check made out to Renter at the address shown above or deliver the payment in person.

## 5. Delivery

[*choose one*]

☐ Renter will pick up the Property from Owner at [*specify address*] _____
_____.

☐ Owner will deliver the Property to Renter ☐ at no charge ☐ for a fee of $ _____
on _____, _____ at [*specify address*] _____
_____
_____.

☐ Other delivery arrangements: _____
_____
_____.

## 6. Late Return

If Renter returns the Property to Owner after the time and date when the rental period ends, Renter will pay Owner a rental charge of $_____ per day for each day or partial day beyond the end of the rental period until the Property is returned. Owner may subtract this charge from the security deposit (if any).

## 7. Condition of Property

Renter acknowledges receiving the Property in good condition, except for the following defects or damage: _____
_____ .

## 8. Damage or Loss

Renter will return the Property to Owner in good condition except as noted in Clause 7. If the Property is damaged while in Renter's possession due to Renter's negligent, reckless, or intentional act, Renter will be responsible for the cost of repair, up to the current value of the Property. If the Property is lost while in Renter's possession, Renter will pay Owner its current value. Owner and Renter agree that the current value of the Property is [*list value of items individually as well as total*]
$ _____ .

## 9. Disputes. (*This clause applies only to disputes regarding damage to the property or failure to return it, not to disputes regarding personal injuries or damage to other property.*)

[*choose one*]

☐ **Litigation.** If a dispute arises, either Owner or Renter may take the matter to court.

☐ **Mediation and possible litigation.** If a dispute arises, Owner and Renter will try in good faith to settle it through mediation conducted by [*choose one*]:

☐ _____ [*name of mediator*].

☐ a mediator to be mutually selected.

Owner and Renter will share the costs of the mediator equally. If the dispute is not resolved within 30 days after it is referred to the mediator, either Owner or Renter may take the matter to court.

☐ **Mediation and possible arbitration.** If a dispute arises, Owner and Renter will try in good faith to settle it through mediation conducted by [*choose one*]:

☐ _____ [*name of mediator*].

☐ a mediator to be mutually selected.

Owner and Renter will share the costs of the mediator equally. If the dispute is not resolved within 30 days after it is referred to the mediator, either Owner or Renter may take the matter to

[*choose one*]:

☐ _____ [*name of arbitrator*].

☐ an arbitrator to be mutually selected.

The arbitrator's decision will be binding and judgment on the arbitration award may be entered in any court that has jurisdiction over the matter. Costs of arbitration, including lawyers' fees, will be allocated by the arbitrator.

Owner's signature: _____ Date: _____

Renter's signature: _____ Date: _____

# Notice of Termination of Personal Property Rental Agreement

To _____ [*name of person to whom notice is being sent*]:

## 1. Notice of Termination

This is a notice that as of _____, _____, I am terminating the following rental agreement:

Name of Owner: _____

Name of Renter: _____

Property covered by agreement: _____
_____

Date agreement signed: _____, _____

## 2. Reason for Termination

The reasons for the termination are as follows [*optional, unless a reason to terminate is required by the rental agreement*]: _____
_____
_____
_____
_____
_____.

## 3. Return of Property

[*choose one*]:

☐ [*for renters*] I will return the Property to Owner on or before _____, _____.

☐ [*for owners*] Please return the Property to Owner on or before _____, _____.

## 4. Return of Security Deposit

☐ Renter has deposited $_____ with Owner. Owner agrees to inspect the Property for damage and refund Renter any unused portion of the security deposit. Within 24 hours of the return of the Property, Owner will deposit in the U.S. mail a refund check made out to Renter at the following address: _____
_____.

Date: _____

Signature: _____, ☐ Owner ☐ Renter

Print name: _____

# Storage Contract

Property Owner: _____

Address: _____

Property Custodian: _____

Address: _____

*If there is more than one owner or custodian, the use of the singular incorporates the plural.*

1. **Property**

    Owner desires to store with Custodian, and Custodian agrees to accept and store for Owner, the following property ("the Property"): _____

    _____

    _____

    _____

    _____

    _____

    Photographs of ☐ some ☐ all of the items are attached.

2. **Storage Location**

    The Property will be stored at the following location: _____

    _____

    Custodian agrees that the Property will not be removed from this location without prior written notice to and written consent of Owner.

3. **Storage Term and Payment**

    [*choose one*]

    ☐ Custodian agrees to store the Property on a _____ [*daily, weekly, or monthly*] basis in exchange for payment of $_____ per _____, payable on the first day of each such period.

    ☐ Custodian agrees to store the Property for payment of $_____. Payment will be made on or before _____, _____.

4. **Beginning and Ending Dates**

    [*choose one*]

    ☐ Storage will begin on _____, _____, and will continue until Owner claims the Property or Custodian serves Owner with a _____-day written notice terminating this storage agreement.

    ☐ Storage will begin on _____, _____, and will continue until _____, _____, or until Owner claims the Property, whichever occurs first.

5. **Use of Property**

   Custodian will not use the Property, or permit it to be used by anyone else, without Owner's prior written consent. Notwithstanding Clause 13, Custodian is liable for any damage to the Property during use without Owner's prior written consent.

6. **Reclaiming Property**

   Owner may reclaim the Property at any time, but not later than the date specified in Clause 4, or the date specified in the Custodian's notice of termination under that clause. Custodian will make the Property available to Owner, but may first require Owner to pay Custodian any unpaid charges allowed by Clauses 3 and 7.

   Custodian may refuse delivery if Custodian has received any notice of attachment, levy, or similar notice and has given notice to Owner under Clause 15, or is instructed to withhold delivery by a court or law enforcement officer.

7. **Failure to Reclaim Property**

   If Owner fails to reclaim the Property on or before the last day of storage indicated in the Custodian's notice of termination or in Clause 4, Custodian will [choose one]:

   ☐ continue to store the Property at the rate of $_____ per _____
   until Owner reclaims the Property. Custodian may require owner to pay accrued storage fees before turning over the Property.

   ☐ send to Owner's last known address by first-class mail a notice to reclaim the Property, and wait 30 days; if Owner does not make arrangements to reclaim the Property during the 30 days, Custodian may deem the Property abandoned, sell it to pay for outstanding storage fees, and hold the balance (minus reasonable costs of sale) for Owner.

8. **Early Reclaiming**

   If Owner reclaims the Property during a period for which payment has been made, no pro rata refund will be made.

9. **Delivery to Someone Other Than Owner**

   Custodian will not deliver the Property to any person other than Owner without prior written permission from Owner. If Owner dies while this agreement is in effect, Owner instructs Custodian to deliver the Property to _____
   upon proper proof of that person's identity and documentation of Owner's death, unless Custodian is instructed otherwise by a court or law enforcement official.

10. **More Than One Owner**

    If more than one Owner is listed at the beginning of this form [choose one]:

    ☐ Custodian may deliver the Property only to all of the Owners.

    ☐ Custodian may deliver the Property to _____
    [state Owner's name] rather than all of the Owners.

## 11. Value of the Property

Owner and Custodian agree that the approximate ☐ replacement value ☐ fair market value of each item of Property on the date this agreement is signed is [*list items and their value*]:

| Item | Value |
|------|-------|
|      |       |
|      |       |
|      |       |
|      |       |
|      |       |
|      |       |
|      |       |
|      |       |
|      |       |
|      |       |
|      |       |
|      |       |
|      |       |
|      |       |

## 12. Condition of the Property

The Property being stored appears to be in good condition except for the following defects or damage [*provide details on each item of property being stored*]: _____
_____
_____
_____
_____.

## 13. Care During Storage Period

Custodian agrees to exercise reasonable care to protect the Property from loss, theft, or damage. Custodian agrees to be liable for loss, theft, or damage to the Property caused by Custodian's negligent, reckless, or intentional act. Owner agrees to be liable for damage to the Property or the storage location caused by inherent or defective condition of the Property.

☐ Owner will insure the Property.

☐ Custodian will insure the Property to the extent allowable under Custodian's homeowners' or other insurance policy.

## 14. Title to the Property

The Owner shall at all times retain title to the Property.

15. **Notice of Attachment**

    Custodian agrees to notify Owner promptly in writing if custodian receives any notice of attachment, levy, or similar notice.

16. **Disputes**

    [*choose one*]:

    ☐ **Litigation.** If a dispute arises, either Owner or Custodian may take the matter to court.

    ☐ **Mediation and possible litigation.** If a dispute arises, Owner and Custodian will try in good faith to settle it through mediation conducted by [*choose one*]:

    ☐ [*name of mediator*].

    ☐ a mediator to be mutually selected.

    Owner and Custodian will share the costs of the mediator equally. If the dispute is not resolved within 30 days after it is referred to the mediator, either Owner or Custodian may take the matter to court.

    ☐ **Mediation and possible arbitration.** If a dispute arises, Owner and Custodian will try in good faith to settle it through mediation conducted by [*choose one*]:

    ☐ _____ [*name of mediator*].

    ☐ a mediator to be mutually selected.

    Owner and Custodian will share the costs of the mediator equally. If the dispute is not resolved within 30 days after it is referred to the mediator, it will be arbitrated by [*choose one*]:

    ☐ _____ [*name of arbitrator*].

    ☐ an arbitrator to be mutually selected.

    The arbitrator's decision will be binding and judgment on the arbitration award may be entered in any court that has jurisdiction over the matter. Costs of arbitration, including lawyers' fees, will be allocated by the arbitrator.

17. **Modification of This Agreement**

    All agreements between the parties related to storage of the Property are incorporated in this contract. Any modification to this contract must be in writing signed by Owner and Custodian.

18. **Additional Terms**

    Additional terms for the storage of the Property are as follows: _____
    _____
    _____
    _____
    _____ .

Owner's signature: _____ Date: _____

Custodian's signature: _____ Date: _____

Form 63

# Home Maintenance Agreement

Homeowner's name: _____

Address: _____

Phone: _____ Email: _____

Contractor's name: _____

Address: _____

Phone: _____ Email: _____

Contractor's license number (if applicable): _____

Homeowner desires to contract with Contractor to perform certain work on property located at:
_____
_____.

1. **Work to Be Done**

   The work to be performed under this agreement consists of the following: _____
   _____
   _____
   _____
   _____
   _____.

2. **Payment**

   In exchange for the work specified in Clause 1, Homeowner agrees to pay Contractor as follows [*choose one*]:

   ☐ $_____, payable upon completion of the specified work by ☐ cash ☐ check ☐ credit card ☐ other.

   ☐ $_____, payable one-half at the beginning of the specified work and one-half at the completion of the specified work by ☐ cash ☐ check ☐ credit card ☐ other.

   ☐ $_____ per hour for each hour of work performed, up to a maximum of $_____, payable at the following times and in the following manner: _____
   _____.

   ☐ Other: _____
   _____.

3. **Time**

   The work specified in this contract shall [*check the boxes and provide dates*]:

   ☐ begin on _____, _____.

   ☐ be completed on _____, _____.

**4. Additional Terms**

Homeowner and Contractor additionally agree that: _____
_____
_____
_____
_____
_____ .

All agreements between Homeowner and Contractor related to the specified work are incorporated in this contract. Any modification to the contract must be in writing.

Homeowner's signature: _____ Date: _____

Contractor's signature: _____ Date: _____

# Home Repairs Agreement

Homeowner's name: _____

Address: _____

Phone: _____ Email: _____

Contractor's name: _____

Address: _____

Phone: _____ Email: _____

Homeowner and Contractor agree that contractor will perform certain work on property located at:
_____
_____ .

1. **Work to Be Done**

    The work to be performed under this agreement consists of the following: _____
    _____
    _____
    _____
    _____
    _____
    _____
    _____
    _____
    _____ .

2. **Payment**

    In exchange for the work specified in Clause 1, Homeowner agrees to pay Contractor as follows [*choose one*]:

    ☐ $ _____ , payable upon completion of the specified work by  ☐ cash
       ☐ check  ☐ credit card  ☐ other.

    ☐ $ _____ , payable by  ☐ cash  ☐ check  ☐ credit card  ☐ other  as follows:
       _____ % payable when the following occurs: _____
       _____ % payable when the following occurs: _____
       _____ % payable when the following occurs: _____ .

    ☐ $ _____ per hour for each hour of work performed, up to a maximum of $ _____ ,
       payable at the following times and in the following manner: _____
       _____
       _____ .

    ☐ Other: _____
       _____ .

3. **Time**

    The work specified in Clause 1 will [*check the boxes and provide dates*]:

    ☐ begin on _____, _____.

    ☐ be completed on _____, _____.

    Time is of the essence.

4. **Licensing and Registration Requirements**

    Contractor will comply with all state and local licensing and registration requirements for the type of activity involved in the specified work [*check one box and provide description*]:

    ☐ Contractor's state license or registration is for the following type of work and carries the following number: _____.

    ☐ Contractor's local license or registration is for the following type of work and carries the following number: _____.

    ☐ Contractor is not required to have a license or registration for the specified work, for the following reasons: _____
    _____.

5. **Permits and Approvals**

    [*check all appropriate boxes*]

    ☐ Contractor  ☐ Homeowner will be responsible for determining which permits are necessary and for obtaining those permits.

    ☐ Contractor  ☐ Homeowner will pay for all state and local permits necessary for performing the specified work.

    ☐ Contractor  ☐ Homeowner will be responsible for obtaining approval from the local homeowners' association, if required.

6. **Injury to Contractor**

    Contractor will carry insurance. If Contractor is injured in the course of performing the specified work, Homeowner will be exempt from liability for those injuries to the fullest extent allowed by law.

7. **Additional Terms**

    Homeowner and Contractor additionally agree that: _____
    _____
    _____
    _____
    _____
    _____.

    All agreements between Homeowner and Contractor related to the specified work are incorporated in this contract. Any modification to the contract must be in writing.

Homeowner's signature: _____ Date: _____

Contractor's signature: _____ Date: _____

Form 65

## Contractor Mid-Job Worksheet

| Date | Issue/Question | Response | Additional cost? | Resolved? | Initials |
|------|----------------|----------|------------------|-----------|----------|
|      |                |          |                  |           |          |
|      |                |          |                  |           |          |
|      |                |          |                  |           |          |
|      |                |          |                  |           |          |
|      |                |          |                  |           |          |
|      |                |          |                  |           |          |
|      |                |          |                  |           |          |

Form 66

# Daily Expenses

Week of _____

| Sunday | | Monday | | Tuesday | | Wednesday | |
|---|---|---|---|---|---|---|---|
| Expenses | Cost | Expenses | Cost | Expenses | Cost | Expenses | Cost |
| _____ | _____ | _____ | _____ | _____ | _____ | _____ | _____ |
| _____ | _____ | _____ | _____ | _____ | _____ | _____ | _____ |
| _____ | _____ | _____ | _____ | _____ | _____ | _____ | _____ |
| _____ | _____ | _____ | _____ | _____ | _____ | _____ | _____ |
| _____ | _____ | _____ | _____ | _____ | _____ | _____ | _____ |
| _____ | _____ | _____ | _____ | _____ | _____ | _____ | _____ |
| _____ | _____ | _____ | _____ | _____ | _____ | _____ | _____ |
| _____ | _____ | _____ | _____ | _____ | _____ | _____ | _____ |
| _____ | _____ | _____ | _____ | _____ | _____ | _____ | _____ |
| _____ | _____ | _____ | _____ | _____ | _____ | _____ | _____ |
| _____ | _____ | _____ | _____ | _____ | _____ | _____ | _____ |
| _____ | _____ | _____ | _____ | _____ | _____ | _____ | _____ |

**Daily Total:** _____   **Daily Total:** _____   **Daily Total:** _____   **Daily Total:** _____

| Thursday | | Friday | | Saturday | | Other | |
|---|---|---|---|---|---|---|---|
| Expenses | Cost | Expenses | Cost | Expenses | Cost | Expenses | Cost |
| _____ | _____ | _____ | _____ | _____ | _____ | _____ | _____ |
| _____ | _____ | _____ | _____ | _____ | _____ | _____ | _____ |
| _____ | _____ | _____ | _____ | _____ | _____ | _____ | _____ |
| _____ | _____ | _____ | _____ | _____ | _____ | _____ | _____ |
| _____ | _____ | _____ | _____ | _____ | _____ | _____ | _____ |
| _____ | _____ | _____ | _____ | _____ | _____ | _____ | _____ |
| _____ | _____ | _____ | _____ | _____ | _____ | _____ | _____ |
| _____ | _____ | _____ | _____ | _____ | _____ | _____ | _____ |
| _____ | _____ | _____ | _____ | _____ | _____ | _____ | _____ |
| _____ | _____ | _____ | _____ | _____ | _____ | _____ | _____ |
| _____ | _____ | _____ | _____ | _____ | _____ | _____ | _____ |
| _____ | _____ | _____ | _____ | _____ | _____ | _____ | _____ |

**Daily Total:** _____   **Daily Total:** _____   **Daily Total:** _____   **Daily Total:** _____

**Total for the Week**   $ _____

# Monthly Income

| Source of income | Description | Amount of each payment | Time period covered by each payment | Monthly income |
|---|---|---|---|---|
| **A. Wages or Salary** | | | | |
| Job 1: _____ | Gross pay, including overtime: | $_____ | | |
| | *Subtract:* | | | |
| | Federal taxes | $_____ | | |
| | State taxes | $_____ | | |
| | Social Security (FICA) | $_____ | | |
| | Medicare | $_____ | | |
| | Union dues | $_____ | | |
| | Insurance payments | $_____ | | |
| | Child support withholding | $_____ | | |
| | Other deductions (specify): | $_____ | | |
| | **Subtotal Job 1** | $_____ | _____ | $_____ |
| Job 2: _____ | Gross pay, including overtime: | $_____ | | |
| | *Subtract:* | | | |
| | Federal taxes | $_____ | | |
| | State taxes | $_____ | | |
| | Social Security (FICA) | $_____ | | |
| | Medicare | $_____ | | |
| | Union dues | $_____ | | |
| | Insurance payments | $_____ | | |
| | Child support withholding | $_____ | | |
| | Other deductions (specify): | $_____ | | |
| | **Subtotal Job 2** | $_____ | _____ | $_____ |
| Job 3: _____ | Gross pay, including overtime: | $_____ | | |
| | *Subtract:* | | | |
| | Federal taxes | $_____ | | |
| | State taxes | $_____ | | |
| | Social Security (FICA) | $_____ | | |
| | Medicare | $_____ | | |
| | Union dues | $_____ | | |
| | Insurance payments | $_____ | | |
| | Child support withholding | $_____ | | |
| | Other deductions (specify): | $_____ | | |
| | **Subtotal Job 3** | $_____ | _____ | $_____ |
| | **Total Wages and Salary** | $_____ | | $_____ |

Form 67

| Source of income | Description | Amount of each payment | Time period covered by each payment | Monthly income |
|---|---|---|---|---|
| **B. Self-Employment Income** | | | | |
| Job 1: _____ | Gross pay, including overtime: | $_____ | | |
| | *Subtract:* | | | |
| | Federal taxes | $_____ | | |
| | State taxes | $_____ | | |
| | Self-employment taxes | $_____ | | |
| | Other deductions (specify): | $ | | |
| | _____ | | | |
| | **Subtotal Job 1** | $_____ | _____ | $_____ |
| Job 2: _____ | Gross pay, including overtime: | $_____ | | |
| | *Subtract:* | | | |
| | Federal taxes | $_____ | | |
| | State taxes | $_____ | | |
| | Self-employment taxes | _____ | | |
| | Other deductions (specify): | | | |
| | _____ | | | |
| | **Subtotal Job 2** | $_____ | _____ | $_____ |
| | **Total Self-Employment Income** | | | $_____ |
| **C. Investment Income** | Dividends | $_____ | _____ | $_____ |
| | Interest | $_____ | _____ | $_____ |
| | Leases | $_____ | _____ | $_____ |
| | Licenses | $_____ | _____ | $_____ |
| | Rent | $_____ | _____ | $_____ |
| | Royalties | $_____ | _____ | $_____ |
| | Other deductions (specify): | | | _____ |
| | _____ | $_____ | | $_____ |
| | **Total Investment Income** | | | $_____ |
| **D. Other Income** | Bonuses | $_____ | _____ | $_____ |
| | Note or trust income | $_____ | _____ | $_____ |
| | Alimony or child support | $_____ | _____ | $_____ |
| | Pension/retirement income | $_____ | _____ | $_____ |
| | Social Security | $_____ | _____ | $_____ |
| | Other public assistance | $_____ | _____ | $_____ |
| | Other (specify): | | | |
| | _____ | $_____ | _____ | $_____ |
| | _____ | $_____ | _____ | $_____ |
| | **Total Other Income** | | | $_____ |
| | **Grand Total Monthly Income** | | | $_____ |

# Monthly Budget

| | Proj. | Jan. | Feb. | Mar. | April | May | June | July | Aug. | Sept. | Oct. | Nov. | Dec. |
|---|---|---|---|---|---|---|---|---|---|---|---|---|---|
| **Home** | | | | | | | | | | | | | |
| rent/mortgage | | | | | | | | | | | | | |
| property taxes | | | | | | | | | | | | | |
| renters' ins. | | | | | | | | | | | | | |
| homeowners' ins. | | | | | | | | | | | | | |
| homeowners' association dues | | | | | | | | | | | | | |
| telephone | | | | | | | | | | | | | |
| gas & electric | | | | | | | | | | | | | |
| water & sewer | | | | | | | | | | | | | |
| cable TV, satellite, streaming services | | | | | | | | | | | | | |
| internet access | | | | | | | | | | | | | |
| garbage | | | | | | | | | | | | | |
| household supplies | | | | | | | | | | | | | |
| housewares | | | | | | | | | | | | | |
| furniture & appliances | | | | | | | | | | | | | |
| cleaning | | | | | | | | | | | | | |
| yard or pool care | | | | | | | | | | | | | |
| maintenance & repairs | | | | | | | | | | | | | |
| **Credit & Loans** | | | | | | | | | | | | | |
| credit card payments | | | | | | | | | | | | | |
| personal loan payments | | | | | | | | | | | | | |
| other loan payments | | | | | | | | | | | | | |
| **Food** | | | | | | | | | | | | | |
| groceries | | | | | | | | | | | | | |
| breakfast out | | | | | | | | | | | | | |
| lunch out | | | | | | | | | | | | | |
| dinner out | | | | | | | | | | | | | |
| coffee/tea | | | | | | | | | | | | | |
| snacks | | | | | | | | | | | | | |
| **Clothing** | | | | | | | | | | | | | |
| clothing, shoes & accessories | | | | | | | | | | | | | |
| laundry, dry cleaning & mending | | | | | | | | | | | | | |
| **Self-Care** | | | | | | | | | | | | | |
| toiletries & cosmetics | | | | | | | | | | | | | |
| haircuts | | | | | | | | | | | | | |
| massage | | | | | | | | | | | | | |
| health club membership | | | | | | | | | | | | | |
| donations | | | | | | | | | | | | | |

Form 68

|  | Proj. | Jan. | Feb. | Mar. | April | May | June | July | Aug. | Sept. | Oct. | Nov. | Dec. |
|---|---|---|---|---|---|---|---|---|---|---|---|---|---|
| **Health Care** | | | | | | | | | | | | | |
| insurance | | | | | | | | | | | | | |
| medications | | | | | | | | | | | | | |
| vitamins | | | | | | | | | | | | | |
| doctors | | | | | | | | | | | | | |
| dentist | | | | | | | | | | | | | |
| eye care | | | | | | | | | | | | | |
| therapy | | | | | | | | | | | | | |
| **Transportation** | | | | | | | | | | | | | |
| car payment | | | | | | | | | | | | | |
| insurance | | | | | | | | | | | | | |
| road service club | | | | | | | | | | | | | |
| registration | | | | | | | | | | | | | |
| gasoline | | | | | | | | | | | | | |
| maintenance & repairs | | | | | | | | | | | | | |
| car wash | | | | | | | | | | | | | |
| parking & tolls | | | | | | | | | | | | | |
| public transit, Uber/Lyft & cabs | | | | | | | | | | | | | |
| parking tickets | | | | | | | | | | | | | |
| **Entertainment** | | | | | | | | | | | | | |
| music | | | | | | | | | | | | | |
| movies | | | | | | | | | | | | | |
| concerts, theater & ballet | | | | | | | | | | | | | |
| museums | | | | | | | | | | | | | |
| sporting events | | | | | | | | | | | | | |
| hobbies & lessons | | | | | | | | | | | | | |
| club dues or membership | | | | | | | | | | | | | |
| books, magazines & newspapers | | | | | | | | | | | | | |
| software & games | | | | | | | | | | | | | |
| subscriptions | | | | | | | | | | | | | |
| **Dependent Care** | | | | | | | | | | | | | |
| child care | | | | | | | | | | | | | |
| clothing | | | | | | | | | | | | | |
| allowance | | | | | | | | | | | | | |
| school expenses | | | | | | | | | | | | | |
| toys | | | | | | | | | | | | | |
| entertainment | | | | | | | | | | | | | |

|  | Proj. | Jan. | Feb. | Mar. | April | May | June | July | Aug. | Sept. | Oct. | Nov. | Dec. |
|---|---|---|---|---|---|---|---|---|---|---|---|---|---|
| **Pet Care** | | | | | | | | | | | | | |
| grooming | | | | | | | | | | | | | |
| vet | | | | | | | | | | | | | |
| food | | | | | | | | | | | | | |
| toys & supplies | | | | | | | | | | | | | |
| **Education** | | | | | | | | | | | | | |
| tuition or loan payments | | | | | | | | | | | | | |
| books & supplies | | | | | | | | | | | | | |
| **Travel** | | | | | | | | | | | | | |
| **Gifts & Cards** | | | | | | | | | | | | | |
| holidays | | | | | | | | | | | | | |
| birthdays & anniversaries | | | | | | | | | | | | | |
| weddings & showers | | | | | | | | | | | | | |
| **Personal Business** | | | | | | | | | | | | | |
| supplies | | | | | | | | | | | | | |
| photocopying | | | | | | | | | | | | | |
| postage | | | | | | | | | | | | | |
| bank & credit card fees | | | | | | | | | | | | | |
| lawyer | | | | | | | | | | | | | |
| accountant | | | | | | | | | | | | | |
| taxes | | | | | | | | | | | | | |
| savings | | | | | | | | | | | | | |
| **Savings and Investments** | | | | | | | | | | | | | |
| deposit to savings | | | | | | | | | | | | | |
| deposit to retirement account | | | | | | | | | | | | | |
| deposit to annuity | | | | | | | | | | | | | |
| purchase of stock | | | | | | | | | | | | | |
| purchase of mutual funds | | | | | | | | | | | | | |
| other | | | | | | | | | | | | | |
| **Total Expenses** | | | | | | | | | | | | | |
| **Total Income** | | | | | | | | | | | | | |
| **Difference** | | | | | | | | | | | | | |

Form 68: Monthly Budget

Form 69

# Statement of Assets and Liabilities

(as of _____)

| Assets | Date of Purchase | Account Number (if relevant) | Current Market Value ($) |
|---|---|---|---|
| **Cash and Cash Equivalents** | | | |
| Cash | _____ | _____ | _____ |
| Checking accounts | _____ | _____ | _____ |
| Savings accounts | _____ | _____ | _____ |
| Money market accounts | _____ | _____ | _____ |
| Other | _____ | _____ | _____ |
| **Subtotal** | | | _____ |
| **Real Estate** | | | |
| House/condo/co-op | _____ | _____ | _____ |
| Vacation home | _____ | _____ | _____ |
| Income properties | _____ | _____ | _____ |
| Unimproved lot | _____ | _____ | _____ |
| Other lot | _____ | _____ | _____ |
| **Subtotal** | | | _____ |
| **Personal Property** | | | |
| Motor vehicles | _____ | _____ | _____ |
| Furniture | _____ | _____ | _____ |
| Home furnishings | _____ | _____ | _____ |
| Electronic equipment | _____ | _____ | _____ |
| Computer equipment | _____ | _____ | _____ |
| Jewelry | _____ | _____ | _____ |
| Clothing | _____ | _____ | _____ |
| Collections (coin, stamp, etc.) | _____ | _____ | _____ |
| Animals | _____ | _____ | _____ |
| Other | _____ | _____ | _____ |
| **Subtotal** | | | _____ |
| **Investments and Miscellaneous Assets** | | | |
| Life insurance (term cash value) | _____ | _____ | _____ |
| Life insurance (whole policies) | _____ | _____ | _____ |
| Stocks | _____ | _____ | _____ |
| Bonds | _____ | _____ | _____ |
| Mutual funds | _____ | _____ | _____ |
| Annuities | _____ | _____ | _____ |
| IRAs | _____ | _____ | _____ |
| Keoghs | _____ | _____ | _____ |
| 401(k) plans | _____ | _____ | _____ |
| Other retirement plans | _____ | _____ | _____ |
| Partnerships | _____ | _____ | _____ |
| Accounts receivable | _____ | _____ | _____ |
| Other | _____ | _____ | _____ |
| **Subtotal** | | | _____ |

## Liabilities

| | Date Incurred | Account Number | Total Balance Due ($) |
|---|---|---|---|
| **Secured** | | | |
| Mortgages or deeds of trust | | | |
| Home equity loans | | | |
| Liens | | | |
| Motor vehicle loans | | | |
| Bank loans | | | |
| Personal loans | | | |
| Other | | | |
| **Subtotal** | | | |
| **Unsecured** | | | |
| Student loans | | | |
| Bank loans | | | |
| Personal loans | | | |
| Credit card balances | | | |
| Judgments | | | |
| Taxes | | | |
| Support arrears | | | |
| Other | | | |
| **Subtotal** | | | |

## Net Worth Summary

**Total Assets**

- Cash subtotal $ _____
- Real Estate subtotal $ _____
- Personal Property subtotal $ _____
- Investments subtotal $ _____

**Total Assets** $ _____

**Total Liabilities**

- Secured subtotal $ _____
- Unsecured subtotal $ _____

**Total Liabilities** $ _____

**Net Worth**

(Assets minus liabilities) $ _____

# Assignment of Rights

Assignor 1's name: _____
Address: _____

Assignor 2's name: _____
Address: _____

Assignee 1's name: _____
Address: _____

Assignee 2's name: _____
Address: _____

If there is more than one assignor or assignee, the use of the singular incorporates the plural.

1. Assignor transfers to Assignee all of the following rights of Assignor [*describe the rights you are assigning*]: _____
_____
_____
_____.

2. Evidence of Assignor's rights can be found in the following document [*describe the document, such as a promissory note, providing details of document name, parties, and date*]: _____
_____
_____.

   Evidence of Assignor's right  ☐ is   ☐ is not   attached to this Assignment of Rights form.

3. This assignment takes effect on: _____.

4. This assignment lasts until: _____ [*specify date or event that ends assignment*].

Assignor 1's signature: _____ Date: _____
Print name: _____
Location [*city or county where signed*]: _____
Address: _____

Assignor 2's signature: _____ Date: _____
Print name: _____
Location [*city or county where signed*]: _____
Address: _____

Assignee 1's signature: _____ Date: _____
Print name: _____
Location [*city or county where signed*]: _____
Address: _____

Assignee 2's signature: _____ Date: _____
Print name: _____
Location [*city or county where signed*]: _____
Address: _____

Form 71

# Notice to Terminate Joint Account

Date: _____

_____

_____

_____

_____

[*name and address of creditor*]

Names on account: _____

Account number: _____

To Whom It May Concern:

With this letter, I am requesting that you close the account referenced above, effective immediately.

I am requesting a "hard close" of the account so that neither party to the account may incur new charges. If you do not hard close the account, please be informed that as of the date of this letter, I will not be responsible for any new charges made to this account.

If my account has an outstanding balance, you may keep the account open for billing purposes only. Nevertheless, I request that you keep the account inactive so that neither party to the account can incur new charges.

Please acknowledge receipt of this notice by signing the duplicate of this letter and returning it to me in the enclosed stamped, self-addressed envelope.

Thank you for your assistance with this matter.

Signature: _____ Date: _____

Printed or typed name: _____

Address: _____

Phone: _____

**Receipt acknowledged by:**

Signature: _____ Date: _____

Printed or typed name: _____

Title: _____

Outstanding balance: _____ As of: _____

**Form 72**

# Notice to Stop Payment of Check

Date: _____

_____
_____
_____
_____

[name and address of financial institution]

Re: Stop payment of check

To Whom It May Concern:

This letter is to confirm my phone request of _____ [date] that you stop payment on the following check:

Name(s) on account: _____
Account number: _____ Check number: _____
Payable to: _____
Date written: _____ Amount of check: _____

Please acknowledge receipt of this notice by signing the duplicate of this letter and returning it to me in the enclosed stamped, self-addressed envelope.

Thank you for your assistance.

Signature: _____ Date: _____
Printed or typed name: _____
Address: _____
_____

Phone: _____

---

**Receipt acknowledged by:**

Signature: _____ Date: _____
Printed or typed name: _____
Title: _____

# Request for Credit Report

Date: _____

_____

_____

_____

_____

[name and address of credit bureau]

To Whom It May Concern:

Please send me a copy of my credit report.

Full name: _____

Date of birth _____ Social Security number: _____

Spouse's name: _____

Telephone number: _____

Current address: _____

_____

Previous address: _____

_____

[check one]:

Because of information in my credit file, _____ took the following action on _____, 20____ (I enclose a copy of the notice I received):

- ☐ Denied me credit.
- ☐ Granted me credit, but not near the amount or on the terms that I requested.
- ☐ Terminated my credit account.
- ☐ Made unfavorable changes to my account (but did not change the terms of all, or substantially all, of the consumer accounts of the same type).
- ☐ Took the following adverse action or determination in connection with my application for _____ _____ [the application and adverse action].
- ☐ Took the following adverse action or determination in connection with _____ _____ [the transaction and the adverse action].

☐ I hereby swear that I am unemployed and intend to apply for a job within the next 60 days. Enclosed is a copy of a document verifying my unemployment.

☐ I hereby swear that I receive public assistance/welfare. Enclosed is a copy of my most recent public assistance check as verification.

☐ I hereby swear that I believe there is erroneous information in my file due to fraud.

**Form 73**

☐ I am unaware of anything that would entitle me to a free copy of my report. Enclosed is a copy of a document identifying me by my name and address and a check for $ _____ .

Thank you for your attention to this matter.

Sincerely,

Signature: _____

# Request Reinvestigation of Credit Report Entry

Date: _____

_____

_____

_____

[name and address of credit bureau]

This is a request for you to reinvestigate the following items that appear on my credit report:

☐ The following personal information about me is incorrect:

| Erroneous Information | Correct Information |
|---|---|
| | |
| | |
| | |
| | |

☐ The following accounts are not mine:

| Creditor's Name | Account Number | Explanation |
|---|---|---|
| | | |
| | | |
| | | |
| | | |

☐ The account status is incorrect for the following accounts:

| Creditor's Name | Account Number | Correct Status |
|---|---|---|
| | | |
| | | |
| | | |
| | | |

☐ The following information is too old to be included in my report:

| Creditor's Name | Account Number | Date of Last Activity |
|---|---|---|
| | | |
| | | |
| | | |

☐ The following inquiries are older than two years:

| Creditor's Name | Date of Inquiry |
|---|---|
| | |
| | |
| | |

Form 74: Request Reinvestigation of Credit Report Entry

☐ The following inquiries were not authorized:

Creditor's Name        Date of Inquiry        Explanation

_____ _____ _____
_____ _____ _____
_____ _____ _____
_____ _____ _____

☐ The following accounts were closed at my request and should say so:

Creditor's Name                                     Account Number

☐ Other incorrect information:

[*Explanation*] _____

I understand that you will check each specified item, above, with the credit grantor reporting the information, remove any information the credit grantor cannot verify, or modify information that is incorrect or incomplete. I further understand that [*choose the one that applies to you*]:

☐ Because I am requesting this reinvestigation after receiving my free annual credit report from you, you must complete your reinvestigation within 45 days of receipt of this letter. (15 U.S.C. § 1681j(a)(3).)

☐ You must complete your reinvestigation within 30 days of receipt of this letter. (15 U.S.C. § 1681i(a).)

Sincerely,

Signature: _____ Date: _____

Printed or typed name: _____

Address: _____

_____

Phone: _____ Social Security number: _____

# Dispute Credit Card Charge

Date: _____

_____
_____
_____
_____

[*name and address of the company or financial institution that issued credit card*]

Re: Account number:
    Names(s) on account: _____

To Whom It May Concern:

I am writing to dispute the following charge that appears on my billing statement dated _____ :
Merchant's name: _____
Amount in dispute: _____
I am withholding payment of $ _____ , which represents the unpaid balance on the disputed item.
I am disputing this amount for the following reason(s): _____
_____
_____
_____
_____
_____.

As required by law, I have tried in good faith to resolve this dispute with the merchant. [*Describe your efforts*]
_____
_____
_____
_____
_____.

[*For purchases made with a credit card, such as Visa or MasterCard, not issued by the seller.*]

☐ This purchase was for more than $50 and was made in the state in which I live or within 100 miles of my home. Please remove the charge for this item, and all associated late and interest charges from my account.

Sincerely,

Signature: _____
Printed or typed name: _____
Address: _____
_____
Phone: _____

Form 76

# Demand Collection Agency Cease Contact

Date: _____

_____

_____

_____

_____

[name and address of collection agency, including name of individual collector, if known]

Name(s) on account: _____

Account number: _____

Creditor: _____

To _____ :

Since approximately _____ [date], I have received several communications, including phone calls and letters, from you concerning my account with the above-named creditor.

Under 15 U.S.C. § 1692c, this is my formal notice to you to cease all further communications with me except for the reasons specifically set forth in the federal law.

Signature: _____

Printed or typed name: _____

Address: _____

_____

Phone: _____

# Child Care Agreement

1. **Parent or Legal Guardian(s)**

    Name(s): _____

    Address(es): _____

    _____

    Home phone number(s): _____

    Work phone number(s): _____

    Cell phone number(s): _____ Email: _____

2. **Child Care Provider**

    Child Care Provider's name: _____

    Address: _____

    _____ Home phone number: _____

    Cell phone number: _____ Email: _____

3. **Children**

    Parent(s)/Guardian(s) desire(s) to contract with Child Care Provider to provide child care for: _____

    _____

    _____ [names and birth dates of the children].

4. **Location and Schedule of Care**

    Care will be provided at: _____

    _____ [your address or other location where care is to be given].

    Days and hours of child care will be as follows (unless Parent(s)/Guardian(s) and Child Care Provider agree to a temporary schedule change): _____

    _____ .

5. **Beginning Date**

    Employment will begin on _____ [date].

6. **Training or Probation Period**

    There will be a training/probation period during the first _____ [length of training/probation period] of employment. At the end of the period, Parent(s)/Guardian(s) will let Child Care Provider know whether they will continue the employment relationship. Neither Parent(s)/Guardian(s) nor Child Care Provider is obligated to continue the employment relationship through the entire probationary period.

7. **Responsibilities**

    The care to be provided under this agreement consists of the following responsibilities [describe and provide details]: _____

    _____

    _____

    _____

    _____ .

## 8. Wage or Salary

Child Care Provider will be paid as follows:

- ☐ $ _____ per ☐ hour ☐ week
- ☐ $ _____ per hour when Child Care Provider is required to do overtime
- ☐ other: _____

Parent(s)/Guardian(s) will withhold federal [*and state, if any*] taxes from Child Care Provider's paychecks.

## 9. Payment Schedule

Child Care Provider will be paid on the following intervals and dates:

- ☐ once a week on _____
- ☐ twice a month on _____
- ☐ once a month on _____
- ☐ other: _____

## 10. Benefits

Parent(s)/Guardian(s) will provide Child Care Provider with the following benefits [*describe and provide details*]:

_____
_____
_____
_____ .

## 11. Termination Policy

Either Parent(s)/Guardian(s) or Child Care Provider may terminate this agreement at any time, for any reason, without notice.

## 12. Confidentiality

Child Care Provider will not share any health, financial, relationship, or other personal matters concerning this family with outsiders.

## 13. Additional Provisions

Parent(s)/Guardian(s) and Child Care Provider agree to the following additional terms: _____
_____
_____
_____ .

## 14. Modifications in Writing

To be binding, any modifications to this contract must be in writing and signed by both parties to the agreement.

### Signatures

Parent/Guardian 1's signature: _____ Date: _____

Parent/Guardian 2's signature: _____ Date: _____

Child Care Provider's signature: _____ Date: _____

# Child Care Instructions

1. **Home and Family Information**

    Name(s) of Parent(s)/Guardian(s) [*list any parents/guardians who live at this address; other parents/guardians may be listed under Emergency Contacts*]: _____

    Names of children: _____

    Address: _____

    _____ Home phone number: _____

    Cell phone number: _____ Email: _____

2. **Parent/Guardian Work Information**

    [*list name and address of employer, work phone number, and regular work hours for each parent/guardian*]

    _____

    _____

3. **Child's Personal and Care Information**

    [*provide the following information for each child*]

    Name of child: _____

    Date of birth: _____

    Allergies and other medical conditions: _____

    Medications: _____

    Meal, nap, and bedtime schedule: _____

    Other comments: _____

    _____

4. **Child's Health Care Providers**

    [*list names, addresses, and phone numbers*]

    Doctor: _____

    Dentist: _____

    Other medical providers: _____

5. **Emergency Contacts**

    [*list names, addresses, and phone numbers of people whom babysitter can contact if unable to reach you in an emergency; specify their relationship to your family, such as children's aunt or neighbor*]

    _____

    _____.

    **IN CASE OF EMERGENCY, CALL 911.**

6. **Other Important Information:** _____

# Elder Care Agreement

1. **Employer**
   Name(s) of employer(s): _____
   Address(es): _____
   _____
   Phone number(s): _____
   Email: _____

2. **Caregiver**
   Caregiver's name: _____
   Address: _____
   _____
   Phone number: _____
   Email: _____

3. **Location and Schedule of Care**
   Caregiver agrees to care for _____ [name of person for whom you're arranging care] at _____
   _____ [address or other location where care is to be given]
   according to the following schedule: _____
   _____.

4. **Beginning Date**
   Employment will begin on _____ [date].

5. **Responsibilities**
   Caregiver's responsibilities will include [provide as much detail as you think is necessary]:
   _____
   _____
   _____.

6. **Compensation**
   Caregiver will be compensated as follows:
   ☐ $ _____ per ☐ hour ☐ week ☐ month
   ☐ other: _____
   Employer will withhold federal [and state, if any] taxes from Caregiver paychecks.

7. **Payment Schedule**
   Caregiver will be paid on the following schedule:
   ☐ once a week on _____
   ☐ twice a month on _____
   ☐ once a month on _____
   ☐ other: _____

## 8. Benefits

Employer(s) will provide Caregiver with the following benefits [*describe and provide details or enter "none"*]:

_____
_____
_____
_____ .

## 9. Termination Policy

Employer(s) or Caregiver may terminate this agreement at any time, for any reason, without notice.

## 10. Additional Provisions

Employer(s) and Caregiver agree to the following additional terms [*specify any other elements of your agreement or enter "none"*]: _____

_____
_____
_____
_____
_____ .

## 11. Modifications in Writing

To be binding, any modifications to this agreement must be in writing and signed by both parties to the agreement.

## Signatures

Signature(s) of employer(s): _____ Date: _____

Signature of Caregiver: _____ Date: _____

# Housekeeping Services Agreement

1. **Employer**

   Name(s) of employer(s): _____

   Address(es): _____

   _____

   Home phone number(s): _____

   Work phone number(s): _____

   Cell phone number: _____ Email: _____

2. **Housekeeper**

   Housekeeper's name: _____

   Address: _____

   _____ Home phone number: _____

   Cell phone number: _____ Email: _____

3. **Location and Schedule of Work**

   Employer(s) desire(s) to contract with Housekeeper to work at: _____

   _____ [*your address*].

   Days and hours of cleaning will be as follows: _____

   _____.

4. **Beginning Date**

   Employment will begin on _____ [*date*].

5. **Housecleaning Responsibilities**

   The services to be provided under this agreement consist of cleaning the following [*describe and provide details*]: _____

   _____
   _____
   _____
   _____
   _____
   _____
   _____
   _____
   _____
   _____
   _____
   _____
   _____.

## 6. Other Responsibilities

Housekeeper also agrees to do the following types of work [*describe and provide details regarding cooking, laundry, and other noncleaning responsibilities*]: _____

_____
_____
_____
_____
_____
_____
_____ .

## 7. Wage or Salary

Housekeeper will be paid as follows:

☐ $ _____ per   ☐ hour   ☐ week   ☐ month

☐ other: _____

## 8. Payment Schedule

Housekeeper will be paid on the following intervals and dates:

☐ once a week on _____

☐ twice a month on _____

☐ once a month on _____

☐ other: _____

## 9. Benefits

Employer(s) will provide Housekeeper with the following benefits [*describe and provide details*]:

_____
_____
_____ .

## 10. Termination Policy

Either Employer(s) or Housekeeper may terminate this agreement at any time, for any reason, without notice.

## 11. Additional Provisions

Employer(s) and Housekeeper agree to the following additional terms: _____

_____
_____
_____ .

## 12. Modifications in Writing

To be binding, any modifications to this contract must be in writing and signed by both parties.

### Signatures

Signature(s) of Employer(s): _____ Date: _____

Signature of Housekeeper: _____ Date: _____

**Form 81**

# Demand Letter

Date: _____

To: _____
_____
_____

[*name and address of person or business to whom you are writing*]

I am requesting compensation and/or a remedy in connection with the following problem: [*Describe in your own words exactly what happened. Specify dates, names of people you dealt with, what was said and done, any harm or damages that resulted, and anything else that might be relevant.*]

_____
_____
_____
_____
_____
_____
_____
_____.

In light of the above, [*choose one*]:

☐ Please send me a check or money order in the amount of $_____ by _____ [*enter date*].

☐ Please _____
_____ [*state exactly what you want done, e.g., "repair my dishwasher properly and fix the damage caused by your faulty work" or "replace the defective television you sold me with a new and properly functioning television of equal or greater retail value"*].

☐ Please send me a check or money order in the amount of $ _____ by _____ [*enter date for payment*]. By _____ [*date for action*], please also _____
_____ [*description of action you're demanding*].

If the problem is not resolved to my satisfaction as outlined above, I will take this dispute to court unless you notify me that you are willing to try to resolve it through mediation. In that case, I am willing to meet with a neutral third party, agreed to by both of us, in a good-faith attempt to resolve the dispute without court action.

[*Note: Use the above paragraph if you are willing to use mediation to resolve your dispute. If you do not want to propose mediation, simply say "If the problem is not resolved to my satisfaction as outlined above, I will promptly take this dispute to court."*]

Thank you for your immediate attention to this matter.

Sincerely,

Signature: _____

Cell phone: _____ Home phone: _____

Email: _____

# Online Auction Buyer Demand Letter

To: _____ [name of seller]
_____
_____ [address]

I am writing to you regarding a dispute over _____
[description of item purchased] for which I was high bidder on the auction at _____
_____ [name of auction site] as Item No.
_____ [number of item at auction site].

A dispute exists because [describe the reason you are dissatisfied with your purchase in as much detail as possible] _____
_____.

I would like to resolve the matter as follows [choose one]:

☐ I will return the item to you via _____ [describe the shipping method] and request compensation from you in the amount of $ _____, which includes the following costs: [list all costs for which you are seeking compensation, for example, shipping item to you, shipping item back to seller, amount paid for item, etc.] _____
_____
_____.

☐ I will keep the item, but I request a partial refund of $_____ for the following reasons: [specify reasons for price reduction, for example, partial damage or not as advertised, and include proof such as photos of item] _____
_____.

☐ I seek a full refund of all monies paid as I never received the item.

Please make payment by [specify the method by which payment shall be made to you. For example, if payment to seller was made by credit card, seek a charge-back. If payment was made by money order, seek a money order, etc.] _____.

If you disagree with my request and would like to resolve the matter through a third-party dispute resolution procedure, I am prepared to use online dispute resolution procedures at:

☐ myADR (www.namadr.com)

☐ other: [list online dispute resolution website] _____

If I do not hear back from you by _____ ,[date] I will conclude that you do not wish to resolve the matter and I will [check as many as apply]:

☐ [if payment was made by credit card] seek a charge-back on my credit card.

☐ file an online incident report at the National Consumer League's Fraud Center (www.fraud.org).

☐ post negative feedback at the online auction site.

Signature: _____
Address: _____
Email: _____

**Form 82: Online Auction Buyer Demand Letter**

# Request for Refund or Repair of Goods Under Warranty

Date: _____

To: _____

_____

_____

_____

[name and address of seller or manufacturer]

ATTN: Customer Service Department

Re: _____

_____ [description of item purchased, including serial number, if any]

To Whom It May Concern:

I am writing to request compensation for the item described above, which I purchased for $_____ on _____ [date] from _____

_____ [specify place of purchase].

    My reason for demanding compensation is as follows [describe the reason you are dissatisfied with your purchase, in as much detail as possible. List anything included with this request, such as a copy of the warranty, purchase receipt, or the item itself]: _____

_____

_____

_____

_____.

    Specifically, I request the following compensation [explain what you want, such as a refund of the full purchase price, a replacement item, or a repair]: _____

_____

_____.

    Please process this request by _____ [specify a deadline for processing your request, such as date within 30 days]. If I don't receive compensation by then, I will take further action, which may include filing a court action.

Thank you for your immediate attention to this matter.

Sincerely,

Signature: _____

Address: _____

_____ Cell phone: _____

Home phone: _____ Email: _____

# Accident Claim Worksheet

## What Happened

Date of accident: _____

Description of accident: _____

_____

Names of parties involved: _____

_____

Names of witnesses: _____

_____

Location of accident: _____

_____

Time of accident: _____

Weather conditions (if outside): _____

## People Responsible for the Accident

Name: _____

Address: _____

_____

Phone (primary): _____  Phone (other): _____

Email: _____

Insurance company: _____

Policy number: _____  Driver's license: _____

What person did: _____

_____

_____

_____

_____

Name: _____

Address: _____

_____

Phone (primary): _____  Phone (other): _____

Email: _____

Insurance company: _____

Policy number: _____  Driver's license: _____

What person did: _____

_____

_____

_____

_____

Name: _____

Address: _____

_____

Phone (primary): _____ Phone (other): _____

Email: _____

Insurance company: _____

Policy number: _____ Driver's license: _____

What person did: _____

_____

_____

_____

_____

_____

## Witnesses

Name: _____

Address: _____

_____

Phone (primary): _____ Phone (other): _____

Email: _____ Date of first contact: _____

Written/electronic statement: ☐ yes ☐ no

What person saw: _____

_____

_____

_____

_____

_____

Name: _____

Address: _____

_____

Phone (primary): _____ Phone (other): _____

Email: _____ Date of first contact: _____

Written/electronic statement: ☐ yes ☐ no

What person saw: _____

_____

_____

_____

_____

_____

Name: _____

Address: _____

_____

Phone (primary): _____ Phone (other): _____

Email: _____ Date of first contact: _____

Written/electronic statement: ☐ yes ☐ no

What person saw: _____

_____

_____

_____

_____

_____

## Medical Treatment Providers

Name: _____

Address: _____

_____ Telephone: _____

Date of first visit: _____ Date of most recent or last visit: _____

Person to be contacted for medical records: _____

Date requested: _____ Date received: _____

Person to be contacted for medical billing: _____

Date requested: _____ Date received: _____

Reason for treatment and prognosis: _____

_____

_____

_____

_____

Name: _____

Address: _____

_____ Telephone: _____

Date of first visit: _____ Date of most recent or last visit: _____

Person to be contacted for medical records: _____

Date requested: _____ Date received: _____

Person to be contacted for medical billing: _____

Date requested: _____ Date received: _____

Reason for treatment and prognosis: _____

_____

_____

_____

_____

Name: _____
Address: _____
_____ Telephone: _____
Date of first visit: _____ Date of most recent or last visit: _____
Person to be contacted for medical records: _____
Date requested: _____ Date received: _____
Person to be contacted for medical billing: _____
Date requested: _____ Date received: _____
Reason for treatment and prognosis: _____
_____
_____
_____
_____.

## Other Party's Insurance Company (First Party)

Company name: _____
Address: _____
_____ Telephone: _____
Claim number: _____ Insured: _____
Adjuster: _____ Date demand letter was sent: _____
Settlement amount: _____ Date accepted: _____

## Other Party's Insurance Company (Second Party)

Company name: _____
Address: _____
_____ Telephone: _____
Claim number: _____ Insured: _____
Adjuster: _____ Date demand letter was sent: _____
Settlement amount: _____ Date accepted: _____

## Communications With Insurer

Date: _____ Name of employee: _____
If oral, what was said: _____
_____
_____
_____.

Date: _____ Name of employee: _____
If oral, what was said: _____
_____
_____
_____.

Date: _____ Name of employee: _____
If oral, what was said: _____
_____
_____
_____
_____ .

Date: _____ Name of employee: _____
If oral, what was said: _____
_____
_____
_____
_____ .

## Losses

Describe damage to your property: _____
_____

Do you have photos showing damage?   ☐ yes   ☐ no

## If Repairable

Estimates for repairs (name of repair shop and amounts of estimates): _____
_____

## Actual

Repair bills (name of repair shop and amounts of bills): _____
_____

## If totaled

Value at the time destroyed: _____ Documentation of value: _____

# General Release

Releasor: _____

Address: _____

_____

Releasee: _____

Address: _____

_____

1. Releasor voluntarily and knowingly signs this release with the express intention of canceling Releasee's legal liabilities and obligations as described below.

2. Releasor hereby releases Releasee from all claims, known or unknown, that have arisen or may arise from the following occurrence: _____

_____

_____.

    Releasor understands that, as to claims that are known to the parties when the release is signed, any statutory provisions that would otherwise apply to limit this general release are hereby waived. Releasor also understands that this release extends to claims arising out of this incident that are *not* known by Releasor at the time this release is signed.

3. In exchange for granting this release, Releasor has received the following payment or other consideration:

    _____

    _____

    _____.

4. By signing this release, Releasor additionally intends to bind Releasor's spouse, heirs, legal representatives, assigns, and anyone else claiming under the Releasor. Releasor has not assigned any claim covered by this release to any other party. Releasor intends that this release apply to the heirs, personal representatives, assigns, insurers, and successors of Releasee as well as to the Releasee.

Releasor's signature: _____ Date: _____

Print name: _____ County of residence: _____

Releasor's spouse's signature: _____ Date: _____

Print name: _____ County of residence: _____

Releasee's signature: _____ Date: _____

Print name: _____ County of residence: _____

Releasee's spouse's signature: _____ Date: _____

Print name: _____ County of residence: _____

[OPTIONAL: ATTACH NOTARY CERTIFICATE]

# General Mutual Release

Party 1: _____

Address: _____

_____

Party 2: _____

Address: _____

_____

1. We voluntarily and knowingly sign this mutual release with the express intention of eliminating the liabilities and obligations described below.

2. Disputes and differences that we both desire to settle exist between us with respect to the following:

   _____
   _____
   _____.

3. The value (consideration) for this mutual release consists of our mutual relinquishment of our respective legal rights involved in the disputes described above.

4. In addition, the following payment or other consideration will be provided or paid [*check and explain any that apply*]:

   ☐ Party 1 will receive from Party 2: _____
   _____.

   ☐ Party 2 will receive from Party 1: _____
   _____.

5. By signing this release, we both intend to bind our spouses, heirs, legal representatives, assigns, and anyone else claiming under us, in addition to ourselves. Each party understands that, as to claims that are known to that party when the release is signed, any statutory provisions that would otherwise apply to limit this general release are hereby waived. Each party also understands that this release extends to claims arising out of this incident that are *not* known at the time this release is signed.

Party 1's signature: _____ Date: _____

Print name: _____ County of residence: _____

Party 1's spouse's signature: _____ Date: _____

Print name: _____ County of residence: _____

Party 2's signature: _____ Date: _____

Print name: _____ County of residence: _____

Party 2's spouse's signature: _____ Date: _____

Print name: _____ County of residence: _____

[OPTIONAL: ATTACH NOTARY CERTIFICATE]

Form 87

# Release for Damage to Real Estate

Releasor: _____
Address: _____
_____

Releasee: _____
Address: _____
_____

1. Releasor is the owner of certain property (Property) located at _____ , which specifically consists of the following: _____ _____ _____ .

2. Releasor voluntarily and knowingly signs this release with the intention of eliminating Releasee's liabilities and obligations as described below.

3. Releasor hereby releases Releasee from all claims, known or unknown, that have arisen or may arise from the occurrence described in Clause 4. Releasor understands that, as to claims that are known to the parties when the release is signed, any statutory provisions that would otherwise apply to limit this general release are hereby waived. Releasor also understands that this release extends to claims arising out of this incident that are *not* known by Releasor at the time this release is signed.

4. Releasor has alleged that Property suffered damage in the approximate amount of $ _____ as a result of the following activity of Releasee: _____ _____ _____

5. By signing this release, Releasor additionally intends to bind Releasor's spouse, heirs, legal representatives, assigns, and anyone else claiming under the Releasor. Releasor has not assigned any claim arising from the transaction described in Clause 4 to another party. Releasor intends that this release apply to the heirs, personal representatives, assigns, insurers, and successors of Releasee as well as to the Releasee.

6. Releasor has received good and adequate value (consideration) for this release in the form of: _____ _____ _____ .

Releasor's signature: _____ Date: _____
Print name: _____ County of residence: _____

Releasor's spouse's signature: _____ Date: _____
Print name: _____ County of residence: _____

Releasee's signature: _____ Date: _____
Print name: _____ County of residence: _____

Releasee's spouse's signature: _____ Date: _____
Print name: _____ County of residence: _____

[OPTIONAL: ATTACH NOTARY CERTIFICATE]

# Release for Property Damage in Auto Accident

Releasor: _____

Address: _____

_____

Releasee: _____

Address: _____

_____

1. Releasor voluntarily and knowingly signs this release with the express intention of eliminating Releasee's liabilities and obligations as described below.

2. Releasor hereby releases Releasee from all liability for claims, known and unknown, arising from property damage sustained by Releasor in an automobile accident that occurred on _____ _____ [date] at _____ _____ [location] involving a vehicle owned by Releasee or driven by Releasee or Releasee's agent. Releasor understands that, as to claims that are known to the parties when the release is signed, any statutory provisions that would otherwise apply to limit this general release are hereby waived. Releasor also understands that this release extends to claims arising out of this incident that are *not* known by Releasor at the time this release is signed.

3. By signing this release, Releasor does not give up any claim that Releasor may now or hereafter have against any person, firm, or corporation other than Releasee and those persons and entities specified in Clause 6.

4. Releasor understands that Releasee does not, by providing the value described below, admit any liability or responsibility for the accident described in Clause 2 or its consequences.

5. Releasor has received good and adequate value (consideration) for this release in the form of: _____ .

6. By signing this release, Releasor additionally intends to bind Releasor's spouse, heirs, legal representatives, assigns, and anyone else claiming under the Releasor. Releasor has not assigned any claim arising from the accident described in Clause 2 to any other party. This release applies to Releasee's heirs, legal representatives, insurers, and successors, as well as to Releasee.

Releasor's signature: _____ Date: _____

Print name: _____ County of residence: _____

Releasor's spouse's signature: _____ Date: _____

Print name: _____ County of residence: _____

Releasee's signature: _____ Date: _____

Print name: _____ County of residence: _____

Releasee's spouse's signature: _____ Date: _____

Print name: _____ County of residence: _____

[OPTIONAL: ATTACH NOTARY CERTIFICATE]

# Release for Personal Injury

Releasor: _____

Address: _____

_____

Releasee: _____

Address: _____

_____

1. Releasor voluntarily and knowingly executes this release with the intention of eliminating Releasee's liabilities and obligations as described below.

2. Releasor hereby releases Releasee from all liability for claims, known and unknown, arising from injuries, mental and/or physical, sustained by Releasor as follows: _____

_____

_____.

   Releasor understands that, as to claims that are known to the parties when this release is signed, any statutory provisions that would otherwise apply to limit this general release are hereby waived. Releasor also understands that this release extends to claims arising out of this incident that are *not* known by Releasor at the time this release is signed.

3. Releasor has been examined by a licensed physician or other health care professional competent to diagnose [*choose one or both*]:

   ☐ physical injuries and disabilities.

   ☐ mental and emotional injuries and disabilities.

   Releasor has been informed by this physician or health care professional that the injury described in Clause 2 has completely healed without causing permanent damage.

4. By executing this release Releasor does not give up any claim that Releasor may now or hereafter have against any person, firm, or corporation other than Releasee and those persons specified in Clause 7.

5. Releasor understands that Releasee does not, by providing the value described in Clause 6 below, admit any liability or responsibility for the above described injury or its consequences.

6. Releasor has received good and adequate value (consideration) for this release in the form of:

_____

_____

_____.

7. By signing this release, Releasor additionally intends to bind Releasor's spouse, heirs, legal representatives, assigns, and anyone else claiming under the Releasor. Releasor has not assigned any claim arising from the accident described in Clause 2 to any other party. This release applies to Releasee's heirs, legal representatives, insurers, and successors, as well as to Releasee.

Releasor's signature: _____ Date: _____

Print name: _____ County of residence: _____

Releasor's spouse's signature: _____ Date: _____
Print name: _____ County of residence: _____

Releasee's signature: _____ Date: _____
Print name: _____ County of residence: _____

Releasee's spouse's signature: _____ Date: _____
Print name: _____ County of residence: _____

[OPTIONAL: ATTACH NOTARY CERTIFICATE]

Form 90

# Mutual Release of Contract Claims

Party 1: _____

Address: _____

_____

Party 2: _____

Address: _____

_____

1. We voluntarily and knowingly sign this mutual release with the intention of eliminating the liabilities and obligations described below.

2. Disputes and differences have arisen between us with respect to an agreement entered into between us on _____ [date], under which we agreed to the following:

   _____
   _____
   _____.

   This agreement is hereby made a part of this release and incorporated by reference. A copy of the agreement (if written) is attached to this release.

3. We each hereby expressly release the other from all claims and demands, known and unknown, arising out of the agreement specified in Clause 2. Each party understands that, as to claims that are known to that party when the release is signed, any statutory provisions that would otherwise apply to limit this general release are hereby waived. Each party also understands that this release extends to claims arising out of this incident that are *not* known at the time this release is signed.

4. This release additionally applies to our heirs, legal representatives, and successors and is binding on our spouses, heirs, legal representatives, assigns, and anyone else claiming under us. Neither of us has assigned to another party any claim arising under or out of the contract specified in Clause 2.

5. The value (consideration) for this mutual release binds our mutual agreement to forgo our respective legal rights with reference to the disputes and differences described above.

6. We also agree that the contract specified in Clause 2 shall be and is hereby rescinded, terminated, and canceled as of _____ [date].

Party 1's signature: _____ Date: _____

Print name: _____ County of residence: _____

Party 1's spouse's signature: _____ Date: _____

Print name: _____ County of residence: _____

Party 2's signature: _____ Date: _____

Print name: _____ County of residence: _____

Party 2's spouse's signature: _____ Date: _____

Print name: _____ County of residence: _____

[OPTIONAL: ATTACH NOTARY CERTIFICATE]

Form 91

# Complaint Letter to a Government Agency

Date: _____

To: _____
_____
_____
_____

[name and address of consumer protection office]

To Whom It May Concern:

I wish to lodge a complaint about the following company:

    Name: _____

    Address: _____
    _____

    Phone number: _____ Website: _____
    Name of person with whom I dealt: _____

    The details of my complaint are as follows [attach additional sheets if necessary]: _____
_____
_____
_____
_____
_____
_____
_____
_____
_____ .

    Please investigate this matter and inform me of the results.

Sincerely,

Signature: _____

Printed name: _____

Address: _____
_____

Email: _____ Cell phone: _____

Home phone: _____

cc: _____
_____
_____

# Notice to Cancel Certain Contracts

To Whom It May Concern:

This letter constitutes written notice to you that I am canceling the following contract:

Seller: _____

Address: _____

_____

Buyer: _____

Address: _____

_____

Contract pertains to the following goods/services purchased: _____

_____ .

Date contract signed for these goods/services: _____ .

Please acknowledge receipt of this letter by signing below and returning the acknowledgment to me in the enclosed envelope. I understand that under the law, you must refund my money within _____ days. Furthermore, if applicable, I understand that you must either pick up the items purchased, or reimburse me within _____ days for my expense of mailing the goods back to you. If you do not pick up the goods within that time, I am entitled to keep them.

Buyer's signature: _____ Date: _____

Print name: _____

## Acknowledgment

Seller's signature: _____ Date: _____

Print name: _____

# Identity Theft Worksheet

**Credit Bureaus**

☐ Experian: www.experian.com

Date of Contact     Type of Contact     Comments

☐ Equifax: www.equifax.com

Date of Contact     Type of Contact     Comments

☐ TransUnion: www.transunion.com

Date of Contact     Type of Contact     Comments

**Financial Institutions**

**Credit Card Companies**

Name of Company     Phone Number or Website     Date of Contact     Contact Person or Method     Comments

**Banks**

Name of Bank     Phone Number or Website     Date of Contact     Contact Person or Method     Comments

**Other Service Providers**

Name of Institution     Phone Number or Website     Date of Contact     Contact Person or Method     Comments

**Law Enforcement Agencies**

**Local Police Department**

Name of Department     Phone Number or Website     Date of Contact     Name of Person or Officer Contacted     Comments

**Federal Trade Commission: www.ftc.gov**

Date of Contact     Contact Method     Comments

# Form 93

## Other Law Enforcement Agencies

| Name of Agency | Phone Number or Website | Date of Contact | Contact Person or Method | Comments |
|---|---|---|---|---|
| | | | | |
| | | | | |
| | | | | |

## Other Contacts

### Postal Inspector: www.uspis.gov

| Phone Number or Website | Date of Contact | Contact Person or Method | Comments |
|---|---|---|---|
| | | | |
| | | | |

### Social Security Administration: 800-772-1213

| Date of Contact | Contact Person or Method | Comments |
|---|---|---|
| | | |

### Debt Collectors

| Name of Collection Agency | Phone Number | Date of Contact | Contact Person | Comments |
|---|---|---|---|---|
| | | | | |
| | | | | |
| | | | | |

### U.S. State Department: 877-487-2778 or https://travel.state.gov/content/travel/en/passports/have-passport/lost-stolen.html

| Date of Contact | Contact Person or Method | Comments |
|---|---|---|
| | | |

### Department of Motor Vehicles

| DMV Location | Phone Number or Website | Date of Contact | Contact Person or Method | Comments |
|---|---|---|---|---|
| | | | | |
| | | | | |
| | | | | |

### Additional Conversations/Correspondence

| Name of Institution | Phone Number or Website | Date of Contact | Contact Person or Method | Comments |
|---|---|---|---|---|
| | | | | |
| | | | | |
| | | | | |

## Expenses Incurred

| Date Expense Incurred | Reason for Expense | Cost |
|---|---|---|
| | | $ |
| | | $ |
| | | $ |
| | | $ |
| | Total Costs: | $ |

# More from Nolo

Nolo.com offers a large library of legal solutions and forms, created by Nolo's in-house legal editors. These reliable documents can be prepared in minutes.

## Create a Document Online

**Incorporation.** Incorporate your business in any state.

**LLC Formation.** Gain asset protection and pass-through tax status in any state.

**Will.** Nolo has helped people make over 2 million wills. Is it time to make or revise yours?

**Living Trust (avoid probate).** Plan now to save your family the cost, delays, and hassle of probate.

## Download Useful Legal Forms

Nolo.com has hundreds of top quality legal forms available for download:

- bill of sale
- promissory note
- nondisclosure agreement
- LLC operating agreement
- corporate minutes
- commercial lease and sublease
- motor vehicle bill of sale
- consignment agreement
- and many more.

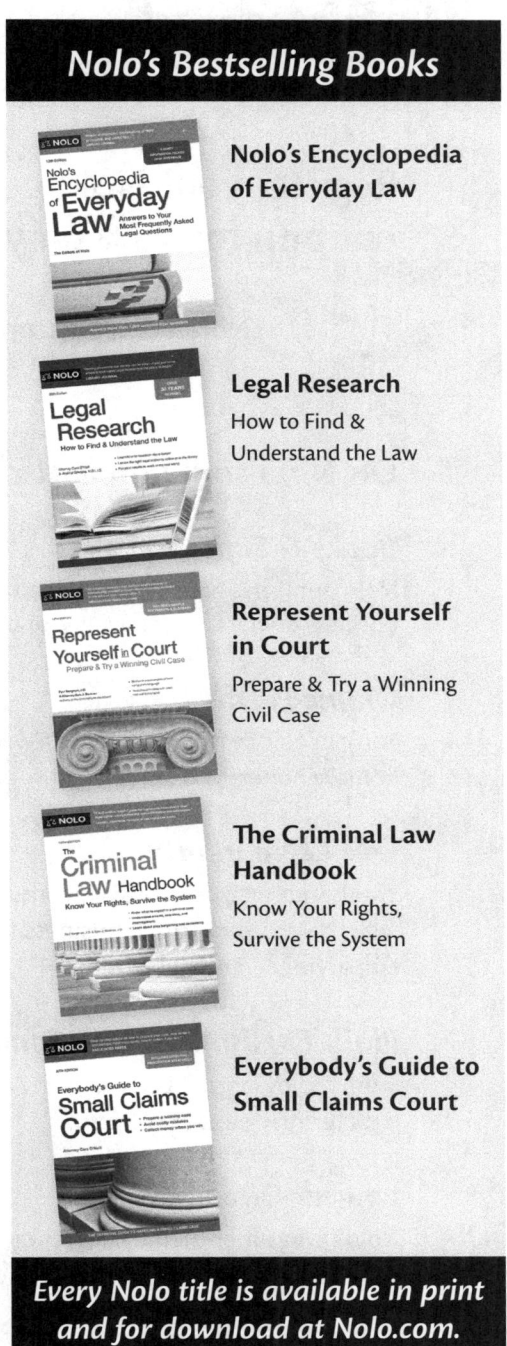

**Nolo's Bestselling Books**

- Nolo's Encyclopedia of Everyday Law
- Legal Research: How to Find & Understand the Law
- Represent Yourself in Court: Prepare & Try a Winning Civil Case
- The Criminal Law Handbook: Know Your Rights, Survive the System
- Everybody's Guide to Small Claims Court

*Every Nolo title is available in print and for download at Nolo.com.*

# www.nolo.com

## Save 15% off your next order

Register your Nolo purchase, and we'll send you a **coupon for 15% off** your next Nolo.com order!

Nolo.com/customer-support/productregistration

## On Nolo.com you'll also find:

### Books & Software
Nolo publishes hundreds of great books and software programs for consumers and business owners. Order a copy, or download an ebook version instantly, at Nolo.com.

### Online Forms
You can quickly and easily make a will or living trust, form an LLC or corporation, or make hundreds of other forms—online.

### Free Legal Information
Thousands of articles answer common questions about everyday legal issues, including wills, bankruptcy, small business formation, divorce, patents, employment, and much more.

### Plain-English Legal Dictionary
Stumped by jargon? Look it up in America's most up-to-date source for definitions of legal terms, free at Nolo.com.

### Lawyer Directory
Nolo's consumer-friendly lawyer directory provides in-depth profiles of lawyers all over America. You'll find information you need to choose the right lawyer.

**SPOT13**